Globalism and Its Critics

The American Foreign Policy Debate of the 1960s

Edited and with an introduction by

William Taubman
Amherst College

D. C. HEATH AND COMPANY
Lexington, Massachusetts Toronto London

CONTENTS

INTRODUCTION

In the middle and late 1960s, as the Indochina War escalated in a frightening and frustrating crescendo, Americans began to ask and attempt to answer some of the most important questions a people can put to itself. What had we been doing wrong (and right) in the world, and why? How, in the light of the Vietnam experience, should our national interests be reevaluated? What, if any, new directions were demanded in foreign affairs, and what changes in the domestic political–economic system might be needed to make new departures possible?

The answering of these questions constituted, this book shall argue, a Great Debate about American foreign policy. It was not, to be sure, a formally organized competition with an officially proclaimed victor. Rather it was an extended and often diffuse national discussion between Presidents Johnson and Nixon and their critics and among critics themselves in the Congress, the press, the universities, a discussion which, in fact, has continued into the 1970s. The debate marked what some call a turning point in American diplomacy. "The postwar era in international relations has ended," declared President Nixon in his 1970 State of the World Message; the report marked, he said, "a watershed in American foreign policy." But the controversy constitutes more than an American problem; it raises as well the most important questions in international relations: What forces move nations? What constitutes the national interest? What jeopardizes national security? How are domestic politics and foreign policies intertwined?

This book distinguishes four broad lines of thought in the foreign policy debate. It analyzes each one's fundamental assumptions about the nature of international relations, as well as its specific recommendations for American policy. This Introduction guides the reader through the major disagreements; head-notes to each selection make finer distinctions among writers who share common overall perspectives. The debate was never pro-versus-con. Yet breaking it down into four perspectives involves problems which should be clear from the start. Did discussion ever fully crystallize into broad sets of answers to the questions posed above? Are such distinctions not arbitrary? Won't writers who prize their uniqueness object? Readers may judge for themselves whether the breakdown makes sense. If, indeed, they are challenged to regroup writers according to different criteria, the book will have accomplished its aim of encouraging further thought and debate.

The debaters who appear in these pages range from "hawkish" former Air Force General Nathan F. Twining to critics on the far left. But one should not imagine that every conceivable position in the debate is presented here, or that those points of view which are included receive attention in proportion to their actual political clout. If clout were the only criterion, then globalism (presently to be defined) and certain of its critics would predominate, while far-left critics would be left out. The editor recognizes another principle— that ideas are important no matter what their political weight.

"Globalism." The term was invented by its critics. It was, they say, the reigning Cold War orthodoxy, the approach which, coming to full flower under Lyndon Johnson, culminated in the escalation in Vietnam. One obvious characteristic of globalism was its world-wide reach. Even more important were the premises which prompted American intervention in Vietnam and elsewhere, in particular the long-standing, many say characteristically American, combination of messianic moralism and calculated self-interest that is the essence of globalism. This blend, this ability to think of America as exceptional in its unselfishness, goes back to Woodrow Wilson and beyond. It led in the 1960s, write critics Edmund Stillman and William Pfaff, to "the general conviction that the affairs of the world are to be understood in terms of a universal conflict of values—between freedom and unfreedom, reason and force, orderly progress and despotism."[1] But globalism was also the conviction, in the words of George Ball, that "our safety as well as our values are at stake."

[1] Quotations from material reprinted in this book are not, as a general rule, footnoted. Citations from other sources are.

Johnson administration spokesmen were fond of interpreting their mission in terms of the highest idealism, as in LBJ's 1966 Commencement Day declaration that "America's only interests in the world today are those we regard as inseparable from our moral duties to mankind." But on less ceremonial occassions there were also signs of self-interest. W. W. Rostow's rule is clear: "It is the American interest to maintain a world environment for the United States within which American society can continue to develop in conformity with the humanistic principles which are its foundation." To which the corollary is not only a requirement for "physical security" (that "no single power or group of powers hostile or potentially hostile to the United States dominate that area [Eurasia] or a sufficient portion of it to threaten the United States and any coalition that the United States can build and sustain"), but an ideological requirement as well—that "all societies . . accept as a goal a version of the democratic value judgments consonant with their culture and their history and that they move toward their realization with the passage of time."

One of the revelations of the *Pentagon Papers* was Assistant Secretary of Defense John McNaughton's breakdown of American interests in Vietnam: "70 percent—to avoid a humiliating U.S. defeat (to our reputation as a guarantor); 20 percent—to keep SVN (and the adjacent) territory from Chinese hands; 10 percent to permit the people of SVN to enjoy a better, freer way of life."[2] Not surprisingly, such arithmetic was not emphasized in public. To probe its roots, one must read a nongovernmental strategist like Johns Hopkins professor George Liska. Liska's fundamental premise is that the world is incorrigibly prone to conflict. For him the enemy is not necessarily communism; it may be "local or regional imperialisms" which threaten "international anarchy or chaos." In such a world, the United States is an inevitable target; it has no choice but to act as world policeman. Yet, by doing so, it can contribute to the establishment of "law and order" at home as well, for "in the last resort whatever order exists in the United States depends on the government's known will and ability to deal firmly with [external] hostile force."

Liska reveals a basic tension in globalism: on the one hand, a

---

[2] Neil Sheehan, Hedrick Smith, et al., *The Pentagon Papers* (New York: Bantam Books, 1971), p. 432.

profoundly pessimistic view of men and nations; but at the same time the optimistic hope that exceptional America can bring order if not law to the world. Liska writes that politics is "first and foremost the hard labor of averting the highest evil before reaching out for the supreme good." But to realist critics, American globalism has reached out for an unattainable good and thereby brought about a preventable evil.

No doubt all the writers included in this book think themselves "realistic." The term "realism" is reserved for a particular "school" because its members draw upon an established tradition of Realist international political analysis. Not all writers grouped under this heading associate themselves with Hans J. Morgenthau's Realist theory of international relations; Stanley Hoffman has been one of its most eloquent critics.[3] Yet those included here share a common complaint: Globalists claim to be "hard-nosed"; Realists think them naive. The world is a nasty place all right; but not as dangerous as Globalists seem to think; nor, in any case, is the United States equipped to set it right. The very nature of world politics has combined with fatal flaws of American political style and process to doom what the Globalists like to call our "role of world responsibility." Our leaders were not wicked, writes Stanley Hoffmann, they were worse; their good intentions, far from mitigating their errors, multiplied them. For, as Hoffmann puts it, "The ethics of political action . . . is an ethics of consequences"[4]; and often "the greatest threat to moderation and peace, and certainly the most insidious, comes from objectives that are couched in terms of fine principles in which the policy maker fervently believes, yet that turn out to have no relation to political realities and can therefore be applied only by tortuous and brutal methods."[5]

According to Realist critics, American foreign policy went off the rails about the time of the Korean War. Western Europe, our primary concern until then, was truly vital to American interests; what's more, it was defensible with the kinds of resources we were able to deploy. Asia, to which Korea turned our attention, was not, as a general

[3] See Stanley Hoffmann, ed., *Contemporary Theory in International Relations* (Englewood Cliffs, N.J.: Prentice-Hall, 1960), pp. 30–38.
[4] Stanley Hoffmann, *Gulliver's Troubles or The Setting of American Foreign Policy* (New York: McGraw–Hill, 1968), p. 127.
[5] Letter to *The New York Review of Books,* March 27, 1969, p. 44.

rule, as vital to America; nor was a country like South Vietnam defensible at cost commensurate with its importance. What led us to indiscriminate global involvement? Failures of understanding stemming from a parochial political style, say Stillman and Pfaff. The very nature of our democratic political process, answer others, harking back to a theme sounded by de Tocqueville. Do these not add up to an insurmountable obstacle to the basic change which Realists seem to be calling for? If so, our dilemma has all the ingredients of tragedy. Except—is it so clear that the change proposed is so basic after all?

Consider Stanley Hoffmann's injunction to be discriminating and respect diversity: "Act in such a way as to let others follow their own course; see to it that they are not pushed off their course and that they can follow the course they choose, but do not set the course for them, and if they stumble and fall you will not be made responsible." Whom will such advice offend? Is it not broad enough to accommodate Globalists who insist that they too operate in its spirit? Or take Hoffmann's more specific recommendation that "the United States can be satisfied with a diverse world in which as few states as possible are under the control of its *main* enemies; the control of many states by national Communists would not be a disaster." Does that not contradict his judgment that "the control of potentially or presently important nations by Communists, even local ones, would be a calamity because it would raise the number of our main foes . . ."?

Realists suggest as standards for future American intervention (1) that the nation or area be truly vital to American security; (2) that it be a victim of overt aggression and not indigenous rebellion; (3) that we feel certain that with a moderate amount of American assistance a legitimate government will prevail. One might object (some critics do) that the fundamental standard—*American* security —is unpardonably selfish. But even granting Morgenthau's axiom about the morality of the *national* interest, there are further problems. Which American interests are truly vital and which merely more or less important? Is it clear even in the 1970s whether the Vietnam conflict began as aggression or civil war? By what criteria shall one judge (1) the legitimacy of a particular government and (2) its chances to prevail with a limited amount of American aid? With Stanley Hoffmann answering these questions, a policy of "Realist restraint" might be the result. But with former Under Secretary of State Eugene V. Rostow?

Rostow accepts the fundamental Realist rule: safety first; virtue second. But safety, he goes on to argue, is in large part a state of the popular mind and as such subject to dangerous fluctuations. "War comes," says Rostow, "when people feel that the moorings are slipping, when the situation is getting out of hand and there's a slide toward chaos which threatens their sense of safety." From which it follows that "foreign policy should not allow such fears to develop, that the best—the only—cure for such fears is to prevent the convulsions in the distribution of power which have always been their cause." From which it further follows that the United States had good reason to get involved and stay so long in Vietnam—for failure in Vietnam could lead to doubts in Japan; which, to the degree they undermined the American-Japanese connection, could threaten a convulsion in the distribution of power; which could prompt Americans to begin feeling insecure and to start lashing out at imaginary enemies without and within.

Or consider Richard Nixon as Realist. Nixon's 1963 speech (reprinted below) was vintage globalism. His 1970 State of the World Message retreated toward a more differentiated approach. But what policies lay beneath the rhetoric? The Nixon Doctrine maintains America's global commitments while reducing military strength. Some say such a strategy means increased reliance on nuclear deterrence; others have called it world-wide Vietnamization. And meanwhile, in Vietnam itself, President Nixon, like his Globalist predecessor, has discerned a vital interest—to show the world and the American people themselves that (George Liska take note!) America is not "a pitiful giant" but can defend itself both at home and abroad.

"Radical-Liberal" has been used by Vice President Spiro T. Agnew as a term of abuse. Philosopher Arnold Kaufman has used the same phrase to praise "a new man in American politics," one who believes that deep-seated social ills in America and in the world "are so great that one cannot be authentically liberal unless he is radical."[6] The line between Realist and Radical-Liberal critiques of globalism is difficult to trace, so much so that it has not been fully appreciated by critics themselves. Stanley Hoffmann once replied to an attack by

6 See Arnold S. Kaufman, *The Radical Liberal: New Men in American Politics* (New York: Atherton Press, 1966).

Noam Chomsky as follows: "He [Chomsky] insists that we disagree on American military intervention and political subversion *in general.* I insist that we do not." Chomsky had cited Hoffmann's belief that " 'the central problem [in Vietnam] does not lie in the *nature* of American objectives,' but rather in 'the relevance of its ends to specific cases,' " and he had challenged Hoffmann's assertion that American objectives in Vietnam were " 'worthy ends.' " It would follow from this, Chomsky continued, "that had our premises about the local situation and our abilities been accurate, and had the means been less corrupting and the costs (as calculated by us) properly balanced, then military intervention would have been legitimate; all the objections Hoffmann raises would be met. To this view I counterposed a very different one: that 'we have no authority and no competence to make such judgments about Vietnam or any other country and to use our military power to act on these judgments.' "[7]

Chomsky's precise wording might not be acceptable to other Radical-Liberal critics. But they would agree, I think, on this—that the main threat to American security comes not from the power of states which call themselves Communist, but rather from two devastating American failures—first, the failure adequately to address America's own pressing crises of poverty, of race relations, of cities, of the environment; and second, a failure to reach out generously and compassionately to downtrodden and underdeveloped nations and so to attempt, however haltingly, to ward off a civil war in the world between the rich nations and peoples of the North and the poor of the South. Like many of the Realist critics, Radical-Liberals bemoan what they describe as America's near-paranoid anticommunism; the fractured Communist camp has been neither as hostile nor as capable of doing us harm as Globalists assumed. But some Radical-Liberals go farther—so far as to say that communism may actually contribute to America's goal of world peace by promoting needed change in the underdeveloped world. According to Robert Heilbroner, some form of communism or left-wing nationalism may be the only way for many developing nations to manage "The Great Ascent." To be sure, it may not; clearly whatever progress communism brings comes at a terrible human cost. But the point is that it should not be for Americans to make the excruciating choice,

[7] The exchange is in *The New York Review of Books,* March 27, 1969, pp. 44–45.

especially when, as in Vietnam, the only way to save a country from communism is to destroy it.

Radical-Liberals move beyond realism on grounds of morality as well as self-interest—which links them, strange though it may seem, with globalism. Hans Morgenthau and George McGovern both condemn the Vietnam intervention; but while the former bases his case primarily on "the national interest," the latter charges moral bankruptcy. Walt Rostow justifies a military crusade against communism; Michael Harrington proposes a massive program of foreign aid; both believe in an American mission which far transcends the bounds of national interest "Realistically" defined. Some Radical-Liberals—those who would pay more attention to America's problems and less to the world's—hark back to an earlier tradition of neutralism and disinvolvement. Their America is also exceptional—in its ability to step back from East-West power politics and lead the way by the force of example. Such critics, it has been argued, deserve to be viewed, but not necessarily to be damned, as "neoisolationists."[8] But it is difficult to see how the aid program that Harrington proposes would constitute withdrawal from the world. On the contrary, such a program, calibrated as Harrington would have it to reach "the people" by bypassing the oligarchs, might well draw America into new and deeper involvements on a global scale.

Would such an aid program be workable or desirable? Hans Morgenthau would surely have grave doubts. Could such a program ever be adopted in America? Heilbroner fears that "the pull of vested interests, the inertia of bureaucracy, plus a lurking fundamentalism that regards communism as an evil which admits of no discussion—the anti-Christ—will maintain America on its present course, with consequences I find frightening to contemplate." Harrington, attributing America's "almost-imperialism" to a "misguided idealism," hopes for the day when "the deep running force of American idealism bursts out of the channels to which the generals and executives have confined it to take its own direction."

Such assessments hardly constitute unbounded optimism. But to Radical critics like Gabriel Kolko and Harry Magdoff, they are too hopeful by half. To Kolko and Magdoff, ours is not an "almost-imperialism"; it is the real thing. It is, they contend, part and parcel

---

[8] See Robert W. Tucker, *A New Isolationism: Threat or Promise* (New York: Universe Books, 1972).

of our capitalist system; it answers that system's needs for export markets, raw materials, and for massive military spending to avoid depression. It can be cast off only when the capitalist system itself is fundamentally altered or discarded. One need not demonstrate, Kolko argues, that all American statesmen have been captains of industry; whatever their backgrounds, their course is set. Often, it is true, that course has been justified as a response to aggressive communism; in reality the "Soviet threat" has been sold to the public as a cover for selfish class interests.

Such a brief summary inevitably oversimplifies the Radical case. Nor is there space to do more than mention some of the hard questions with which Radicals have been challenged. How to explain the fact that the vast bulk of American investment has been in advanced industrial nations and not in less-developed countries into which America has militarily intervened? How to explain the fact that the mass of American voters have regularly voted into power the leaders who, according to Kolko, serve class and not mass interests? How to explain the fact that the Soviet Union, a country in which the state owns the means of production, has carried out its own brand of imperialism?

One reason criticism of the Radical critique need not be pursued here is that Realists and Radical-Liberals in effect do so while offering alternative explanations of globalism. Globalism is of course at the farthest end of the spectrum from the Radical position and yet —there is one more unexpected commonality which closes the circle of the foreign policy debate. George Liska, it will be remembered, argues on political-psychological grounds that to remain liberal at home, America must be imperialist abroad. Gabriel Kolko, though understanding the roots of the matter differently, would agree. Liska, of course, proceeds to support a continuation of imperial policies, while Kolko hopes that an American defeat would open the way to a better world. But where does that leave the rest of us? More Vietnams or a violent upheaval at home? After the experience and debate of the 1960s, not only Realist and Radical-Liberal writers, but many other Americans as well will hope and work for a middle way.

GLOBALISM

FIGURE 1. A Globalist view. (Courtesy, Albany *Knickerbocker News*)

Kennedy, Nixon, Ball, Johnson, Rusk

THE STATESMEN SPEAK

The following selections, in chronological order, present major Globalist voices speaking out for the public record. Whether President John F. Kennedy should be included among them is a matter of controversy (about which see Suggestions for Additional Reading). Certain passages in his Inaugural Address (". . . we shall pay any price, bear any burden, meet any hardship, support any friend, oppose any foe to assure the survival and the success of liberty.") have been cited, by Henry Kissinger among others, as the essence of Globalist excess. Yet the reader will note as well Kennedy's readiness for negotia ions with Communist powers and his offer of aid to the developing nations. Of the Globalist sweep of Richard Nixon's 1963 speech, there can be no doubt. In 1965, Under Secretary of State George Ball was a secret dove counseling deescalation of the war. But Ball's public stance differed little from those of President Johnson and Dean Rusk.

JOHN F. KENNEDY, 1961

Vice President Johnson, Mr. Speaker, Mr. Chief Justice, President Eisenhower, Vice President Nixon, President Truman, Reverend Clergy, fellow citizens:

We observe today not a victory of party but a celebration of freedom—symbolizing an end as well as a beginning—signifying renewal as well as change. For I have sworn before you and Almighty God the same solemn oath our forebears prescribed nearly a century and three quarters ago.

The world is very different now. For man holds in his mortal hands the power to abolish all forms of human poverty and all forms of human life. And yet the same revolutionary beliefs for which our forebears fought are still at issue around the globe—the belief that the rights of man come not from the generosity of the state but from the hand of God.

We dare not forget today that we are the heirs of that first revolution. Let the word go forth from this time and place, to friend and foe alike, that the torch has been passed to a new generation of Americans—born in this century, tempered by war, disciplined by a

John F. Kennedy, Inaugural Address, January 20, 1961. In *Public Papers of the Presidents of the United States, John F. Kennedy, 1961* (Washington: Government Printing Office, 1962), pp. 1–3.

hard and bitter peace, proud of our ancient heritage—and unwilling to witness or permit the slow undoing of those human rights to which this nation has always been committed, and to which we are committed today at home and around the world.

Let every nation know, whether it wishes us well or ill, that we shall pay any price, bear any burden, meet any hardship, support any friend, oppose any foe to assure the survival and the success of liberty.

This much we pledge—and more.

To those old allies whose cultural and spiritual origins we share, we pledge the loyalty of faithful friends. United, there is little we cannot do in a host of cooperative ventures. Divided, there is little we can do—for we dare not meet a powerful challenge at odds and split asunder.

To those new states whom we welcome to the ranks of the free, we pledge our word that one form of colonial control shall not have passed away merely to be replaced by a far more iron tyranny. We shall not always expect to find them supporting our view. But we shall always hope to find them strongly supporting their own freedom —and to remember that, in the past, those who foolishly sought power by riding the back of the tiger ended up inside.

To those peoples in the huts and villages of half the globe struggling to break the bonds of mass misery, we pledge our best efforts to help them help themselves, for whatever period is required—not because the Communists may be doing it, not because we seek their votes, but because it is right. If a free society cannot help the many who are poor, it cannot save the few who are rich.

To our sister republics south of our border, we offer a special pledge—to convert our good words into good deeds—in a new alliance for progress—to assist free men and free governments in casting off the chains of poverty. But this peaceful revolution of hope cannot become the prey of hostile powers. Let all our neighbors know that we shall join with them to oppose aggression or subversion anywhere in the Americas. And let every other power know that this hemisphere intends to remain the master of its own house.

To that world assembly of sovereign states, the United Nations, our last best hope in an age where the instruments of war have far outpaced the instruments of peace, we renew our pledge of support —to prevent it from becoming merely a forum for invective—to strengthen its shield of the new and the weak—and to enlarge the area in which its writ may run.

Finally, to those nations who would make themselves our adversary, we offer not a pledge but a request: that both sides begin anew the quest for peace, before the dark powers of destruction unleashed by science engulf all humanity in planned or accidental self-destruction.

We dare not tempt them with weakness. For only when our arms are sufficient beyond doubt can we be certain beyond doubt that they will never be employed.

But neither can two great and powerful groups of nations take comfort from our present course—both sides overburdened by the cost of modern weapons, both rightly alarmed by the steady spread of the deadly atom, yet both racing to alter that uncertain balance of terror that stays the hand of mankind's final war.

So let us begin anew—remembering on both sides that civility is not a sign of weakness, and sincerity is always subject to proof. Let us never negotiate out of fear. But let us never fear to negotiate.

Let both sides explore what problems unite us instead of belaboring those problems which divide us.

Let both sides, for the first time, formulate serious and precise proposals for the inspection and control of arms—and bring the absolute power to destroy other nations under the absolute control of all nations.

Let both sides seek to invoke the wonders of science instead of its terrors. Together let us explore the stars, conquer the deserts, eradicate disease, tap the ocean depths and encourage the arts and commerce.

Let both sides unite to heed in all corners of the earth the command of Isaiah—to "undo the heavy burdens . . . [and] let the oppressed go free."

And if a beach-head of cooperation may push back the jungle of suspicion, let both sides join in creating a new endeavor, not a new balance of power, but a new world of law, where the strong are just and the weak secure and the peace preserved.

All this will not be finished in the first one hundred days. Nor will it be finished in the first one thousand days, nor in the life of this administration, nor even perhaps in our lifetime on this planet. But let us begin.

In your hands, my fellow citizens, more than mine, will rest the final success or failure of our course. Since this country was founded, each generation of Americans has been summoned to give testimony to its national loyalty. The graves of young Americans who answered the call to service surround the globe.

Now the trumpet summons us again—not as a call to bear arms, though arms we need—not as a call to battle, though embattled we are—but a call to bear the burden of a long twilight struggle, year in and year out, "rejoicing in hope, patient in tribulation"—a struggle against the common enemies of man: tyranny, poverty, disease and war itself.

Can we forge against these enemies a grand and global alliance, North and South, East and West, that can assure a more fruitful life for all mankind? Will you join in that historic effort?

In the long history of the world, only a few generations have been granted the role of defending freedom in its hour of maximum danger. I do not shrink from this responsibility—I welcome it. I do not believe that any of us would exchange places with any other people or any other generation. The energy, the faith, the devotion which we bring to this endeavor will light our country and all who serve it —and the glow from that fire can truly light the world.

And so, my fellow Americans: ask not what your country can do for you—ask what you can do for your country.

My fellow citizens of the world: ask not what America will do for you, but what together we can do for the freedom of man.

Finally, whether you are citizens of America or citizens of the world, ask of us here the same high standards of strength and sacrifice which we ask of you. With a good conscience our only sure reward, with history the final judge of our deeds, let us go forth to lead the land we love, asking His blessing and His help, but knowing that here on earth God's work must truly be our own.

RICHARD M. NIXON, 1963

We should always have a concern for the sensitivities and opinions of our friends in other nations. But, as the strongest nation in the

From Richard Nixon, "American Policy Abroad: Analysis and Recommendations,"
Vital Speeches of the Day, June 1, 1963, pp. 487, 489–490. Used by permission.

world, it is our responsibility to lead, not follow, the forces of freedom. Our policies should never be compromised to the level that only the weak and timid may approve.

We should have respect for the right of any nation to be neutral but in developing the defense and foreign policies of the United States we should remember that if it were not for the power of the United States no nation in the world today could enjoy the luxury of neutrality.

*   *   *

Red China and Russia are having their differences. But we cannot take too much comfort in the fact that what they are debating about is not how to beat each other but how to beat us. They are simply arguing about what kind of a shovel they should use to dig the grave of the United States.

Communism has its troubles. But we must face up to the fact that in 40 years it has extended its power to over a billion people and a third of the world and it has yet to give up an inch of territory anyplace in the world.

Communism is on the move. It is out to win. It is playing an offensive game. Where in the world today do we expect trouble? In the Communist satellites of Eastern Europe? No, in the free nations of Latin America, Africa, and Asia.

What is the administration's policy for dealing with this great Communist offensive? A common theme runs through the policy statements: we shall hold the line against further Communist gains in the hope that communism will eventually wither and die. As President Kennedy put it January 25, "The West has the power to hold back the expansion of communism until the time it loses its force and momentum." The basis for this strategy is that we assume time is on our side and that if we can only hold what we have we will win the struggle for the world because the Communists will lose it.

This is not a policy of appeasement but it is a policy of containment. Because it is essentially defensive in character, it is doomed to failure.

We can regain the initiative only by adopting a strategy of victory for freedom to meet the strategy of victory for communism.

*   *   *

Three elements are essential for a victory of strategy, all based on maintaining the military superiority of the West: (1) Reestablishment of unity among the Western Allies; (2) more effective assistance for the struggling free nations of Asia, Africa, and Latin America who are threatened by Communist subversion; (3) developing a new program to extend freedom to match the Communist efforts to extend slavery.

*   *   *

Communism's strength and appeal is not primarily its military power, its economic productivity, or its materialist philosophy, but in the spirit of those who become infected with the Marxist virus. Call it drive, dedication, will to win, anything you like, Communist leaders have a conviction that they should win and that they will win. No risks, no defeats seem to discourage or weaken that will and it is this spirit that they pound into their people. On hundreds of billboards on the highways in the Soviet Union I saw the slogan, "Work for the Victory of Communism." And on thousands of placards in every factory I visited the same message was repeated. People in other countries are naturally attracted to such a message because they want to be on the winning side and simply through conviction and repetition the Communists convince them that theirs is the winning side.

This vital, dynamic drive has been characteristic of all great revolutionary movements, including our own. We must not forget that it was Thomas Jefferson who said at the time of the signing of the Declaration of Independence, "We act not for ourselves alone but for the whole human race." And Woodrow Wilson, just before World War I, said, "A patriotic American is never so proud of his flag as when it comes to mean to others as well as to himself a symbol of hope and freedom."

I would not deny for one moment that much of this spirit exists in America today. President Kennedy caught it when he said in his inaugural address, "Ask not what your country can do for you but what you can do for your country."

But now the impression is gaining ground that we seem to be running out of steam. We hear too many Americans talk of our goal being to hold our own, of not taking risks, of welcoming neutralism in other countries. . . .

I say that it is time for us proudly to declare that our ideas are for export. We need not apologize for taking this position. In two World

Wars, one million Americans lost their lives and since World War II we have generously given $100 billion in foreign aid to other countries. For what purpose? Not for an acre of territory or to gain domination over any other people but because we believe in freedom, not just for ourselves but for others as well.

It is this kind of spirit that must inspire us now. To the Communists who say that their goal is a Communist America, we must answer our goal is nothing less than a free Russia, a free China, a free Eastern Europe, and a free Cuba.

Only such a great goal, deeply believed in, constantly repeated, selflessly worked for, is worthy of the efforts of a great people in this gigantic struggle. Only such a goal will blunt the Communist ideological offensive and regain the initiative for the cause of freedom.

GEORGE BALL, 1965

Modern Americans have no taste for imperialism, and few would challenge the desirability of reducing our commitments if we could be assured that this would not jeopardize the vital interests of ourselves and our friends. Certainly no American in a position of responsibility today wishes to extend United States commitments farther than is essential for the safety of the free world. But is any substantial curtailment of responsibilities possible without undermining the structure of world security we have worked so hard to construct?

President Johnson has stated on more than one occasion that the state of the Union depends, in large measure, upon the state of the world. In recognition of this fact we have during the postwar period undertaken three major responsibilities:

> *First,* to provide a major share of the defense of free-world interests against Communist aggression.
>
> *Second,* to contribute technology and resources to the economic and political development of the free nations that have arisen from the ashes of old colonial systems.
>
> *Third,* to use our prestige and moral leadership to prevent internecine quarrels between other free-world states and to bring about their settlement if they cannot be prevented.

From George Ball, "The Dangers of Nostalgia," *Department of State Bulletin,* April 2, 1965, pp. 533–537.

The argument that we should retreat from these responsibilities—that the United States should withdraw its power and attention from many parts of the world—goes to the heart of our proven policies. These policies have served us well in the postwar years, and they should not be lightly discarded. For if we do disengage from our responsibilities, who is there to assume them? And if they are not assumed, can we be certain that America itself will be secure?

*   *   *

Nor can America withdraw, as some have suggested, from a high measure of responsibility for the maintenance of order and stability throughout the free world. We can never again return to a day when the world was policed by the British Fleet and order was kept over large portions of the earth by diligent proconsuls of colonial powers.

For, in addition to the drawing of the Iron Curtain and the narrowing of the Atlantic, a third great change has occurred in the past 20 years which has altered the structure of world powers almost beyond recognition. Prior to 1940, at least 1 billion people were controlled by a handful of nations, mostly in Western Europe, that held dominion over vast colonial systems. The sun never set on the British Empire—and only intermittently on the empire of the French. Holland held vast possessions in the East Indies, Belgium, a great territory in Africa.

But today almost all of this is gone. In place of a world system of colonial dependencies, there are 50 new nations—a few perhaps born prematurely, almost all born weak. The great industrial nations of Europe and North America have accepted the fact that never again will they exercise power through the control of subject peoples.

One cannot dismantle a vast and highly developed power structure such as prewar colonialism in the brief period of a quarter century without creating power vacuums and power dislocations of major dimensions. Out of necessity, out of idealism, out of a mature sense of reality, the United States has acted in many of these situations to safeguard the liberty of free peoples from Communist aggression. We have assumed responsibility—not because we abhorred vacuums but because we abhorred tyranny.

Today, as a consequence, we find ourselves in a position unique in world history. Over the centuries a number of nations have exercised world power, and many have accepted at least some of the responsibilities that go with power. But never before in human history has a nation undertaken to play a role of world responsibility except in defense and support of a world empire. Our actions have not been motivated by pure altruism; rather we have recognized that world responsibility and American security are inseparably related. But, nevertheless, what America has done is an achievement of which the American people can be justly proud.

Concept of World Involvement

Those who advocate a progressive withdrawal of American power have, it seems to me, never made clear where or how a withdrawal, once begun, could end without great damage to freedom. They have never acknowledged the fact that in today's interdependent world no action by a global power can ever be taken in isolation. They do not seem to understand that what we do in South Vietnam will have a profound meaning for people in the other outposts of freedom.

Our power cannot and should not be exercised in the same fashion and to the same degree in every trouble spot throughout the world. We must measure and weigh the nature and extent of each involvement. But it is hardly useful to call for the wholesale withdrawal of American commitments without a careful examination of the consequences in each case.

In view of the ever-present threat of Communist aggression, no one can responsibly urge the removal of United States strength unless convinced that the military, economic, and political needs of the peoples of the area will be met from other free-world sources. In practical terms this can come about only through the resumption of world responsibilities by our Western allies.

The United States has long sought to encourage the Western European nations to play a greater role in world affairs. But, based on the experience of recent years, only a few have been prepared to apply the full strength derived from their economic prosperity to the effective sharing of farflung responsibilities. . . .

Western European nations have had little experience in the exercise of responsibility divorced from the defense of territories or the advancement of quite narrow and specific national interests. . . .

And so, while it would be comforting to think that our postwar tasks around the world were largely over—that we could now withdraw our attention from the far corners of the globe with the satisfying feeling of a job well done—that our massive responsibilities could all be shifted to other shoulders—this is simply not the case. For, like it or not, we live in a world that will almost certainly remain for a long time to come turbulent, difficult, frustrating, and complex.

What we dare not do is to turn our backs on the world as it is—and wish it were something different.

The late T. S. Eliot once wrote that "Human kind cannot bear very much reality." But Americans are a people who take pride in being realistic. Now, if ever, we must demonstrate that quality.

LYNDON B. JOHNSON, 1965

The strength of our society does not rest in the silos of our missiles nor lie in the vaults of our wealth, for neither arms nor silver are gods before which we kneel. The might of America lies in the morality of our purposes and their support by the will of our people of the United States.

It was Jefferson who said that "Our interests . . . will ever be found inseparable from our moral duties." That standard guides us still. For America's only interests in the world today are those we regard as inseparable from our moral duties to mankind.

This is the truth—the abiding truth—about your land, America. Yet all through this century, men in other lands have, for reasons of their own, elected to discount moral duty as the motivation that moves America.

In its place they have erected and embraced myths of their own creation—the myths of American isolationism and imperialism, the myths of American materialism and militarism.

*   *   *

If we cannot persuade other men to disbelieve their own persistent, persuasive, and unrealistic myths about America's motivations, we, at least, can urge them to seek after the truth—for the truth about America has been chronicled on every continent in this century.

From Lyndon B. Johnson, "The Morality of Nations," *Department of State Bulletin* June 28, 1965, pp. 1026–1028.

Twenty-one years ago today—on the 6th day of June 1944—it was neither isolationism nor imperialism that sent our sons ashore in Normandy to intervene in the destiny of the continent of Europe, where our culture was cradled.

Nor was it materialism that moved this nation to the works of the postwar world—committing her crops to the care of the hungry, dedicating her dollars and determination to reconstruct the ruined lands of friend and foe, sharing her skills and resources to strengthen the foundations for emerging nations all around the globe.

Neither was it militarism that motivated this nation to dismantle her arms in good faith when victory was won and offer up the atom in good faith for control by all nations. Nor is it militarism now that motivates America to stand her sons by the sons of Europe and Asia and Latin America in keeping a vigil of peace and freedom for all mankind.

What America has done, and what America is doing around the world, draws from deep and flowing springs of moral duty, and let none underestimate the depth of flow of those wellsprings of American purpose.

*   *   *

Sure of its moral purposes—surer of its own moral performance—America shall not be deterred from doing what must be done to preserve this last peace man shall ever have to win or lose. We have—as our forefathers had—a decent respect for the informed opinions of mankind, but we of this generation also have an abiding commitment to preserve and perpetuate the enduring values of mankind. And we shall keep that commitment.

Cherishing the Right of Free Choice

Our purpose, our policy—our constant and continuing commitment—was set forth just 18 years ago this weekend by the then great Secretary of State, George C. Marshall. In a speech the world will never forget, that great citizen of war and peace said this for the United States:

> . . . Our policy is directed not against any country or doctrine but against hunger, poverty, desperation, and chaos. Its purpose should be . . . to permit the emergence of political and social conditions in which free institutions can exist.

Well, that is America's purpose now—our only purpose—in the hungry and poor and desperate and chaotic lands to the farthest corners of this earth. In the policies that guide us abroad—as in the principles that govern us at home—we of the United States cherish the right of others to choose for themselves what they shall believe and what their own societies and institutions shall be.

On this right rests all morality among nations, and we intend to guard and defend this right for others as for ourselves.

DEAN RUSK, 1965

Let me turn to certain other more positive points which the intelligent citizen will keep in mind:

—Peace, in the world as it is, must be protected—if necessary by force. It is not maintained by declarations of good intent.

—Aggression feeds on success. The appeasement of powerful aggressors leads either to surrender or to a larger war. The least costly time to stop aggressions is in their early stages—and preferably before they begin. Because free peoples ignored these elementary points a generation ago, the world suffered the disaster of a great war. The penalty for ignoring them now could be catastrophe.

—The surreptitious infiltration of arms and trained men across frontiers is no less an aggression because it proceeds gradually over a period of time. The infiltration from North Vietnam into South Vietnam is as much of an aggression as was the overt Communist march into the Republic of Korea.

—In the Communist lexicon "peaceful coexistence" means perhaps the avoidance of armed conflicts which the Communists cannot win. The Soviet leaders themselves endorsed in principle what the Communists, in their upside-down language, call "wars of national liberation." . . .

—Nothing in international law or morality confers on an aggressor immunity against reprisal. There can be no privileged sanctuary if we are to organize a decent world order.

—International agreements are made to be kept. *Pacta sunt ser-*

From Dean Rusk, "Guidelines of U.S. Foreign Policy," *Department of State Bulletin,* June 28, 1965, pp. 1032–1034.

vanda—unless the world is to succumb to the law of the jungle. Right does not lie part way between those who break the law and those who are trying to enforce it, between the robber and the policeman.

—We ourselves have no desire to be, and cannot be, gendarmes for the entire world. But we do know that our security is bound up with the security of other free societies. We have very great economic and military strength, which should inspire us with a deep sense of responsibility. Much as we should like to do so, we cannot always escape involvement in disputes between nations within the free world. For the parties to such disputes seek our support and sometimes ask for our good offices. Local disputes divert energies and resources which should be devoted to constructive tasks. And, unless settled, local disputes may lead to small wars and thence to bigger ones. And so we are often obliged to intervene in quarrels in which we have no direct interest—except that they be settled—and in the process find ourselves the object of grumbling by both sides in the dispute.

*   *   *

—Our central goal is the kind of world sketched in the preamble and articles 1 and 2 of the United Nations Charter. And if you have not read those sections recently, I hope you will again very soon because those articles talk about a world community of independent states, each with its own institutions but cooperating with one another to promote their common interests and banding together to resist aggression, a world increasingly subject to the rule of law, a world of freedom and opportunity for the entire human race. We believe that that is also the goal of a great majority of mankind. This identity of basic purpose gives us friends and allies in many nations which are not formally aligned with us—and friends even among the peoples behind the Iron and Bamboo Curtains.

—Innovation for its own sake is not necessarily a virtue. The new ideas of today are often old ideas which were discarded yesterday as unsound. Sound policies should be adhered to even when they do not produce quick and dramatic results. Often the principal requirement for success is persistence. In any event, the United States is so powerful that our conduct must be predictable on the basis of well-understood policies if others around the earth are to find a basis for arranging their own relations with us and others.

—We have vital national interests in the economic and social progress of the developing nations. For a world composed of a few rich and many poor is neither stable nor just. It is not in our power to make all nations rich. But it is in our power to work with them to achieve regular forward momentum. And confidence that the lives of the children will offer more opportunities than were open to their parents is the basis for political and social stability.

—All free nations should understand that power and responsibility go together. Those who seek for more consultation and a larger share in decisions must be prepared to shoulder a fair share of the burden of carrying out the decisions.

—In our dealings with our adversaries we must search unceasingly for common interests. An international agreement does not necessarily mean that one side loses while another gains. The most useful agreements are those through which all the parties gain. We believe that the Soviet Union recognizes a common interest with us, for example, in avoiding a thermonuclear holocaust. And from that should stem various corollary common interests.

*   *   *

—The burdens we carry in protecting and building the strength of the free world are not light. But they are well within our capacity. We cannot afford not to carry them.

—The basic bipartisan foreign policies which we have evolved and which have been pursued over the last 20 years have produced good results for the cause of freedom. Perhaps we erred sometimes by being slow to act. We have not erred when we have stood firm against aggression and when we have assisted other free nations to make economic and social progress.

Personal Commitment to Freedom

If I could conclude on a personal word to each of you—I was very much interested in the point which Mr. Heclo [Hugh Heclo, graduating class speaker] made so eloquently on a matter of commitment. I do hope that you will take away with you from this great university some of the great humane content of the story of man in which the American people played an important part.

I hope that you will not be timid or bored about committing yourself to the simple notion that governments derive their just powers from the consent of the governed. For that is the most powerful and explosive political force at work in the world today. This should not be surprising, because men simply do not like to be pushed around too much. It is a simple idea which we share with ordinary men and women in every corner of the earth even though they may articulate that notion to themselves in somewhat different terms.

W. W. Rostow

DEFINING THE NATIONAL INTEREST

W. W. Rostow, eminent political economist, served in the White House and the State Department as advisor to Presidents Kennedy and Johnson. His book, The United States in the World Arena, *was first published in 1960, then reissued unchanged ten years later. This is not an unusual procedure. But it is interesting that far from qualifying his earlier conception of the national interest in the light of the experience of the 1960s, Rostow went out of his way to affirm it as "a general view that I am not inclined to alter." Note particularly the passage suggesting that flights of Globalist rhetoric have a special instrumental value for a nation which "cannot be effective in its military and foreign policy unless it believes that both its security interests and its commitment to certain moral principles require the nation to act."*

Note: The [author's] concept of the national interest . . . is so central to the author's judgments that it appears worth while to state it explicitly, permitting the reader to isolate the author's presuppositions for critical examination.

A Definition

It is the American interest to maintain a world environment for the United States within which American society can continue to develop in conformity with the humanistic principles which are its foundation.

From W. W. Rostow, *The United States in the World Arena* (New York: Simon and Schuster, 1969), pp. 543–552. Reprinted by permission of the M.I.T. Press, Cambridge, Massachusetts. Copyright © 1960, 1969 by Massachusetts Institute of Technology.

This definition, in terms of the progressive development of the quality of American society, would, of course, include the physical protection of the country; but the protection of American territory is viewed essentially as a means to a larger end—the protection of a still-developing way of life.

The operative meaning of this definition derives from the geographic position of the United States. For no substantial period in the nation's history has the American interest been automatically assured by geographic isolation. Contrary to a mythology which still strongly affects American attitudes and the nation's performance, the American interest has been chronically in danger from the late eighteenth century forward. This danger arose and continues to arise from the simple geographic fact that the combined resources of Eurasia, including its military potential, have been and remain superior to those of the United States—Eurasia being here defined to include Asia, the Middle East, and Africa as well as Europe.

The United States must be viewed essentially as a continental island off the greater land mass of Eurasia. Various combinations of power in Eurasia have been and remain a potential threat to the national interest. American independence was achieved in the eighteenth century only because Americans could exploit a conflict between Britain and France. A united Britain and France could have stifled the American Revolution. During the nineteenth century the nation expanded and consolidated American power on the North American continent and in the Western Hemisphere by exploiting the power conflicts of Eurasia; and in the twentieth century the United States has been thrice placed in jeopardy, and instinctively sensed that jeopardy, when a single power or combination of powers threatened to dominate Western Eurasia, Eastern Eurasia, or both.

There is, then, much in the whole sweep of American history which denies the notion of an America safely isolated by act of God and geography; and there is nothing fundamentally new in taking the American relationship to the power balance in Eurasia as central to the nation's security problem.

The Dual American Interest in Eurasia

If the problem of the national interest is viewed as a question of protecting not only the nation's territory but also its basic values as a society, it follows that the United States has two distinct but connected interests in Eurasia. Since the combined resources of Eurasia could pose a serious threat of military defeat to the United States, it is the American interest that no single power or group of powers hostile or potentially hostile to the United States dominate that area or a sufficient portion of it to threaten the United States and any coalition the United States can build and sustain. But under modern conditions of communication, there is a second threat to the nation's interest. Whatever the military situation might be, a Eurasia coalesced under totalitarian dictatorships would threaten the survival of democracy both elsewhere and in the United States. It is, therefore, equally the American interest that the societies of Eurasia develop along lines broadly consistent with the nation's own ideology; for under modern conditions it is difficult to envisage the survival of a democratic American society as an island in a totalitarian sea.

Three Clarifications of the American Ideological Interest

This proposition must be immediately clarified in three respects.

First, the United States need not seek societies abroad in its own image. The United States does have a profound interest that societies abroad develop and strengthen those elements in their respective cultures that elevate and protect the dignity of the individual as against the claims of the state. Such elements of harmony with the Western democratic tradition exist in different forms everywhere; and they have been strengthened by the attractiveness of the Western democratic example at its best, notably by the example of British parliamentary government, the American Revolution, and the values on which American society was erected. But the forms of legitimately democratic societies can vary widely.

Second, the democratic process must be viewed as a matter of aspiration, trend, and degree, not as an absolute. The value judgments which underlie the political, social, and economic techniques of Western societies might be summarized as follows:

1. Individual human beings represent a unique balancing of motivations and aspirations which, despite the conscious and unconscious external means that help shape them, are to be accorded a moral and even religious respect. The underlying aim of society is to permit these individual complexes of motiva-

tions and aspirations to have their maximum expression compatible with the well-being of other individuals and the security of society.

2. Governments thus exist to assist individuals to achieve their own fulfillment, to protect individual human beings from the harm they might do one another, and to protect organized societies against the aggression of other societies.

3. Governments can take their shape legitimately only from some effective expression of the combined will and judgments of individuals on the basis of one man, one vote.

4. Some men aspire to power over their fellow men and derive satisfaction from the exercise of power aside from the purposes to which power is put. This fundamental human quality in itself makes dangerous to the well-being of society the concentration of political power in the hands of individuals and groups even where such groups may constitute a majority. *Habeas corpus* is the symbol and, perhaps, the foundation of the most substantial restraint—in the form of due process of law—men have created to cope with this danger.

From Plato on, political scientists have recognized that men may not understand their own best interest, and, in particular, that they may be shortsighted and swayed by urgent emotions in their definition of that interest. As between the individual's limitation in defining wisely his own long-run interest and his inability wisely to exercise power over others without check, democratic societies have broadly chosen to risk the former rather than the latter danger in the organization of society, and to diminish the former danger by popular education, by the inculcation of habits of individual responsibility, and by devices of government which temper the less thoughtful political reactions of men.

From this definition the democratic element within a society emerges as a matter of degree and of aspiration. The pure democratic concept is compromised to some extent in all organized societies by the need to protect individuals from each other, by the need to protect the society as a whole from others, and by the checks required to protect the workings of the society from man's frequent inability wisely to define his own long-run interest. Even when societies strive for the democratic compromise, the balance between liberty and order which any society can achieve and still operate effectively, and the particular form that balance will take, are certain to vary. They will vary not only from society to society but also within each society in response to the state of education of its citizens and the nature of the specific problems it confronts as a community at different stages in its history.

It is evident that some present societies have not had and do not now have the capability of combining effective communal action with a high degree of what is here called the democratic element. Both history and the contemporary scene offer instances of governments in which the balance of power is heavily in the hands of the state rather than in the hands of the individual citizens who comprise it.

The legitimate American ideological interest is not that all societies become immediately democratic in the degree achieved in the United States or Western Europe, but that they accept as a goal a version of the democratic value judgments consonant with their culture and their history and that they move toward their realization with the passage of time.

Now a third clarification of the American ideological interest. Since the American interest does not require that all societies at all times accept democratic values and move toward their achievement, the nation is concerned not with total ideological victory, somehow defined, but with the balance and trend of ideological forces in Eurasia. Therefore, the application of the limited, but real, margin of American influence on the course of other societies can and should be selective. Given the nation's geographic circumstance, its history, and the quality of its society, the American interest demands, in a sense, that Americans be crusaders; but the American ideological crusade must be tolerant, long term, and directed toward areas of importance where the nation's margin of influence may be effective. The United States is concerned not with absolutes but with the direction of political trend in Eurasia.

Current Threats from Eurasia

In more specific geographic terms, it is a persistent interest of the United States that no single power or power grouping militarily dominate either Western or Eastern Eurasia.

In Western Eurasia the threat of such an outcome is posed by the possible absorption within the Soviet empire of East Germany and Eastern Europe. The threat would become a reality should West Germany be drawn into the Soviet power orbit; and the threat would be made acute by the ideological defection of Italy, France, or both. In the East the threat of such an outcome is posed by the close alliance of the Soviet Union and Communist China. In Asia there are two major centers of power, Japan on the one hand and India on the other, the latter being key to the complex stretching from Indochina around to Pakistan. In Asia the threat to the American interest would become virtually a reality should either Japan or India be lost to the Free World.

At the present time the intentions and capabilities of the Communist Bloc pose two threats to the United States—a military threat and an ideological threat. These threats are clearly related; the ideological loss of India, for instance, would raise important military problems; the military loss of northern Indochina has raised important problems of ideological orientation throughout Southeast Asia. But the two American interests are not and should not be considered identical. The time necessary and the kind of effort required to cope with the military threat are likely to differ from those required by the ideological threat. The military threat to South Korea was dealt with in a few years; defeating the ideological threat to South Korea may prove a creative Free World task for a generation.

The Interweaving of Power and Ideological Interests

If this view of the American interest is correct, the debate which has been proceeding in the United States over recent years as to whether the nation's interests should be defined in power terms or in terms of the ideological principles to which American society is attached is a somewhat misguided debate. This is so in two respects.

First, if the essential American interest is to preserve a world environment within which its chosen form of democratic society can persist and develop, then the nation's stake in the ideological and political balance in Eurasia is as legitimate as its interest in the military balance of power in Eurasia. Two national efforts, one military and the other political, interacting intimately, must go forward together as part of a total effort to protect the interests of American society.

There is a second sense in which the debate appears misguided. It appears to be a characteristic of American history that this nation cannot be effective in its military and foreign policy unless it believes that both its security interests and its commitment to certain moral principles require the nation to act. From the Spanish-American War to the present, the nation has acted effectively only when both strands in its interest were believed to be involved—in the Spanish-American War itself, in the First and Second World Wars, in the effort to reconstruct and defend Western Europe in 1947–1950, in the early phases of the Korean War.

When idealism alone seemed to be the basis for the positions taken, the nation did not back its play, as, for example, in Wilson's ideological formulation of the American interest at Versailles. Equally, the nation has not been effective when confronted with situations where its power interests might be involved but where a persuasive moral basis for American action was not present. The notion of American imperialism, popular in certain American circles at the turn of the century, died quickly when it confronted the abiding American instinct in support of political independence in the case of the Philippines and elsewhere. Similarly, a major reason why the United States was ineffective in the Indochina crisis of 1954 was that it was then extremely difficult simultaneously to deal with the Communist menace and to disengage from French imperialism in that area; and in the summer of 1956 the United States was gravely inhibited in dealing with Nasser because, among other reasons, his claim to national sovereignty over the Suez Canal had a certain resonance in the American image of its historic meaning on the world scene as the friend of those struggling for independence.

The wisdom of American policy in Indochina and at Suez is, of course, debatable. Moreover, a nation's belief that its ideals are or are not involved is by no means an unambiguous criterion for performance. Nevertheless, it is unrealistic to expect American society —given its history and values—to perform in terms of pure power criteria.

The components in the American ideological interest can, then, be distinguished and summarized in the following three propositions:

1. The ideological loss of key areas in Eurasia would have major military consequence for the United States.
2. Apart from its military consequences, the ideological loss of the balance of power in Eurasia would, under modern conditions, have major adverse consequences for the quality of

American society and for the viability of the humanistic principles which underlie it.

3. Among the qualities of American society threatened by the loss
   of the ideological balance of power in Eurasia would be the
   historic sense of American democratic mission on the world
   scene, present since the nation's founding, which has given
   to American life much of its moral worth, its distinction, and
   its forward momentum.

The art of American statesmanship is to formulate and to sustain
courses of action which harmonize in specific settings abiding American interests and abiding American ideals, steadily preserving the
dual power balance in Eurasia, preventing by forehanded effort the
emergence of such crises as those which hitherto have been required
to evoke a major American effort at self-preservation.

The requirements of protecting the military balance of power and
developing the ideological balance of power will not always converge. Foreign policy is full of painful choices. There may be times
when in order to maintain military positions action must be taken
which will conflict with the norms of the American ideological interest; and there may be occasions when it will be proper to take military risks to permit movement toward ideological objectives. But in
the world of 1958 and beyond there are many more points of convergence than are now being exploited. If the dual character of the
national interest—as a democratic island off a potentially threatening
Eurasian mainland—is accepted, and if the interrelations of the two
objectives are perceived, courses of action still appear open to the
United States which will protect and sustain the quality as well as
the existence of the nation's life in the face of current and foreseeable challenges.

The United States and the Decline of Nationhood

Among those challenges is the problem of using American power and
influence to tame military force by effective international accord; for
the nature of modern weapons in a context other than American
monopoly is a danger to the national interest sufficiently grave to
justify acceptance of important constraints on the nation's sovereignty. Put another way, it is a legitimate American national objective to see removed from all nations—including the United States—

the right to use substantial military force to pursue their own interests. Since this residual right is the root of national sovereignty and
the basis for the existence of an international arena of power, it is,
therefore, an American interest to see an end to nationhood as it has
been historically defined.

The pace at which means of communication are now under development argues, further, that the present nations of the globe will
move into relations of increasing intimacy and interaction.

Between them, the urgent imperative to tame military force and
the need to deal with peoples everywhere on the basis of an accel-
erating proximity argue strongly for movement in the direction of
federalized world organization under effective international law. And,
should effective international control of military power be achieved,
it might prove convenient and rational to pass other functions upward
from unilateral determination to an organized arena of international
politics.

It is not easy or particularly useful to peer far beyond the time
when this great human watershed is attained. Nevertheless, it can
be said that the American regional interest would still continue to
embrace elements from the long sweep of the past. Convergent and
conflicting relationships of geography, of cultural connection, of economic interest would in substantial measure be simply transferred
from a setting where military force enters the equation of negotiation
to one of global domestic politics. When the great conference has
ended and the freely moving inspectors take up their initial posts
from one end of the world to the other and the nightmare passes,
the agenda of international politics will look not unfamiliar. Much in
the historic relation of the United States to the balance of affairs in
Eurasia will remain. There will be, however, a special dimension to
global politics with special meaning for Americans—the problem of
so conducting the world's affairs as to avoid a dissolution of the federal machinery and civil war.

General Nathan F. Twining
CRITIC ON THE RIGHT

Most of the critics included in this book charge that America overextended itself in opposing Communist power. Yet, if such was indeed the case, a major reason (see Suggestions for Additional Reading*) was the constant and often vociferous pressure from right-wing critics demanding more, not less, crusading against communism. Richard Nixon's 1963 speech is an example of a warning from the right. So is the 1966 book by General Nathan F. Twining, Chairman of the Joint Chiefs of Staff between 1957 and 1960. Twining rejects a policy of containment, and calls instead for the defeat of communism. His moralistic fervor and readiness for world-wide action qualify Twining as an extreme right-wing Globalist. He goes far beyond others in viewing virtually any compromise with the major Communist powers as appeasement, and in recommending termination of diplomatic relations with the Soviet Union.*

Terms of reference and adjustments of basic national security policy within the foreseeable future will be profoundly affected by the American government's judgment as to the intent and capabilities of the various Communist governments which exist throughout the world today.

It may be that in the process of governmental evolution, the Communist system can become sufficiently civilized to believe in a world that guarantees freedom and the dignity of man and subscribes to the rule of law and order. Certainly, the basic peaceful attitudes of the majority of the men and women behind the Iron Curtain indicate that such evolution would be inevitable. However, the leadership of a nation, as vividly demonstrated by Adolf Hitler, can coerce millions of people into circumstances, ideologies, and actions which they do not really desire. This can easily happen with respect to the militant, frustrated, narrow, and conspiratorial leadership characteristic of the Communist world. All civilized men on both sides of the Iron Curtain hope that this will not happen. However, it might happen.

The political-military problem of the United States and the Free World has become more complex because of what appears, at least on the surface, to be a gradual breakup of what we once referred

From *Neither Liberty Nor Safety* by Nathan F. Twining, pp. 271–281, 288–294, 297–298. Copyright © 1966 by Nathan F. Twining. Reprinted by permission of Holt, Rinehart and Winston, Inc.

to as the "monolithic Communist world" or sometimes as the "Sino-Soviet Bloc." We now seem to have three general types of Communist governments:

1. The governments of the Eastern European satellites—Poland, Hungary, Czechoslovakia, Bulgaria, Rumania, and East Germany.
2. The Red Chinese government, allied with such fanatic and inconsequential nations as Albania, North Korea, and North Vietnam.
3. The Russian government itself.

There are other Communist governments, quasi-Communist governments, and opportunistic governmental leaders scattered throughout the world, of course—Egypt, Algeria, Cuba, Indonesia, and some of the foundling states in Africa. However, these entities have no real power base with which to seriously threaten the security of the United States for many years to come.

The U.S. Joint Chiefs of Staff, in their constant study of the national defense problem, list and analyze all countries of the world, small or large, friend, foe, or neutral, as one of the many factors pertinent to their responsibilities for national security planning. However, I will confine myself to the three general types of major Communist powers which exist, as a matter of fact and as a matter of serious military concern in today's world.

The governments of the Eastern European Soviet satellites (Albania excluded), while generally communistic in nature, are not militant protagonists of the theory that the Marxist-Leninist concept should dominate the entire world. We could probably get along with them if they did not have an economic-political-military gun at their heads. Nevertheless, they usually vote against Free World objectives in the forum of the United Nations, and their military forces constitute a potential threat to Western Europe as an augmentation of Soviet power in event of general war. However, if I were a Russian strategic planner, I would consider these countries as unreliable allies.

Red China under its present leadership seems to me at this writing to be practically a hopeless case. Naked force seems to be the only logic which the leadership of that unfortunate nation can comprehend. The ultimate objectives of China's leaders are certainly the subjugation and communization of all Southeast Asia, the Indonesian area, the Philippines, and Australia. However, their time schedule for conquest is probably not fixed—simply because they now lack the physical power to accomplish the objective. The aggressiveness and boldness of the Red Chinese government will undoubtedly increase as their nuclear stockpile and means of delivery continue to grow. At the moment, however, Red China is a paper tiger and constitutes no real military threat to the United States. In any war with mainland China in the near future we could knock them out practically overnight if we chose to use nuclear weapons. The Chinese Communists know this fact of life and will undoubtedly be careful during the near future. However, their ultimate objective is *Conquest*—and the future we face will become increasingly dangerous as their nuclear power develops. Consequently, in dealing with that government, I would have a very short fuse on the problem. If we are to prevent the present Red Chinese leadership from pursuing a pattern of violence and conquest, we should be prepared to identify the issues before that nation has developed an atomic arsenal.

With respect to Russia itself, the basic question is: Do we, or *do we not* now have a cooperative enemy?

If I were about to presume that the Russian government had gentled and modified its character to include earnest regard for human dignity and a world of law and order, I would ask for some substantial proof before accepting the premise. The proof would be easy to come by. It would involve the four points I have mentioned on earlier pages.

1. The elimination of the Iron Curtain and the establishment of an open society such as that existing in the Free World.
2. The elimination of the ruthless controls which still enslave the Eastern European satellites, and concurrent permission for these enslaved ethnic groups to determine their own destiny.
3. The elimination of organized subversion throughout the world and the tampering of that subversive apparatus with the internal security affairs of other nations.
4. A governmental pronouncement, adopted as a matter of real policy, that the Communist movement no longer is dedicated to the destruction of all other forms of civilized society.

If the present leadership of the Communist conspiracy were sincere about "coexistence" and actually desired elimination of tensions between East and West, these four steps could be taken with no delay. In the absence of even one demonstrated move in this direction,

I must doubt the sincerity of the apparent "coexistence" program and the peaceful intentions of the Sino-Soviet bloc.

I use the obsolete term "Sino-Soviet bloc" deliberately, even though much has been said recently about the ideological schism which exists between Russia and China. I cannot take this schism too seriously, or believe that it necessarily works in our own behalf, because two things are clear: if it does exist, the United States now has two enemies instead of one, both with the same announced objective—the destruction of the institutions and values of the Free World. And, when the chips are down, there can be no real doubt that the two would join forces to eliminate Western values, and then settle their own differences at a later time in history. So, in looking toward the future, the military establishment must assume that the objectives of the Communist credo remain *as stated by that conspiracy*. There has been no convincing evidence provided to the contrary.

If the United States were to assume the contrary viewpoint, it should disarm at once. If it does not make the assumption that the Russian Bear has gentled its fierce appetites during an evolutionary domestication, elementary prudence would indicate that America had better keep her guard up. Keeping the guard up, in this world of modern technology, means the elimination of constraints on our technological progress, gaining the lead, and remaining technologically ahead of the enemy at any point in time in actual fighting hardware. Actually, what is occurring is that this government has not made a clear decision with respect to either premise. It does not have sufficient trust in the enemy to disarm completely, nor will it allow the fullest preparation for the eventuality of deceit.

Because the government fretfully clings to indecision, it has imposed constraints on vital areas of U.S. technological development which can be capitalized upon by the enemy, if he so chooses, at some future time. As specific examples, U.S. nuclear weapons programs, nuclear propulsion and power programs, aircraft programs, and national military space programs are moving along at a rate far below that which is attainable through the full application of the scientific genius and the industrial know-how of the Free World.

The Basic Premise

I can summarize my views on national security planning into two sentences. The leaders of an organized conspiracy have sworn to destroy America and the Free World by one means or another, and there is no real evidence available at this time to indicate that their objective has been changed. Therefore, we had better be prepared to fight to maintain our liberty.

The Initiative

Having made the assumption that we do in fact live in a dangerous world and that we do confront an organized system dedicated to our destruction, the first element of national security policy would appear to be, in terms of elementary logic, the elimination or neutralization of that system.

Elimination, destruction, or neutralization requires initiative. In its definition of any of these nouns, the U.S. government should not constantly be in a position of defensive reaction to the subversion, probing, thrusts, and overt military actions initiated by its opponents. We should have a plan of our own which is focused on consciously and consistently probing and implementing actions to neutralize the enemy.

We may say that we have done some of the things necessary to take the initiative through such operations as economic and military aid and the Peace Corps, but these programs have had very limited objectives. As a nation, we have still said that we will "contain" rather than "neutralize." As a consequence, the United States seems to be fighting a battle in which it constantly retreats on the political, on the geographic, and on the technological fronts of war.

The power of the initiative might be related to the principle of surprise. Without initiative, the best one can do is to hold one's own. With the power of initiative, the opposition can be destroyed. It would therefore seem axiomatic that the first principle of our national security policy would be to seize and maintain the initiative in all dimensions of modern war; to include the economic, psychological, political, military, and the technological.

If the government were to implement a policy involving initiative for America, the first logical step would not be to start an indiscriminate nuclear war. But, the nation might be able to revert to some of its earlier judgments with respect to the nature of communism. Over a period of years, in its attempts toward accommodation and creation of a peaceful world, our government has gone a long way toward accepting the basic immorality of the Communist system. Americans might now ask their government if it had the moral right to agree to a world in which millions of people were kept in a condition of slavery, and to accept such condition through continued recognition of the Soviet Union as a legitimate government. Many people have rationalized the recognition by the United States of the U.S.S.R. as a legitimate government with the argument that the United States obtains more from the relationship than does the U.S.S.R. The argument is that in the absence of recognition of the present Russian government, America would not have access to vitally needed intelligence information. I have never taken this argument seriously because, first, while a person is behind the Iron Curtain he sees mostly what has been determined for him to see, and second, because there are other intelligence techniques available which can provide us with much of the vital security information which we need. From this viewpoint it would appear thoroughly logical to *break diplomatic relations* with the U.S.S.R. and to insist on the payment of its overdue indebtedness to the United Nations of some sixty million dollars.

How can our government really rationalize the economic boycott against Cuba and our failure to recognize Communist China as a legitimate government when the United States maintains diplomatic relationships with the original villain, the U.S.S.R. The might of Cuba constitutes no threat, in a purely military sense, to the United States. Cuba cannot destroy this country and the United States could destroy that entire little island. Red China, likewise, constitutes no immediate military threat. At the present time, America could destroy the power base of Communist China in one overnight blow by utilizing only the power of the U.S. Navy's 7th Fleet which is already deployed in Pacific waters. Red China *will* constitute a threat, in the near future, if allowed to continue with the development of nuclear weapons, and the development of means of delivery of these weapons. This can happen much quicker than most wishful thinkers are inclined to believe. However, at the moment, Red China constitutes no real military threat to the security of the power base of the United States, and could not defend itself effectively if we decided to attack with nuclear weapons.

The U.S.S.R. does constitute such a threat. And yet, by some curious quirk of logic, policy, and circumstance, the United States persists in exercising the diplomatic niceties usually reserved for cooperative and civilized nations.

Economic and Military Aid

A policy embodying initiative would affect our allies and the so-called "neutral" nations of the world, as well as our enemies. The ordinary citizen might say, with some evidence of substantiation in history, that you are either "for me" or "against me." This type of hard-boiled judgment could profoundly affect the worldwide application of U.S. military and economic aid.

I find it extremely difficult to rationalize the expenditure of United States taxpayers' dollars on aid to countries which align themselves with the enemy and which consistently vote against the principles of civilized behavior in the United Nations. If America believes that there is a conspiracy dedicated to her destruction, how can she really rationalize the vast expenditure of United States treasure in Poland and Yugoslavia, and how can America rationalize the subsidy of the U.S.S.R. through the provision of millions of tons of wheat to feed populations which are the victim of its own conspiracy? Such efforts seem to me to be a subsidy of communism and living proof to the peoples of those countries that the Communist system is working.

Even against this backdrop of self-contradiction and anomaly, the strictly military viewpoint would require a totally different treatment of so-called neutral nations than has been our practice during the last decade. The State Department argument for military and economic assistance to neutral nations is always premised with the conviction that if "you don't help them, you will drive them into the arms of the enemy."

I remember so vividly when, in the aftermath of World War II, the Chinese Communists were labeled by many people in the State Department as simple "agrarian" reformers. According to them, the Red Chinese leaders were really not Communists, they simply wanted a reform of the Chinese Nationalist government. I can also remember so vividly that at many National Security Council meetings, which I attended, the problem of the emergence of Castro in Cuba was discussed and his ultimate objectives were debated. The argument against firm United States action in Cuba, to prevent the establishment of a Communist beachhead in this hemisphere, was usually countered by the statement that "Castro is not a Communist, he is simply a patriot attempting to overthrow the dictator Battista; do not push him too far, because you will push him into the arms of communism." History shows what happened to both China and Cuba.

It is therefore difficult to understand the favored treatment of neutrals, as opposed to the positive help which might be given to real friends who actually oppose communism. In the face of the stark realities of the world in which we live, my judgment would be against squandering the wealth of the United States in support of neutralist governments. Let them alone until they make up their minds. If they want to "go Communist," let the U.S.S.R. support them, rather than the United States taxpayer, because, after all, most of them can contribute very little to defense of the Free World.

The question of colonialism and support of our Western Allies, of course, presents somewhat the same problem. Colonialism is an ugly word these days in most of the press of the world, but unfortunately, it has never been subjected to the type of critical analysis that our government is attempting to employ through the cost/effectiveness procedure with respect to its own weapons of war. I have never seen a State Department "white paper" on the subject of colonialism.

This problem might be reduced to a single question as follows: do human beings want to live in a primitive society, or do we prefer the values of civilization? After all, colonialism developed because some people of the earth, living in a land of splendid natural resources, did not develop the genius nor the inspiration to capitalize upon the fruits of a bountiful nature. It was only through the genius and the work of the colonialists that the latent capabilities of these areas of the world were brought into a reality. Now that his genius has been successful, in some cases for many generations, the colonialist is suddenly "an unwanted oppressor" holding down the people who inhabited the area before he arrived. The point is that justice would indicate that the colonialist should have some rights.

As a nation we have not done very well in supporting some of our allies with military aid in respect to the colonial issue. We have gone along with the concept that the vote of one man or the vote of one nation in world affairs (that one man or that one nation having no real responsibility) is as good as that of the vote of a responsible, creative, people. We have thereby abdicated the world of reality and the world in which power factors are still important.

Apologists for our aid policy insist that the United States should give economic and military aid "without strings attached." I do not understand this philosophy. Why shouldn't we have strings, yattached," as a *quid pro quo,* for the resources and the wealth which our government takes away from our people, and our own industrial development, and gives to others? "Strings attached" seems to have some kind of an obnoxious political connotation. However, I see absolutely no point in giving either economic or military aid to neutral countries who do not care to support our fundamental beliefs before the United Nations. I see even less reason for providing economic and military aid to Communist countries that conspire toward our ultimate destruction. We are digging America's grave when we permit our government to rescue Communist countries from the pitfalls and failures of their own economic system, feeding them and giving them other material aid paid for out of the pockets of the American taxpayers.

A reversal of American policy toward neutral countries would, of course, generate a violent emotional reaction around the world. However, no one seems to love us anyhow. We cannot buy love, but at least we might reestablish respect.

*   *   *

In this summary of contemporary military affairs, as I have reported them, it has been necessary to move from the area of purely military affairs into the area of political-military affairs. This has been necessary because the two areas are inseparable and mutually interacting and I have been in a position to see, very vividly, the impact of political action on the capability of our military forces to ensure and maintain the physical security of this free land. After all, America maintains a military establishment for a single purpose—to defend and maintain our freedom.

People see the events of the times from their own limited perspective. Mine is a military perspective—it was my life and my career for forty-four years. I am aware that there is no special virtue necessarily associated with long service in any kind of an organization. Quite to the contrary, an organization may frequently become ineffective if the "Old Guard" stays too long and the young, the fresh are held in check, are not allowed to emerge when changing times and circumstances demand change. However, when dealing with the most vital problem of humanity—freedom itself—some reasonable continuity of responsibility, in terms of logic, would seem to have merit. I do not know whether a man in uniform should stay on for one war or three wars, or for twenty years, thirty years, or forty years —but I do know that men and women both in uniform and as career civil servants in government generally have a greater sense of continuity of responsibility than do transients on the scene. Nevertheless I am compelled to view the current trends of national security organization and planning with some apprehension.

Heritage

The next four years can be very critical years of our brief life as a nation. President Johnson has inherited, among other problems, the following circumstances:

1. The results of this nation's post-World War II compromises, including the loss of China to communism, the German problem, De Gaulle, and the enslavement of the Eastern European satellites.
2. The growth to significant power of the world-wide Communist movement.
3. The policy of containment; the progressive loss of freedom in Southeast Asia; the Congo, Cuba, and still unresolved stalemate in Korea, South Vietnam, Laos, Cambodia, and hostile Indonesia.
4. The emerging dominance of the new, small, and sometimes irresponsible members of the United Nations.
5. The U.S.S.R. as a massive nuclear and technological power.
6. The emergence of Red China as a nuclear power.
7. The deterioration of solidarity in NATO, SEATO, and CENTO.
8. The results of the 1958 uninspected moratorium on nuclear weapons testing and the Test Ban Treaty of the Kennedy Administration.
9. The precedent of governmental fear of escalation and proliferation.
10. A highly centralized defense establishment under a single civilian Chief of Staff and a civilian General Staff.
11. International economic problems of great difficulty and great importance, sometimes referred to as the "Gold Flow Problem."
12. The basic orientation of our national space program to "space for peaceful purposes."

*   *   *

Current Trends

It is much too early, as this book goes to press, to judge the performance of the Johnson Administration from a national security viewpoint or, for that matter, from any other viewpoint. It can easily be observed, however, that the policies of this Administration will not be a blueprint of those of the Kennedy years; changes are in process. I will not comment on the fabric of legislative and executive actions which relate to the current emphasis on the Great Society, but the more significant trends in political-military affairs should be mentioned.

Policy With Respect to Vietnam

It is probably fair to observe that the increased pressure on North Vietnam, through air strikes against targets on North Vietnamese territory and through build-up of American ground forces in the area, is a form of escalation which the policy makers of the Kennedy Administration would have been extremely reluctant to undertake. The Johnson Administration apparently is not going to give up easily in Vietnam.

It was only a few short years ago that American military personnel (ordered by their government into Vietnam as "Military Advisors") were not allowed to wear the United States uniform, and even the commanding general was officially known as "Mister." Our government has discarded this practice and the Johnson Administration has gone part way in carrying the war to the enemy.

On the negative side, sanctuaries are still granted to the seat of government of North Vietnam and to logistic support lines leading into Red China. And, of course, detailed control of tactical military operations by the White House still persists. Additionally, our government has advised the enemy that Hanoi is safe and that the United States will not use even small nuclear weapons tactically.

Therefore, at this writing, while it seems that the Johnson Administration has been bolder in Vietnam than the Kennedy Administration, still the Johnson Administration has not gone full out in the change of policy. The United States continues to operate under self-imposed restrictions and seems to be getting mired down in a man-to-man war of attrition on the Asian land mass. (A war in which for many years we have said we would never become involved.)

The Chinese Communist Camp

Behind the North Vietnamese invasion of the territory and the sovereign rights of the South Vietnamese lies Red Communist China. The Viet Cong could not possibly undertake the types of operations which have been employed without both political and matériel support from Red China. During the latter days of the Korean War, under the Administration of President Eisenhower, this nation shied away from direct involvement with Red China. U.S. military forces could neutralize sufficient military targets in Red China overnight and set that nation back to an industrial and technical base more consistent with its medieval concept of government, law, and order. If ever there was a "paper tiger" in fact, it was not the United States of America. It was Red China—and still is.

However, Red China is moving with more than the bluff and the bluster which is only the current tactic of its irrational and suspicious leadership. If we give the Hitler-type mentality which now dominates Red China a little more time, we will have a real problem. Up to this writing, the current Administration has done nothing about this clearly developing threat.

In short, the Johnson Administration has thus far given no assurance that it will face up to the Red Chinese leadership at places and times which are most favorable to the destiny of free men.

The Dominican Republic

In April, 1965, the United States moved military forces into the Dominican Republic during a situation of civil revolt. The prompt action by the Johnson Administration in quelling another Communist takeover in the Caribbean deserves mention and credit. As usual, the Communist nations issued bitter denunciations of the action, but they did nothing more in an overt military sense. Our own domestic grouping of left-wing pacifists, compromisers, appeasers, and ill-informed adolescent students also objected to the act. If these American groups could only think in terms of the power factors which exist in the world today, they would realize that they were supporting Communist policy in their criticism of the actions of our own government.

The facts of the case appear to indicate quite clearly that the President's actions were fully justified and were necessary to the long-term preservation of freedom in this hemisphere. It is one thing to have true wars of national liberation, such as our own War for Independence; a totally different circumstance exists when a foreign power uses a smaller nation to engineer a revolution which will be controlled from the outside. Such revolutions lead only to slavery, to communism, and to the loss of free institutions. No proof of this allegation need be made other than the simple question: "Where are the plebiscites which would give self-determination to the Eastern European satellites?"

*   *   *

Decisions Facing the Administration

The thirty-sixth President of the United States is confronted with a monumental task in leading this nation through the labyrinth. Some leading and possibly prophetic questions might be asked as follows:

1. How will he reverse the ever-growing "status quo" philosophy, the "no-win" philosophy and again make the United States the master of its own destiny?
2. Will he retain the appeasers in government, and in some of the advisory committees to the White House, or will he discard them?
3. What will be his continuing attitude toward escalation, proliferation, and safe sanctuaries to enemy forces which are engaged in or are supporting aggression?
4. What will be his attitude toward giving aid to those nations who oppose America's principles and/or constantly vote against America in the United Nations?
5. What will be his attitude toward this nation's alliances and how will he strengthen and unify the forces of freedom throughout the world?
6. What will be his attitude toward civil defense measures, super-megaton nuclear warheads (now possessed by the U.S.S.R. but not by the United States), military activities in space, a follow-on bomber to replace the B-52, and modernization of the Navy?
7. Will he keep the United States task force for nuclear-weapons testing ready to go in event of a Soviet abrogation of the nuclear test ban treaty?
8. What will he do to reestablish the legitimate freedom of speech of the uniformed members of the armed forces?

9. What will he do about the "building block" philosophy of technological development of military weapons systems?
10. What can he, or will he, do about restoring the prestige of the professional military establishment and placing military decisions on weaponry and tactics back into professional military hands?

Probably no man, in four years, can take actions which can compensate adequately for the mistakes of a generation. But he may be able to reverse the trend of the past five years.

George Liska
WAR AND ORDER

What sort of world view inspires an analyst to write "The destruction in South and North Vietnam becomes more bearable when one regards the war as . . . an increasingly symbolic contest, with both global and long-range significance for the cause of order. . . . Suffer as they do and must, the peoples of Vietnam are not the first or the last small people to render such a service to the larger commonweal"?

These are the words of George Liska, Research Associate with the Washington Center of Foreign Policy Research and Professor of Political Science at Johns Hopkins University. Professor Liska's writing makes for difficult reading but is worth the effort. In contrast to other Globalists, he begins by denying American uniqueness. Rather, he argues, we are only the latest in a long line of imperial powers who have performed the vital function of preserving the international order. Liska's hope is not unlike that of Realist critic Stanley Hoffmann—to keep "the flow of international life moving in the direction of an authentic, multiregional system." Not only, however, are his means different, but in the end Liska's hopes, like those of other Globalists, turn out to depend on Americans' exceptional quality as "a people which is less of an inbred tribe than any other in existence," and on the hope that "if only the United States, its people, and its leaders, could find in themselves the insight and resolve to apply the weary wisdom of the ages while retaining a leavening dose of original innocence, they might start something genuinely new and authentically revolutionary in the affairs of men."*

My argument is simple. American foreign policy has conformed to the evolutionary pattern of other major nations as the United States has moved from the favored conditions surrounding its origins into the full complexity of mature international life. Only a home-bound historiography, lacking in sympathetic understanding of the foreign policy predicaments of other (especially European) nations, can hold otherwise. Only such a self-centered outlook can continue to perceive the sweep of American foreign policy as categorically different from that of, say, Spain, France, or Britain, the other nations which at one point or another aspired to the privilege and submitted to the exigencies of paramount power.

From George Liska, *War and Order* (Baltimore: The Johns Hopkins Press, 1968), pp. 3–4, 15–18, 26–30, 49–53, 87–88, 92–95. Reprinted by permission.

* *War and Order*, pp. 108, 112.

It may be difficult to equate the ideas and ideologies underlying the Cortés of Castile and the U.S. Congress, the Crown of Rheims and the Constitution of Philadelphia, or even the Magna Carta and the Bill of Rights. It may be equally hazardous to compare the personal world-views of a Thomas Jefferson and a Philippe-Auguste, of a Clive and a Clay, or of a Medina Sidonia and a George Marshall, who, following upon the consolidators and the expansionists, wielded their sovereign's sword at crucial moments between supremacy and a balance of power. But it is possible to place in a single perspective the parallel sweep of the foreign policies of great nations in the proper temporal sequences. In such a perspective American foreign policy can be viewed as going through certain typical phases which, with an acceptable degree of interpretive distortion and actual discontinuities, marked other nations' policies in comparable international conditions. Similarities in overall development and dynamic then appear as more significant than the peculiarities of situation and style.

*   *   *

The imperial role of the United States should be perceived as a consequence of two converging conditions. On the one hand, we have the mature state of American foreign policy in its present phase, which is characterized by tension between a concern with the balance of power and an inclination toward supremacy. On the other hand, we have the present state of the international system, where there is the need for a modicum of order, if only as a condition of orderly long-term internal developments in critical countries, including the United States. The emphasis in evaluating the imperial role can be on the subjective aspect, stressing the actor's readiness or propensity to act expansively in terms of power, or it can be on the objective aspect, stressing the conditions of order and asserting responsibility. The emphasis is crucial, since it will influence or even determine one's attitude toward the involvement of the United States in military conflict. Such involvement is the unavoidable consequence of any but a parasitic or formal participation (be it exploitative, auxiliary, mediatory, or institutional) in much of contemporary international politics.

Conflict is still the distinctive feature of international politics outside the developed states of Europe and Japan, which are either

temporarily exhausted and demoralized or perhaps lastingly reformed. In the vaster unreclaimed areas, rampant with unsatisfied
grievances, the choice is one between structured conflict and un-
structured chaos. In practice this means that interventions may use
and oppose violence at different levels of deployment, utilizing different kinds of force. It also means that interventions may occur at different stages of both the disintegration of existing order and the
expansion of forces and powers committed to another vision of eventual order. In simpler terms, this means that a salient power like the
United States is rather restricted in its options. It can choose to fight
important but still limited engagements, such as that in Vietnam, at a
relatively early stage of dislocation in the regional structure of power
and will. Or it can choose to retrench until such time as it may have
to fight a bigger war or face more diffuse and even less coercible
elements of disorder under still less favorable conditions. The United
States chose to fight in Vietnam while there was still an authority
that was willing to supply manpower, a battleground, and a rationale
for the contest. It avoided the risk of having to fight later in conditions of spreading subversion by some and self-protective effacement
by others, on the mainland and possibly in the island realms of Asia.

The essence of the anti-interventionist or anti-imperial position is
to deny the dangers of inaction, while interventionists are inclined
to favor timely action even against "hypothetical" dangers. One side
believes in the automatic erosion (by local developments) and reciprocal paralysis (by conflicting ambitions and aspirations) of actual or
potential threats—Chinese, North Vietnamese, Communist, or other—
before they reach the point of clearly endangering the national security of the United States. The other side gives higher credence to
the probability, given the distribution of power and will in the world
generally and in Asia particularly, of a snow-balling momentum of
unchecked hostile forces—deemed disordering from the American
perspective—and of supine or submissive local responses to them.

The accuracy of the more pessimistic view cannot be convincingly
established even in retrospect if it is acted upon. All one can say for
pessimism about the predicament of men and states is that it forms
the basis of the traditional approach to statecraft. Only the pessimistic approach has been tested historically, and those adhering to it
have usually been successful in averting the particular age's idea of
supreme evil, even if often at considerable cost. To take the more

pessimistic position, to act to avert possible catastrophe where there might have been only the annoyance of local turbulence and inter- mittent terror, is to come to terms with a dreary prospect for this country: recurrent American use of force, even if, one may hope, in a more limited and manageable form than in Vietnam. Before deciding whether this prospect is tolerable, let us first look at the problem of conflict a little more closely. Then, after a review of feasible types of international order, we shall examine the elements of continuity and the conditions of possible change in international relations.

If participation in conflict is to be truly discretionary, the incidence of force must be shown to vary as a function of good intentions and prudent policies. The facts of the matter do not clearly support this particular kind of human omnipotence in international politics. The rough impression emerging from history is of a relatively constant sum of used force in different periods that are sufficiently short to be significant for an individual lifetime. Such a diagnosis, if correct, makes the use of force by the United States more acceptable. If conflict is inherent in any period of international politics, and if there is no sure way to escape from it, it makes sense for a major country to control the scale and distribution of conflict by timely engagement. Provided that the ordering power learns how to endure recurrent con- flicts, the tendency for the sum of conflict to remain constant will save it from being overwhelmed by too many concurrent engage- ments.

* * *

To accept an imperial role for the United States is to make proper adjustments in one's view of the present era's dominant conflict. In a world seen as bipolar, the principal function of the United States was (and may again become) to contain the Soviet Union or its successor to the role of the challenger. In a world seen as having a single focus in America's salient power, the key preoccupation and related American function has to do with a growing number of more varied threats.

The containment of the more assertive of the Communist great powers is still necessary; but it may well be secondary to the con- tainment of disorder caused ultimately by some form of insufficient power. Despite the nonfulfillment of the key expectation underlying the cold war—the ability of the Soviets to move toward material parity—the Soviet Union will go on trying to improve its position relative to the United States. It will stage comebacks as a global competitor from an improved position in nuclear deterrence and respectable diplomacy. It may even improve its conventional military resources, which are required for sustained intervention in areas remote from the home base. The best prospects for Soviet achievements would seem to be in Europe and in areas contiguous to the Eurasian heartland, including the traditional and traditionally frustrating Russian penetration in the Near and Middle East. In the Europe-centered orbit, Russia has a potentially beneficial role to play in preventing the United States from either arrogance or somnolence. But no readily visible effort at countercontainment is likely to nullify America's global material and military primacy, specifically in the non-European world, in the near future. Any reduction in American sway can result only frcm acts of self-denial which, fostered by self-doubt, may result in partial or complete self-debasement.

The second function of the United States, that of maintaining imperial order, rather than containing a rival power, bears on two types of disorder. At this point we shall indicate them only briefly. One class of disorders—in evidence in Vietnam—consists of acts controlled by an identifiable political will and intelligence; if unchecked, they give rise to international anarchy. The other class of disorders—displayed in the Congo—consist of actions which are in effect uncontrolled by an accountable agent; if allowed to spread, they give rise to chaos. Controlled disorder is intrinsically manageable, while diffuse disorder may become uncontrollable. The latter represents an even greater source of uneasiness than the first, since it threatens not only local positions but also the general predictability of behavior and calculable responsiveness to counteraction, including counterforce. The first threat is to a specific order; the second to the possibility of any order. The first arouses apprehensions; the latter generates a propensity to panic which can spread to otherwise stable bodies politic.

All order, just or unjust, rests in the last resort, if in different degrees, on force. This force—municipal, imperial, or multilateral community force—is employed in conflict with agents defined as those of disorder. Apart from the Communist states and the European powers, there are two available instruments for ordering force in the world today: the armed forces of the United States, in principle available for action anywhere, and the few cohesive and usable national armed forces of the lesser states, in principle available only for internal action or, at best, for multilateral peacekeeping operations which are strategically safeguarded by the United States. Where national military force is sufficient to insure order, the United States can abstain from intervening. Where it is not, as was the case in Vietnam, the United States will either have to fight (as the force behind a preferred order) or permit the substitution of a different order or of disorder. There do not seem to be other alternatives.

If this is true, it is not very significant to say that the insertion of American imperial power has made local insufficiencies still more pronounced. The relevant question is whether the American military and related input did or did not more than compensate for the aggravation. Nor is it pertinent to argue that revolutionary disorders succeed only where conditions are favorable to them, especially if the conditions isolated as determining are said to be governmental competence, popular will and support, traditions of submissiveness or sturdiness, and similar broad and ambiguous notions. So phrased the argument is circular and the judgment can only be retrospective. In most cases, conditions will actually be indeterminate and behavior will be susceptible of being swayed toward one or another outcome by the timely application of force. To argue, finally, that each situation of disorder is particular unto itself, responding to local conditions and resources, is to ignore what can be overemphasized but also unduly discounted: the presence or absence in the total environment of a power which, on the basis of precedents, may be regarded as having set the outer limits to tolerated disorder.

Such power, purposefully applied, can at present only be American power. To commit American power to a general role of upholding order would entail not only specific commitments (which may be tacit), but also specific performances (which must be visible). All three—role, commitment, performance—sharpen the position of the United States as the target of contrary and countered forces. But the position itself derives originally more from the fact that internationally the United States, like any powerful or wealthy group in an unstable and turbulent community, is the inescapable target of all those who are uninterested in legitimacy and express themselves in revolts against the existing order. It is, therefore, unrealistic to try to differentiate specific American interests, in separation from America's position, as the basis for policy; just as it is unrealistic to speculate about America's relation to violent change and revolution as the determinant of wider support for American policy. The position is largely given; the role derives from it with implacable logic; it may only be carried out with variable skill and achieve a variable degree of acceptance as preferable to available alternatives.

*   *   *

. . . Elementary order is at stake if violence or other coercive pressure is exerted in ways and for ends tantamount to international anarchy or chaos. International anarchy must not be equated with war. Rather, it entails an erosion or debasement of the standards of international behavior and interstate conflict. It is generated by deliberate and controlled employment of force or other coercive pressure which is locally disproportionate in magnitude, unmanageable or demoralizing in mode, and indeterminate in thrust. If left unchecked, such use of force can escalate to the point where it would be too costly for any ordering influence, individual or collective, to master.

The criteria of anarchy concern both goals and means. If the goals are expansive or indeterminate, they will require the backing of major force if they are to have a chance to succeed. The resulting local or regional imperialism, when unchecked or apparently irresistible, is the principal source of international anarchy. With regard to means, anarchy threatens when the mode of relevant behavior and the kind of force or coercion employed are difficult or impossible to oppose without resort to equivalent measures—such as infiltration, subversion, assassination of leaders, terrorization or deportation of politically passive populations.

The magnitude and the methods of locally employed power are, it would seem, the decisive criteria from the perspective of world order. It is, consequently, not a decisive consideration for the United States whether the local or regional imperialism is Communist or non-Communist: it can be engaged in by Sukarno's Indonesia, by Ho Chi Minh's Vietnam, by Communist China, or by Gandhian India. Expansion can be pursued, by Egypt in the name of Pan-Arabism or Arab socialism and by Israel in the name of Zionism or Israeli security, by Cuba on behalf of Castroism, or by a future Argentina on behalf of an updated variety of Peronism. There is, however, one aspect of expansion which is especially relevant for the United States as the power with the greatest stake in the existing degree of world order. This is the ultimate thrust of such expansionism, whatever its averred goal. The key concern is whether the drive to overthrow the existing distribution of power, authority, and rights, or to preclude its natural evolution, also aims at obstructing U.S. access to the area by means short of massive force.

The regime in North Vietnam qualified for American opposition by these standards. Independently or in collusion with Communist China it set out to destroy, first by sponsorship of subversion and later directly, any future chance for a balance of relatively autonomous power among the lesser states of former Indochina and, by plausible extension, of Southeast Asia. The related goal was to bar American access and participation in the shaping of such a balance or balances. It is because Sukarno had a similar and apparently self-perpetuating ambition, first against West New Guinea and then against Malaysia, that he too ought to have been overtly "confronted" by the United States rather than deviously countered by way of support for internal and British opposition.

American action against non-Communist expansionism is also mandatory because it alone can demonstrate ideological impartiality and, therefore, the credibility of the larger American purpose and of its predictability in implementation. For these reasons—the acceptance and thus legitimacy for its imperial role—the United States will have to curb Israel's present ambitions and some of its practices in the Near East, should they continue unabated.

International order also has a domestic dimension, in that tribal, class, regional, or communal strife can easily become unpredictable in the magnitude, mode, and ultimate thrust of violence. To differentiate this type of disorder from international anarchy, we call it here, in its extreme form, chaos. World order is at stake when this type of turbulence does not remain confined and isolated, but instead ramifies abroad, either by the design and doing of other states or by its own internal dynamic. Involvement of extraneous powers in internal disorders can in turn vary in intensity. It has been greater in the 1960s in the Belgian Congo and Yemen than in Nigeria or Colombia, for instance. When, by contrast, internal disorders spread to other countries or generate a pervasive atmosphere conducive to violence by their own momentum, external ramification is less immediately explosive but may be more difficult for international or extraneous agents to cope with. Although international involvement in the Congo was on the whole contained, propensity to violence spread to other African countries, most prominently to Nigeria, on a scale which has justified international concern even if it did not warrant any but indirect counteraction. Actual or potential breakup in and of new countries that often perpetuate accidental colonial boundaries—for example, the Congo, Nigeria, Indonesia—ought to be judged individually. Significant criteria are the prospective viability of the dissident group in terms of its size and the intensity of its opposition to the central authority—an intensity which is apt to reflect the strength of the group and of its grievances.

The two types of disorder—chaos and anarchy—converge when a grossly inadequate economic performance leads to attempts to compensate externally for internal stagnation and instability. Nkrumah's Ghana and Sukarno's Indonesia fall into this category. By contrast, other unstable and inadequately developing countries like Burma and India have been satisfied with reflecting their internal conditions in foreign policies that are no more than wayward. They are almost as difficult to fit into a coherent structure of world order.

Unchecked international ramifications of internal decay and turbulence affect the United States and its role in the maintenance of order in several ways. They tend, first, to inhibit American access to the area because they give rise to anti-Americanism. Second, they are likely to compel the United States to share whatever access it retains. Third, internal breakdown of public order in one country can set off cumulative international chaos in areas where order is always precarious. Somewhat like international anarchy, such chaos is not to be equated with just any violence. It stands rather for a chain reaction of uncontrollable violence which makes conventional ordering power inadequate once the turbulence has been allowed to exceed a certain intensity or scope. The Congo is in this category—a fact which was responsible for two American unilateral interventions in that country after the U.N.'s withdrawal.

If acted upon with some consistency and a judicious mix of instruments, these broad criteria of elementary order and action against disorder do not cast the United States in the role of an omnipresent policeman. For the United States the criteria imply no more (if no less) than continuous readiness for policing action wherever it is necessary to keep the flow of international life moving in the general direction of an authentic, multiregional system. The goal is a self-sustaining global system rather than one sustained by the power of a single state or by the ramifying conflict of the two most powerful states. To this end, in the vital, formative period of the system some entity must preserve the basic conditions for individual or collective self-help by those organized groups (states, factions, or parties) threatened by international anarchy or chaos. Once one admits the need for such an ordering function, it becomes a matter of expediency whether a policing action is carried out by the leading world power in cooperation with other powers and the United Nations, whenever possible and sufficient, or unilaterally, whenever necessary as an alternative to collective failure.

* * *

The domestic implications of the controversy over Vietnam are equally important. The key domestic issue is the racial crisis. There is an interdependence between affirmation of American prestige and power vis-à-vis Hanoi and its allies and the prospect for a semi-orderly integration of American society in the face of Black Power. In the last resort, whatever order exists in the United States depends on the government's known will and ability to deal firmly with hostile force. A collapse of this reputation abroad would strengthen the appeal and increase the credibility of domestic advocates of violence as a safe and profitable way to "racial equality." Any administration conspicuously thwarted abroad would be bound to have the greatest difficulty in dealing with domestic crises. The consequence of default in the exercise of the imperial role might very well be a Second American Revolution for the "independence" of a hitherto "colonized" group. An internationally discredited American government might have as much trouble mastering the second revolution as a similarly handicapped British government had with the first, or as the Russian regime had with the revolutions of 1905 and 1917.

Historical analogies of this kind may seem inapplicable to the United States. Also, new potentialities for managing domestic conflict—plus compulsions for avoiding international entanglements—may seem inherent in expansive industrial societies. Yet the traditional wisdom that encourages the display of fortitude wherever most feasible or least painful cannot be fully ignored. . . .

The debate over American foreign policy which has boiled up as a result of the Vietnam war has been fraught with conflicting affirmations and conceits. . . .

[An important issue] concerns the relation of internal and external effort. All are in favor of coming to grips with social and urban problems in the United States. But whereas the internationalists of yesterday were all for large-scale foreign economic aid, the liberal anti-interventionists have more recently been comparing the billions allegedly wasted abroad and those presently needed for domestic programs. In doing so they seem to forget that a domestic "giveaway," like the foreign expenditure, would not have the desired effect unless it occurred within the right political framework; unless economic aid is matched with authoritative administration, compassion with control, commitment to progress with capacity to foster order, and commitment to order with a capacity to control and resolve internal conflict.

It may be that, in the very short run, even a rich nation like the United States has to determine its priorities when allocating resources either for a war on the Vietcong or on poverty. But it is doubtful that this dichotomy applies to the really crucial underlying issues of social and political integration of a dynamic body politic. Social integration in conditions of order and an expansive foreign policy are actually interdependent in the longer run. Generally considered, the degree to which it is harder to predict, control, and recreate conditions and events in the international arena than in the realms of domestic policy will promote foreign-policy activism and interventionism on the part of states which can at all have an active foreign policy. This will offend those who resent the natural and contrary tendency to inertia in domestic politics. But, a failure to accommodate policy to the special needs of the foreign arena is apt, sooner or later, to lead to crises blamed on prior inaction which will adversely affect conditions in the domestic arena as well.

There is a more basic aspect to the interdependence of domestic and foreign policies. A successful past foreign policy, like America's, which helped create the conditions of an expanding body politic beset with unavoidable competition among established and rising group interests, will acquire a momentum of its own. Such momentum will have to be maintained if peaceful adjustment of internal group conflicts is to be facilitated over time by the continuing expansion of outlets and targets for political attention and controversy. If there can be too little concern with internal issues, there can be an overconcentration on them; the dispersal of interest and resources is often preferable to their polarization and confrontation.

Any active, far-reaching foreign policy will go beyond the "bread" of foreign aid and the "games" of U.N. debates and cultural diplomacy. It will involve armed action which, once it assumes the form of protracted war, will unavoidably create the impression of conflict between sociopolitical integration and foreign-policy intervention. The impression is false. Whereas a growing state is typically drawn into expansive foreign action by conflicts involving the international balance of war-making power, at a later stage such a state will be more typically led to perpetuate an expansive policy as a condition of peacefully balancing the interests of relatively receding and advancing subjects of interest and power within the body politic itself. When this happens, and it is happening in and for the United States, national security as the principal motive and warrant for expansive foreign-policy action is superseded by national stability and cohesion. The two add up to something like national integrity when, next to the gratification of more prosaic drives and needs, one assigns a proper place to the satisfaction of the higher need for meaningful individual and collective political function, abroad as well as at home, and comes to terms with the fact that each arena attracts actors with a different (and potentially antagonistic) conception of worthwhile political action and thus, in the last resort, of the good life.

The crisis normally attending transition from a parochial to an imperial body politic, often in a frustrating first imperial war, reflects the difficulties implicit in reassessing the interrelation between domestic and external needs and efforts in the domain of action, and in effecting the switch from national security to national integrity in the domains of motivation and justification for action abroad. Without such reevaluation, however, it is impossible to generate either the consent or the authority for adapting domestic group demands to external obligations. International obligations are denied validity as long as they are seen as obstacles to material satisfactions, hindering efforts to implement the obligations in such a way as to heighten their potential utility as an avenue and a precondition to a wider range of satisfactions. The debate and the contest are diverted from the valid and essential qualitative question of how to implement a recurrent constant of involvement to the quantitative question of how much to retain and discard of a presumably variable and optional commitment. The basic condition of implementing the imperial role in a sustained manner is to shield the critical and persistent foreign-policy modes from carping and changeable domestic moods. An updated organization of national power and public powers might conduce to that end. The legitimizing basis for a partial disconnection between domestic and foreign politics in a democratic society is the acceptance of the underlying interconnection between international and domestic stability in the longer run. For the public to accept recurrent external involvement, as an alternative to concurrent internal and external anarchy, is a vital condition to be fulfilled if the United States is to continue its evolution from a middle-class democracy to an imperial democracy multiracially structured, socially and economically mobile, and internationally responsible.

II REALIST CRITICS

FIGURE 2. A Realist view. (Editorial cartoon by Pat Oliphant; copyright, *The Denver Post.* Reprinted with permission of Los Angeles Times Syndicate.)

Hans J. Morgenthau

THE MORALITY OF THE NATIONAL INTEREST

Hans J. Morgenthau, for many years Albert A. Michelson Distinguished Service Professor of Political Science and Modern History at the University of Chicago, is the leading contemporary Realist theorist of international relations. His classic text, Politics Among Nations, *elaborates his view that the key to international politics is "the concept of interest defined in terms of power." The task of the statesman, according to Morgenthau, is to pursue the national interest with a decent regard for others doing the same. The danger to peace in our time has been the rise of "nationalistic universalism," different varieties of which have animated the foreign policies of both great powers in the Cold War. The first selection, taken from a volume published in 1952, contains the core claim of Professor Morgenthau's approach. The second reading, reprinted from a book published in 1969, offers a bill of particulars against globalism.*

THE MORAL DIGNITY OF THE NATIONAL INTEREST

The fundamental error that has thwarted American foreign policy in thought and action is the antithesis of national interest and moral principles. The equation of political moralizing with morality and of political realism with immorality is itself untenable. The choice is not between moral principles and the national interest, devoid of moral dignity, but between one set of moral principles divorced from political reality, and another set of moral principles derived from political reality.

The moralistic detractors of the national interest are guilty of both intellectual error and moral perversion. The nature of the intellectual error must be obvious from what has been said thus far, as it is from the record of history: a foreign policy guided by moral abstractions, without consideration of the national interest, is bound to fail; for it accepts a standard of action alien to the nature of the action itself. All the successful statesmen of modern times from Richelieu to

Churchill have made the national interest the ultimate standard of their policies, and none of the great moralists in international affairs has attained his goals.

The perversion of the moralizing approach to foreign policy is threefold. That approach operates with a false concept of morality, developed by national societies but unsuited to the conditions of international society. In the process of its realization, it is bound to destroy the very moral values it sets out to promote. Finally, it is derived from a false antithesis between morality and power politics, thus arrogating to itself all moral values and placing the stigma of immorality upon the theory and practice of power politics.

There is a profound and neglected truth hidden in Hobbes's extreme dictum that the state creates morality as well as law and that there is neither morality nor law outside the state. Universal moral principles, such as justice or equality, are capable of guiding political action only to the extent that they have been given concrete content and have been related to political situations by society. What justice means in the United States can within wide limits be objectively ascertained; for interests and convictions, experiences of life and institutionalized traditions have in large measure created a consensus concerning what justice means under the conditions of American society. No such consensus exists in the relations between nations. For above the national societies there exists no international society so integrated as to be able to define for them the concrete meaning of justice or equality, as national societies do for their individual members. In consequence, the appeal to moral principles by the representative of a nation vis-à-vis another nation signifies something fundamentally different from a verbally identical appeal made by an individual in his relations to another individual member of the same national society. The appeal to moral principles in the international sphere has no concrete universal meaning. It is either so vague as to have no concrete meaning that could provide rational guidance for political action, or it will be nothing but the reflection of the moral preconceptions of a particular nation and will by that same token be unable to gain the universal recognition it pretends to deserve.

Whenever the appeal to moral principles provides guidance for political action in international affairs, it destroys the very moral principles it intends to realize. It can do so in three different ways. Universal moral principles can serve as a mere pretext for the pursuit of national policies. In other words, they fulfill the functions of those ideological rationalizations and justifications to which we have referred before. They are mere means to the ends of national policies, bestowing upon the national interest the false dignity of universal moral principles. The performance of such a function is hypocrisy and abuse and carries a negative moral connotation.

The appeal to moral principles may also guide political action to that political failure which we have mentioned above. The extreme instance of political failure on the international plane is national suicide. It may well be said that a foreign policy guided by universal moral principles, by definition relegating the national interest to the background, is under contemporary conditions of foreign policy and warfare a policy of national suicide, actual or potential. Within a national society the individual can at times afford, and may even be required, to subordinate his interests and even to sacrifice his very existence to a supra-individual moral principle—for in national societies such principles exist, capable of providing concrete standards for individual action. What is more important still, national societies take it upon themselves within certain limits to protect and promote the interests of the individual and, in particular, to guard his existence against violent attack. National societies of this kind can exist and fulfill their functions only if their individual members are willing to subordinate their individual interests in a certain measure to the common good of society. Altruism and self-sacrifice are in that measure morally required.

The mutual relations of national societies are fundamentally different. These relations are not controlled by universal moral principles concrete enough to guide the political actions of individual nations. What again is more important, no agency is able to promote and protect the interests of individual nations and to guard their existence—and that is emphatically true of the great powers—but the individual nations themselves. To ask, then, a nation to embark upon altruistic policies oblivious of the national interest is really to ask something immoral. For such disregard of the individual interest, on the part of nations as of individuals, can be morally justified only by the existence of social institutions, the embodiment of concrete moral principles, which are able to do what otherwise the individual would

have to do. In the absence of such institutions it would be both fool-
ish and morally wrong to ask a nation to forego its national interests
not for the good of a society with a superior moral claim but for a
chimera. Morally speaking, national egotism is not the same as individual egotism because the functions of the international society are
not identical with those of a national society.

The immorality of a politically effective appeal to moral abstractions in foreign policy is consummated in the contemporary phenomenon of the moral crusade. The crusading moralist, unable in the
absence of an integrated national society to transcend the limits of
national moral values and political interests, identifies the national
interest with the manifestation of moral principles, which is, as we
have seen, the typical function of ideology. Yet the crusader goes
one step farther. He projects the national moral standards onto the
international scene not only with the legitimate claim of reflecting
the national interest, but with the politically and morally unfounded
claim of providing moral standards for all mankind to conform to in
concrete political action. Through the intermediary of the universal
moral appeal the national and the universal interest become one and
the same thing. What is good for the crusading country is by definition good for all mankind, and if the rest of mankind refuses to accept such claims to universal recognition, it must be converted with
fire and sword.

There is already an inkling of this ultimate degeneration of international moralism in Wilson's crusade to make the world safe for democracy. We see it in full bloom in the universal aspirations of Bolshevism. Yet to the extent that the West, too, is persuaded that it
has a holy mission, in the name of whatever moral principle, first to
save the world and then to remake it, it has itself fallen victim to the
moral disease of the crusading spirit in politics. If that disease should
become general, as well it might, the age of political moralizing
would issue in one or a series of religious world wars. The fanaticism
of political religions would, then, justify all those abominations un-
known to less moralistic but more politically minded ages and for
which in times past the fanaticism of other-worldly religions provided
a convenient cloak.

THE UNITED STATES: PARAMOUNT OR EQUAL?

Isolation and Globalism

American foreign policy has tended, in this century, to move back and forth between the extremes of an indiscriminate isolationism and an equally indiscriminate internationalism or globalism. While the two positions are obviously identified with utterly different foreign policies —indiscriminate involvement here, indiscriminate abstention there— it is important to note that they share the same assumptions about the nature of the political world and the same negative attitudes toward foreign policy correctly understood. They are equally hostile to that middle ground of subtle distinctions, complex choices, and precarious manipulations which is the proper sphere of foreign policy.

Both deny the existence of priorities in foreign policy which are derived from a hierarchy of interests and the availability of power to support them. For both extremes, it is either all or nothing, either total involvement or total abstention. Both refuse to concern themselves with the concrete issues of foreign policy on their own merits—that is, in terms of the interests involved and the power available. While isolationism stops short of these concrete issues, globalism soars beyond them. Both assume the self-sufficiency of American power to protect and promote the American national interest either in indiscriminate abstention or indiscriminate involvement. While the isolationist used to say, "We don't need to have anything to do with the world, for we can take care of our own interests on our own terms," the Globalists say, "We shall take on the whole world, but only on our own terms." In short, isolationism is a kind of introverted globalism, and globalism is a kind of isolationism turned inside out. To stigmatize a position that falls short of such indiscriminate globalism as "neo-isolationism" is a polemic misuse of terms; it derives from the globalist assumption that indiscriminate involvement is, as it were, the natural stance of American policy.

Both attitudes, in different ways oblivious of political reality, substitute for the complex and discriminating mode of political thought

From *A New Foreign Policy for the United States* by Hans J. Morgenthau, pp. 15–18, 124–129. Copyright © 1969, by Praeger Publishers, Inc., New York. Reprinted by permission of Praeger Publishers, Inc., and the Pall Mall Press Ltd.

a simple approach, which in its simplicity is commensurate with the simplicity of their picture of the political world: the moral crusade. The isolationist's moralism is naturally negative, abstentionist, and domestically oriented; it seeks to protect the virtue of the United States from contamination by the power politics of evil nations. Wilsonian globalism endeavored to bring the virtue of American democracy to the rest of the world. Contemporary globalism tries to protect the virtue of the "free world" from contamination by communism and to create a world order in which that virtue has a chance to flourish. The anti-Communist crusade has become both the moral principle of contemporary globalism and the rationale of our world-wide foreign policy.

The anti-Communist crusade has its origins in the Truman Doctrine, formulated in President Truman's message to Congress of March 12, 1947. His message assumed that the issue between the United States and the Soviet Union, from which arose the need for aid to Greece and Turkey, must be understood not as the rivalry between two great powers but as a struggle between good and evil, democracy and totalitarianism. In its positive application this principle proclaimed the defense of free, democratic nations everywhere in the world against "direct or indirect aggression," against "subjugation by armed minorities or by outside pressure." In its negative application it postulated the containment of the Soviet Union everywhere in the world. Thus, the Truman Doctrine transformed a concrete interest of the United States in a geographically defined part of the world into a moral principle of worldwide validity, to be applied regardless of the limits of American interests and of American power.

The globalism of the Truman Doctrine was not put to the test of actual performance. . . .

The contrast between crusading pronouncements and the actual policies pursued continued, and was even accentuated, under the stewardship of John Foster Dulles, owing, on the one hand, to his propensity for grandiose announcements and, on the other, to his innate caution and President Eisenhower's common sense. The only major practical tribute the Eisenhower administration paid to the anti-Communist crusade was alliances, such as the Baghdad Pact and SEATO, which were supposed to contain communism in the Middle East and Asia, respectively.

Under President Kennedy, the gap between crusading pronounce-ments and actual policies started to narrow, because of the intellec-tual recognition on the part of the Kennedy administration that com-munism could no longer be defined simply, as it could in 1950, as the "spearhead of Russian imperialism." Thus the crusading spirit gave way to a sober, differentiating assessment of the bearing of the newly emerged, different types of communism on the American na-tional interest.

The Doctrine of American Paramountcy

Under President Johnson, pronouncements and policies were, for the first time since the great transformation of American policy in 1947, very nearly in harmony. What President Johnson only implied, the Secretaries of State and Defense clearly stated: We are fighting in Vietnam in order to stop communism throughout the world. And the President stated with similar clarity that "we do not propose to sit here in our rocking chair with our hands folded and let the Commu-nists set up any government in the Western Hemisphere." What in the past we had said we were doing or would do but never did, we were now in the process of putting into practice: to stop the expan-sion of communism on a global scale by force of arms.

*   *   *

The interventions of the United States in Cuba, the Dominican Re-public, and Vietnam, and other less spectacular ones, have been jus-tified as reactions to Communist intervention. This argument derives from the assumption that communism everywhere in the world is not only morally unacceptable and philosophically hostile to the United States, but also detrimental to the national interests of the United States and must therefore be opposed on political and military as well as moral and philosophic grounds. I shall assume for the pur-poses of this discussion that, as a matter of fact, Communist inter-vention actually preceded ours in all these instances, and shall raise the question as to whether our national interest required our inter-vention against the Communist one.

Ten or twenty years ago, this question could have been answered in the positive without further examination. For then communism anywhere in the world was a mere extension of Soviet power, controlled and used for the purposes of that power. Since we were committed to the containment of the Soviet Union, we were also committed to the containment of communism anywhere in the world. Today however, we are faced not with one monolithic Communist bloc controlled and used by the Soviet Union, but with a variety of communisms, whose relations with the Soviet Union and China change from country to country and from time to time and whose bearing upon the interests of the United States requires empirical examination in each instance. Communism has become polycentric, with each Communist government and movement, to a greater or lesser extent, pursuing its own national interests within the common framework of Communist ideology and institutions. The bearing which the pursuit of those interests has upon the policies of the United States must be determined in terms not of Communist ideology but of their compatibility with the interests of the United States.

Subjecting our interventions in Cuba, the Dominican Republic, and Vietnam to this empirical test, one realizes the inadequacy of the simple slogan "Stop Communism" as the rationale of our interventions. While this slogan is popular at home and makes only minimal demands upon discriminating judgment, it inspires policies that do either too much or too little in opposing communism, and can provide no yardstick for a policy that measures the degree of its opposition to the degree of the Communist threat. Thus, on the one hand, as part of the settlement of the missile crisis of 1962, we pledged ourselves not to intervene in Cuba, which is today a military and political client of the Soviet Union and seeks to become the fountainhead of subversion and military intervention in the Western Hemisphere, and as such directly affects the interests of the United States. On the other hand, we have intervened massively in Vietnam, even at the risk of a major war, although the Communist threat to American interests emanating from Vietnam is at best remote, and in any event infinitely more remote than the Communist threat emanating from Cuba.

As concerns the intervention in the Dominican Republic, even if one takes at face value the official assessment of the facts that the revolution of April 1965 was controlled by Cuban Communists, it appears incongruous that we intervened there in a revolution that was, according to that same assessment, a mere symptom of the disease, while the disease itself—Cuban communism—remained exempt from effective intervention.

This type of intervention against communism per se naturally tends to blend into intervention against revolution per se. We tend to intervene against all radical revolutionary movements because we are afraid lest they be taken over by Communists, and conversely we tend to intervene on behalf of all governments and movements opposed to radical revolution, because they are also opposed to communism. Such a policy of intervention is unsound on intellectual grounds for the reasons mentioned in our discussion of contemporary communism; it is also bound to fail in practice.

Many nations of Asia, Africa, and Latin America are today objectively in a prerevolutionary stage, and it is likely to be only a matter of time until actual revolution breaks out in one or the other of these nations. The revolutionary movements that will then come to the fore are bound to have, to a greater or lesser degree, a Communist component—that is, they run the risk of being taken over by communism. Nothing is simpler, in terms of both intellectual effort and, at least initially, practical execution, than to trace all these revolutions to a common conspiratorial source, to equate all revolutionary movements with world communism, and to oppose them with indiscriminate fervor as uniformly hostile to the interests of the United States. Under this rationale, the United States would be forced to intervene against revolutions throughout the world because of the ever-present threat of a Communist take-over and would transform itself, in spite of its better insight and intentions, into an antirevolutionary power per se.

Such a policy of intervention might succeed if it had to deal with nothing more than isolated revolutionary movements that could be smothered by force of arms. But it cannot succeed, since it is faced with revolutionary situations all over the world; for even the militarily most powerful nation does not have sufficient usable resources to deal simultaneously with a number of acute revolutions. Such a policy of indiscriminate intervention is bound to fail not only with regard to the individual revolution to which it is applied, but also in terms of its own indiscriminate anticommunism. For the very logic that would make us appear as the antirevolutionary power per se would surrender to communism the sponsorship of revolution everywhere. Thus indiscriminate anticommunist intervention achieves what it aims to prevent: the exploitation of the revolutions of the age by communism.

If this analysis of our policy of intervention is correct, then we have intervened not wisely but too well. Our policy of intervention has been under the ideological spell of our opposition to communism and to potentially Communist-led revolutions. While this ideological orientation has continued to determine our policy of intervention, the Soviet Union has continued to pay lip service to the support of "wars of national liberation" but has in practice relegated these wars to a secondary place in the struggle for the world. This softening of the Soviet ideological position has become one of the points of contention in the ideological dispute between the Soviet Union and China. In a statement of June 14, 1963, the Chinese Communist Party declared that "the whole cause of the international proletarian revolution hinges on the outcome of revolutionary struggles" in the "vast areas of Asia, Africa, and Latin America" that are today the "storm centers of world revolution dealing direct blows at imperialism." Conforming to this doctrine, China has almost indiscriminately intervened throughout the world on behalf of subversive movements, very much in the manner in which the Bolshevist government under Lenin and Trotsky tried to promote world revolution. In their reply of July 14th of the same year, the Soviet leaders opposed the " 'new theory' according to which the decisive force in the struggle against imperialism . . . is not the world system of socialism, not the struggle of the international working class, but . . . the national liberation movement." The Soviet Union's recent practice of restraint in fomenting and supporting revolution has matched this theoretical position. This ideological "revisionism" has of course not prevented the Soviet Union from intervening—as in Egypt, Somalia, and Czechoslovakia—when its national interest appeared to require intervention.

One factor that cannot have failed to influence the Soviet Union in toning down its ideological commitment to intervention has been the relative failure of ideological intervention. The United States, China, and Cuba have joined the Soviet Union in the experience of that failure. The uncommitted nations have been eager to reap the benefits of intervention, but have also been very anxious not to be tied with ideological strings to the intervening nation. After making great efforts, expending considerable resources, and running serious risks, the participants in this world-wide ideological competition are still approximately at the point from which they started: Measured against their ambitions and expectations, the uncommitted third of the world is still by and large an ideological no man's land.

This experience of failure is particularly painful, and ought to be particularly instructive, for the United States. For since the end of the Second World War we have intervened in the political, military, and economic affairs of other countries at a cost far in excess of $100 billion, and we have for some time been involved in a costly, risky war in order to build a nation in South Vietnam. Only the enemies of the United States will question the generosity of these efforts, which have no parallel in history. But have these efforts been wise? Have the commitments made and risks taken been commensurate with the results to be expected and actually achieved? The answer must be in the negative. Our economic aid has been successful in supporting economies that were already in the process of development; it has been by and large unsuccessful in creating economic development where none existed before because the moral and national preconditions for such development were lacking. Learning from this failure, we have established the principle of giving aid only to the few nations who can use it rather than to the many who need it. While this principle of selectivity is sound in theory, its consistent practical application has been thwarted by the harsh political and military realities that sometimes make it necessary to give aid when it is not economically justified, as well as by political and military considerations derived from the ideological concerns discussed above.

This principle of selectivity must be extended to the political and military sphere as well. We have come to overrate enormously what a nation can do for another nation by intervening in its affairs even with the latter's consent. This overestimation of our power to intervene is only a counterfoil to our ideological commitment, which by its very nature has no limit. Committed to intervening against Communist aggression and subversion anywhere, we have come to assume that we have the power to do so successfully. But in truth, both the need for intervention and the chances for successful intervention are much more limited than we have been led to believe. Intervene we must where our national interest requires it and where our power gives us a chance to succeed. The choice of these occasions will be determined not by sweeping ideological commitments or by blind reliance upon American power, but by a careful calculation of the interests involved and the power available. If the United States applies this standard, it will intervene less and succeed more.

Edmund Stillman and William Pfaff

THE SOURCES OF POWER AND IMPOTENCE

Edmund Stillman and William Pfaff, both of the Hudson Institute, addressed their 1966 study to "the failure of American foreign policy." They found the roots of that failure in what has been called the American style in international relations. That style reflects, say Stillman and Pfaff, America's traditional isolation from and hence lack of realism about world affairs. It also reflects a democratic faith that since all men are created equal, they will all ultimately be receptive to being governed more or less on the American pattern. Explicit in Stillman and Pfaff's analysis is the contention that such an approach contained the seeds of its own failure in Vietnam. Implicit is the fundamental and disturbing question: If it is true that "unrealism's" roots go so deep into the American experience, what hope can there be for a more sensible approach?

The real source of danger to America in today's world is not so much the Soviets, or Chinese communism, or the nuclear weapon, as that present policy is mired in illusions—and these illusions express the deepest beliefs which Americans, as a nation, hold about the world. The discouraging truth is that the defects of present American policy are not merely defects of technique, of detail, to be cured by one or another refinement of our programs. They are fundamental errors that spring from defects of the national style and political intelligence. . . .

An Isolated Nation

There is no single American philosophy, no one and inescapable view of politics and history, which condemns us as a nation to a single style of foreign policy. There is always tension and conflict in what Americans believe, most of all in what we believe about ourselves. But when this is said, it remains true that there has been, on the evidence of the last fifty years, a characteristic American style of foreign policy—a way of looking at the world and a characteristic belief about what political action can and should accomplish abroad. The sources of this style lie in the experience of isolation, in the beliefs which went into our definition of the Republic and in our development of this country's political society in the nineteenth and early twentieth centuries. But the fact that our style of foreign policy can be explained in terms of the American historical experience does not mean that this style is a good one, or even that it expresses the best tradition of this country. There are ways in which it expresses the worst of us—our most self-indulgent beliefs about ourselves unchecked by the constraints and known limits that operate to give our domestic politics some sense of scale and restraint.

*   *   *

In international affairs we are not so well off. Abroad, our knowledge is sketchy and our skepticism deserts us. Tocqueville thought that democracies would do badly in foreign affairs because "foreign politics demand scarcely any of those qualities which are peculiar to a democracy; they require, on the contrary, the perfect use of almost all those in which it is deficient. Democracy is favorable to the increase of the internal resources of a state; it diffuses wealth and comfort, promotes public spirit, and fortifies the respect for law in all classes of society: all these are advantages which have only an indirect influence over the relations which one people bears to another. But a democracy can only with great difficulty regulate the details of an important undertaking, persevere in a fixed design, and work out its execution in spite of serious obstacles. It cannot combine its measures with secrecy or await their consequences with patience. These are qualities which more especially belong to an individual or an aristocracy; and they are precisely the qualities by which a nation, like an individual, attains a dominant position."[1]

This has not proved to be entirely true. The United States has been capable of pursuing fixed designs with considerable patience and

[1] Alexis de Tocqueville, *Democracy in America,* Vintage edition, ed. by Phillips Bradley (New York, 1958), Vol. I, pp. 243–244.

restraint—when those designs have been concrete. Yet often the designs themselves have proved defective for the reason that as policy changed from a defense of concrete American interests, at which men like Jefferson, Polk, and Lincoln were superb, to international action in remote quarters, at which Wilson and Franklin Roosevelt, for all the decency of their vision, were less successful, America has lacked a deep and dense experience of what it was about. There has been only a slight American involvement in the world's history—and crimes. And it is experience that makes accurate perception possible, as well as a sound judgment of what can be accomplished. It is extraordinary that a nation that understands perfectly well what money and National Guard action can and cannot accomplish to change the minds of Mississippians believes what it does about the efficiency of aid and military intervention abroad.

*   *   *

And today? For all the loudly proclaimed coming-of-age of American foreign policy, our imposing goals hardly differ—as goals, at least—from the evangelical visions of the past, those of Wilson *and* the isolationists. Our mission is to create, according to Mr. Rostow, the State Department's Chief Planning Officer, "no matter how long it may take, a world community in which men and nations can live at peace. No less is required of us for the safety of the nation and the continuity of civilized life on this small planet."[2] Mr. Rusk has added that "our goal . . . is a world in which human rights are secure, a world of better life for all. . . ."[3] Not only is this our objective, but it is, as Mr. Rostow says, our responsibility to achieve it. Vice-President Humphrey has added: "Let there be no doubt about it . . . [America's] capacity . . . to help build a cooperative and progressive international community based on common interest is unique in this world and unique in history."[4] It is the sustained quality of the present American world intervention which distinguishes it from the Wilsonian intervention. It is the confidence in the efficiency and naturalness of

[2] W. W. Rostow, "Peace: The Central Task of Foreign Policy." *D.S. Bulletin,* July 5, 1965, p. 27.
[3] Dean Rusk, "The Unseen Search for Peace." *D.S. Bulletin,* November 1, 1965, p. 690.
[4] Hubert H. Humphrey, "National Power and the Creation of a Workable World Community." *D.S. Bulletin,* June 28, 1965, p. 1049.

America's world involvement which provides the chief difference between present policy and the discredited beliefs of the isolationists.

For who in America today is an isolationist? Now that the enemy, as in Vietnam, is communism, and is further identified with Chinese communism, even Republican conservatives are largely silenced. But does this kinship of moral spirit between isolationism and globalism, between Wilsonianism and globalism, demonstrate much more than a continuity of idealism in America's foreign outlook that transcends party? Is it not, in fact, an expression of a valid interest in bringing the conflicts of nations into some kind of organized check? We would argue that however genuine the idealism, this American spirit goes far beyond reasonable ambition, demonstrating a view of political possibility that has dominated, and distorted, American foreign policy for too long. The continuity in American foreign policy—seriously challenged only in the realistic and limited programs briefly followed in the late 1940s—is essentially a continuity of illusion. It is a continuity with a tradition of self-indulgence and sentimentality in foreign affairs which today has brought the United States into dangers more serious than most Americans are prepared to acknowledge. It may be that it is within our power to change this. The practical virtues of our domestic politics are equally valid for foreign policy, and we are an intelligent and resourceful society. But we need to translate our domestic realism and restraint into foreign affairs.

Ideology and International Action

The current fallacies of American foreign policy can be described individually, but in the end they all reflect a single problem, a generalization from the isolated, and immeasurably lucky, American experience and a tendency to believe (and insist) that America's wants and values are universal. Nearly all sectors of American society hold the belief that American history—particularly the success of federalism and material prosperity in damping down social discord—provides a proto-typical solution for the world's disorders. This is a belief of nearly theological intensity, and it is no exaggeration to label it an American ideology. It is an evangelical belief which argumentation and chronic failure can hardly shake.

*   *   *

George Kennan observes that

> *the mind of American statesmanship, stemming as it does in so large a part from the legal profession in our country, gropes with unfailing persistence for some institutional framework. . . . Behind all this, of course, lies the American assumption that the things for which other peoples in this world are apt to contend are for the most part neither creditable nor important and might justly be expected to take second place behind the desirability of an orderly world, untroubled by international violence. To the American mind, it is implausible that people should have positive aspirations, and ones that they regard as legitimate, more important to them than the peacefulness and orderliness of international life. From this standpoint, it is not apparent why other people should not join us in accepting the rules of the game in international politics. . . .*[5]

To this it must be added that Kennan's is a conservative statement which is concerned with the conflicting but reasonable impulses of other nations that lead to war. There are, as well, forces of irrationality and emotion, of egoism, pride, passion, messianism, and ideological ambition, of cultural shock, racism, vengeance, even of nihilism, which have made themselves felt dramatically in the last five decades of world politics.

The American approach to international affairs typically regards the actions which such impulses produce as "outlawry"—crimes which the international community will wish to suppress. But these forces are not always so easily localized and identified. When they manifest themselves in an institution like the Nazi regime, they are, comparatively speaking, the easiest to deal with. What happens when they show themselves less dramatically among our friends, or even among ourselves, is another matter. It is, for instance, a sad commentary on the perversity of human affairs—to say nothing of the relationship between idealism and violence—that no Administration in American history intervened so often, and sometimes brutally, in Latin American affairs as the Wilson Administration. It has been well said of Wilson that rejecting economic imperialism, he practiced a kind of moral imperialism. He began his Administration by devising thirty treaties, of which twenty-two were signed, that abjured the use of force in favor of arbitration. "I am going to teach the South American republics to elect good men," Wilson asserted to a visiting English-

---

[5] George Kennan, *American Diplomacy 1900–1950,* Mentor edition (New York, 1952), pp. 83, 84.

man in 1914.[6] But the practical effect of his noble intentions was to
bombard Vera Cruz and to sanction military interventions in Mexico,
Haiti, Santo Domingo, and Nicaragua—all notably without teaching
the South American republics anything of the kind.

The Faith in Law

The desire for a system of law which will define "the duties and obligations" of all nations reflects three factors in the parochial American experience. First of all is the success of legal and organizational
remedies in our own history. But next and more important is the intellectual appeal of schematic solutions as short-cutting politics—
"power politics." Last is the effect upon us of an imprecise but very
influential historicism—a deep belief in material progress—which
sees men slowly but inevitably improving their lot, and in political
affairs moving toward a universal constitutionalism and peace.

*   *   *

In the United States our success in achieving a kind of consensus
on law and government reflects as much the lucky fact of geograph-
ical isolation and cultural homogeneity in our early national life as
it does the fact that this country was founded as a free act of organization and legal compact. The theory of politics in this country,
moreover, has always betrayed its origins in the Enlightenment faith,
which became a Populist faith—the belief in reasonable action to
improve things. The effects of this belief had been felt even before
the Revolution and before the Constitution was adopted—in the native habit of democratic decision developed in townships and pro-
vincial assemblies. It was possible for this habit to develop, and a
federal system to be established on its basis, to quote Tocqueville,
not only because "the states have similar interests, a common ori-
gin, and a common language, but . . . they have also arrived at the
same stage of civilization. . . . I do not know of any European nation,
however small, that does not present less uniformity in its different
provinces than the American people, which occupy a territory as extensive as one-half of Europe. The distance from Maine to Georgia is
about one thousand miles; but the difference between the civilization

[6] Interview with Samuel G. Blythe. *Saturday Evening Post,* May 23, 1914, p. 3.

of Maine and that of Georgia is slighter than the difference between the habits of Normandy and those of Brittany."[7]

All this ought to be self-evident: America is not Europe, still less Afro-Asia. But it is another American article of faith that all men are at bottom the same. The experience of uniformity has created a belief in uniformity, just as the values of national homogeneity resulted in making the United States into a vast assimilative machine that absorbed the great immigrations of Slavs, Italians, Jews, Irishmen, and Scandinavians of the latter nineteenth century. . . .

That the United States should then turn outward the assimilationist assumptions that have guided our domestic politics is perhaps not surprising. Our founding beliefs and our subsequent historical experience prompt us to assert a belief in an eventual world union—first consciously constitutional and legalist, and later, we assume, proceeding from this phase by an assimilative process which will at last create "world citizens" out of selfish parochialists and nationalists.

But to believe in this peaceful world process, by analogy to our own past, is not even to understand that past well. It is to forget the implications of the Southern challenge of 1861—a revolt of the agrarian, aristocratic, precapitalist South against the industrial, middle-class, and commercial ethos of the North. In that titanic conflict, in which nearly half a million died, one "consensus" crushed another by force. This is no optimistic prototype for a nuclear world.

The Faith in Unification

We have, of course, been taught by recent history, notably the collapse of the wartime alliance with the Soviets and the outbreak of the Cold War, and the impotence of the United Nations, to give up much of that naive faith in an immediate world law which Stimson expressed and Taft faithfully endorsed. We have substituted another version—another schematic solution which may, we believe, organize the world in a way that will outlaw conflict. Now we see regional federations of nations as the first move in a process whose implied development will be the coming together of United Europe with America into a union of the Atlantic world, and of the Atlantic world even-

[7] Tocqueville, *op. cit.,* Vol. I, p. 176.

tually with the advanced industrial countries of Asia or with a prospective political system of the Americas.[8] On the horizon—and nearly all now concede this is a distant horizon, decades away—is the assimilation into this great federation of constitutional and habitually democratic countries of the newer and less experienced states of Asia and Africa. Nevertheless, as Secretary Rusk has said, the "distant stars" of American foreign policy today remain these goals: that all peoples eventually enjoy Jeffersonian government, the powers of governments to be derived from the consent of their peoples; and that all states should eventually be members of a constitutional world federation—"a world community of independent states, each with its own institutions but cooperating with one another to promote their common interest and banding together to resist aggression, a world increasingly subject to the rule of law. . . . We believe that that is also the goal of a great majority of mankind. This identity of basic purpose gives us friends and allies in many nations. . . ."[9]

Yet the chasm between the American experience of union, constitution, and an assimilative culture, and the prospective world experience is seldom grasped. Even in the limited conceptions of a regional federation of Europe—a society, surely, of profound cultural unity as well as common experience and tradition, of high intelligence and a recent and terrible experience of nationalist self-destructiveness —there has perhaps been too little understanding of the chasm be-

[8] Daniel Boorstin remarks that the implied thesis of the American plan for a League of Nations after World War I was that "the peoples of France, Germany, Italy, and of many lesser nations would seize the opportunity to deal with each other in the manner of Massachusetts, New York, and California. Wilson's program was not merely an embodied idealism, it was a projection of the American image onto Europe. Many of our historians have shared the Wilsonian illusions. Therefore many of them have written the history of the Peace as if there was something perverse in the unwillingness of the Senate and the American people to go along with Wilson's program for Europe. In the long perspective of our history what is surprising is the opposite: that even a considerable minority of Americans were ready to give up their traditional image of Europe and to begin to think of it as a potential America" (see Daniel J. Boorstin, *America and the Image of Europe,* New York, 1960, p. 22). The particular forms or plans for European unification which were enthusiastically supported by the United States after World War II again were those which followed the American model (and which clearly provided for an American role in the new Europe). We have resisted—with some bitterness—schemes which reject this model and substitute for American-style federalism and moderation older European traditions which appeal to Europe's pride and sense of grandeur, and include a component of anti-Americanism, excluding America from a major European role.
[9] Dean Rusk, "Guidelines of U.S. Foreign Policy." *D.S. Bulletin,* June 28, 1965, p. 1033.

tween constitutional forms which have grown organically and federal schemes which are theoretically conceived.

*   *   *

The Faith in Reason

The emotional force behind organizational and constitutional solutions to political conflict derives from the fact that they are simple, and they are simple because they beg the question of the ordeal of common experience and of the coming together of communities. They function from the top down, imposing a scheme upon humanity which humanity is expected to recognize as in the common interest. . . .

Mr. Johnson has said: "If world conditions were largely satisfactory, it would not be difficult to evolve a rule of law. But we do not live in a satisfactory world. It is stained with evil and injustice, by ruthless ambition and passionate conflict. Only by fighting these forces do we help build a base on which the temple of law may rest."[10] This seems like a post-Wilsonian realism, holding to the ideal of world reform but humbler before the conditions which reform must overcome. Yet the validity of the political realism must still be doubted; in fact, it reflects an American historicism, a faith in the millennial victory of reason, a conception of evil as identifiable and as ultimately subject to defeat—and all of these are beliefs which few, except Americans, can today sustain.

The Faith in Progress

We are all historicists, and an oddly naive historicism is the third element underlying the characteristic American approach to foreign affairs. Whether we acknowledge them or not, each of us holds opinions about the meaning of history and the destiny of the human race, though the way we order our practical affairs may contradict the beliefs we would seriously profess. But even the practical historicism of the United States is progressive and optimistic. It stems primarily from the eighteenth-century Enlightenment belief in the imminent feasibility of a perfectly reasonable form of human society in which the old crimes and injustices of history are progressively eliminated

[10] Lyndon B. Johnson, "The Atlantic Community: Common Hopes and Objectives," *D.S. Bulletin,* December 21, 1964, p. 867.

by intelligent reforms and a just ordering of interests, with an allied influence of perfectionist sectarian Protestant Christianity. The success of the American Republic, combined with that sense of moral separateness and superiority we have already mentioned, supported this faith in America's becoming steadily better and better—not merely richer, but *morally* better.

* * *

At the conceptual level this naive faith in progressive improvement is supported by simple analogies between politics and technology. Americans are passionate in their love for technology, and in their mastery of it. Technology is taken as the normative activity of society, so that what man has accomplished in ridding society of grinding labor is thought to presage what can now be done to rid society of cruelty and greed. What is needed, the American faith holds, is a new "science of society" which will match the physical sciences in its certainty and technical mastery. But who will then use this knowledge and for what purpose is not always asked.

* * *

Yet the outcome of the particular belief in techniques is evident in the repeated attempts—notably in Pentagon appraisals—to find "systems," that is, organizational or technological solutions, capable of achieving political ends. In the political sphere modern America harnesses enormous sophistication of technique to goals which are derived largely from unanalyzed tradition. Thus the government has persistently sought to deal with Vietnam in terms of essentially engineering or organizational solutions. The conviction is that Vietnam's crisis can somehow be remedied by the right combination of military and administrative reforms: new tactics, new systems of rural regroupment and security, new methods for Saigon's leaders to "get through to the people," a new emphasis on civic action by military units, new "quick-response" security forces, new village information and indoctrination programs. American critics of our current policy are just as often convinced of the merit of programmatic solutions, except that they are inclined to see these in terms of new structures of government or administration, a new "commitment to democracy" in Saigon, an aid program to make South Vietnam a "showplace of democracy," schemes for "democratic revolution." All of these are intended to isolate the Viet Cong and win the allegiance of the Vietnamese peasants by outbidding the Viet Cong in what is taken to be the peasantry's quest for justice, prosperity, and free political institutions. Both sides believe that America's values and aims in Vietnam are self-evidently valid and relevant, and that our troubles must stem from failures in translating these into practical action and popular appeal. Obviously there is some truth in the specific critiques both sides make, and in many of the proposed remedies, but both ignore the possibility that Vietnam's upheaval is too deeply rooted, too passionate and particular in its sources, for "reasonable" solution—the possibility that one element in the upheaval might, in fact, be what we would regard as a revolt against "reason," against the meliorist and pragmatic methods of a foreign system, and against its values and goals.

*   *   *

The Projection of American Values and Perceptions

We fail to understand this seeming resistance to reason and progress, first of all because no nation can expect to comprehend another; few individuals can approach even a limited and insecure grasp of the motives of others. That much is common experience; those, even in personal life, whom we know best are also those whose ultimate mystery is most evident to us. Who really knows his parents, his wife, his children?

*   *   *

There is, however, a particular American problem here. America is an impressively capable society, but we are also a peculiarly parochial society with a poor record of deep or comprehensive interest in other societies. The reason lies perhaps in the intensity of our own national experience, the need we have had to concentrate upon *making* ourselves into a nation. (The states of Western Europe, after all, became modern nations by virtue of being what they already were; the continuity of the British or Italian nation is a continuity of place and society thousands of years old, whereas the continuity of America is less than a few hundred years old; and the American people is a phenomenal in-gathering from the entire world.) One might think that our worldwide origins would have produced an unparalleled knowledge or sympathy for others. Yet this has not been true. Our isolationism manifests itself here too, perhaps as a matter of hardly conscious yet deliberate choice, part of our repudiation of the old world. America, after all, is the creation of men who did not truly like it elsewhere; this, too, is our tradition. So that whatever it is that America is fated to be in world history, we are not well suited to be the world's mentor.

*   *   *

Here again is the moral passion that dominates our belief about the world. But setting that aside—assuming that we are indeed "better," "purer," more advanced on a "way" which leads toward truth and peace, as well as toward material wealth and industrial power— the problem remains: how accurately do we see the world, and how valid are our judgments when we interpret not the ultimate longings, but the immediate realities and motives of those others, the peoples with whom our foreign policy must deal? Do we really grasp what sends thirteen-year-old boys and grandmothers into battle with U.S. Marines in Vietnam? We speak of the enemy's ideological fanaticism or of men drugged before battle, but what moves the Buddhist priest in South Vietnam to die terribly, or a "reactionary" like Ngo Dinh Diem stubbornly to create the kind of self-defeating mandarin and sectarian government he did establish, and to struggle against our sensible, pragmatic counsels and our material threats until, rather than give in, he met his death?

Our inadequacies in Vietnam might be interpreted as mere tactical errors, but they are not. They spring from deeper causes. Optimistic American society is fundamentally different from most of the world's cultures.

Stanley Hoffmann

TOWARD A MULTIPOLAR WORLD

Stanley Hoffmann's mixed metaphors contain his message about a realistic role for America in world politics: not "like a tennis player who rushes to the net in order to stop every ball," but rather one who plays "farther back in the court . . . letting many of those balls fall as they will outside the court"; not "like a beast burrowing its head in the ground," but like "a man secure in house, or a captain steering his ship through changing weather." Hoffmann, Professor of Government at Harvard, would have Washington work toward the formation of "a multi-hierarchical," or multipolar international system, that is, one in which various middle powers play larger roles, thus delivering the United States from the temptation to act as world policeman. But, writing in 1972, Hoffmann warned against confusing "a set of worthy goals—the establishment of a moderate international system, new relations with our adversaries, the adjustment of our alliances to the new conditions of diplomacy and economics—with a technique—a balance of five powers,"[1] as suggested by President Nixon.

Insofar as America's freedom of action is concerned, there is a difference in kind between the world of the late 1940s and the world today. In record time, there has been a switch from a period in which the United States' margin of indeterminacy was very narrow but its capacity to affect events great, to a period in which the margin seems broader and the capacity less. In 1947–48, the United States had to consider the collapse of British power in the Middle East, the political and economic demise of Europe, the opportunities opened by misery and civil strife for Communist success, and the skill with which Stalin played his cards. It had a simple choice between abdicating from leadership, which would have been a refusal to act as a great power, and deciding to play such a role: "Rarely has freedom been more clearly the recognition of necessity, and statesmanship the imaginative exploitation of necessity."[2] The rescue of Greece and

From *Gulliver's Troubles, Or The Setting of American Foreign Policy* by Stanley Hoffman, pp. 4–6, 210–212, 345–348, 356–372. Copyright © 1968 by the Council on Foreign Relations, Inc. Used by permission of McGraw-Hill Book Company.

[1] Stanley Hoffmann, "Weighing the Balance of Power," *Foreign Affairs* (July 1972), p. 643.

[2] See my *The State of War* (New York: Frederick A. Praeger, 1965), p. 163. I agree with the idea of Arthur Schlesinger, Jr. (in "Origins of the Cold War," *Foreign Affairs*, October 1967, pp. 22–52) that the Cold War "was the product not of a deci-

Turkey, the economic restoration of Western Europe, the beginnings of European cooperation, the consolidation of West Germany, the signing of the North Atlantic Treaty, the use of the United Nations as an instrument against North Korean aggression, the launching of foreign-aid programs—these were acts that transformed and defined the international reality. There were failures and frustrations, especially in the Far East; but many argued that they were due, not to the external limits placed on America's power there, but to America's failure to apply its power. Now, the bipolar contest was not its choice, the ideological battles of communism against the West and anticolonial nationalism against Western empires were not its initiatives, the nuclear race was not its preference. But, where power was applied, despite the sharp constraints of a world America had not at all desired, the United States' capacity to affect events was undeniable.

This world imposed an imperative: the resistance to Soviet imperialism. American leaders, scarred or scared by the experience of the 1930s, were moved by the "vital 'myth' "[3] of the Munich analogy to contain "Communist aggression" with militant fervor. What had to be worked out was the strategy: where to resist and with what means in areas where the threat was already present, and how best to deter it wherever it was absent or only latent. With multiple answers to the many questions raised by this single imperative, America shaped much of the postwar world. Today, the world is both more comfortable and more frustrating, for there is no longer any simple command. The split between Russia and China has deeply affected the nature of communist imperialism; military technology has created an imperative of its own, which has helped to transform the main enemy in part at least into a reluctant partner. In many areas of the world, the old imperative provides no yardstick for policy, either because it is only

sion, but of a dilemma," and that today's "revisionists" underestimate the degree to which the Soviet Union, in 1945, was "not a traditional national state." Even apart from its ideological nature, Cold War between the two superpowers would have erupted for traditional power reasons—those of bipolar confrontation. Settlements would have been difficult in any case, but of course, the ideological nature of the contest ruled them out. To say that the contest was unavoidable short of appeasement by the United States is *not* to see the Cold War "as a pure case of Russian aggression and American response." America's moves were often clumsy and excessive, and the Soviets' policy was a mix of ideological messianism, defensive concerns, national ambitions and flexible prudence. What is clear to this writer is that the Cold War was unavoidable then—which is no reason to condone its earlier excesses or its deadly grip over the different realities of today.

[3] Robert E. Osgood and Robert W. Tucker, *Force, Order, and Justice* (Baltimore: The Johns Hopkins Press, 1967), p. 171.

slightly relevant, or because it is hard to see in advance how *any* policy will help keep trouble away, or because to shape policy according to its dictates could lead to diametrically opposed policies. In other words, today's world dictates no single imperative to the United States, and it does not suggest so many possibilities that the area of choice is noticeably enlarged. The achievements of recent years do not compare with those of the earlier period. It is as if the clay which statesmen have to shape had suddenly hardened.

*   *   *

Because it is too static, because it has too little room for middle-range goals defined in political terms, the United States' approach to international affairs has a way of being unsettled by occurrences which suggest (as they continually do) that the forces of evil are stronger and more cunning, the forces of progress weaker and less active, the forces of surprise and genuine change richer and more imaginative than America had expected. Consequently, we must tinker, to make sure that nothing will prevent our ultimate vision from becoming reality. A vision that looks forward to the dissipation of clouds, but does not tell us much about the way clouds are formed or are actually moving, obliges one to treat every passing mist as a threat of storm that has to be chased away. Only a philosophy of history or a clear-cut vision of the main trends (or a moderate system with well-established rules of the game and players with limited stakes) enable a nation to discriminate between the events that require its intervention and those that do not. But this nation has no clear-cut vision other than its utopia and no philosophy of history other than the static one I have described, and the game is played for the highest stakes ever known, with rules hammered out in trial and error. As a result, it behaves, not like a man secure in his house, or a captain steering a ship through changing weather, but like a beast burrowed in the ground. Its past, its principles, its pragmatism either provide it with or reflect a colossal need for security; hence so many assertions of faith in the direction taken by history. But in the absence of a compass, it is gripped by a fear of insecurity commensurate with its desire for safety, and anticommunism becomes both the expression of that fear and the substitute for a compass.

For a nation so hopeful about the benefits of time, the United States is singularly unwilling to let time operate, to trust "the force of circumstances"; it is as though we knew we were whistling in the dark. A noise hits us from Lebanon: we land Marines; a tremor reaches us from Santo Domingo: we send troops. Russians appear in Conakry or Chinese in Brazzaville: we shudder. The Communists help the rebels in the Congo: we think all is lost. We overestimate the capacity of distant powers to ignite subversive fires. Yet the more we act and overact, the more we endow others with the same capacity to affect events that we attribute to ourselves. And when events show that their capacity is indeed limited, we exaggerate in the opposite direction, seeing in each tactical test a decisive contest that will determine the future. Then, when we have won the test, we proclaim that the fight is all over and primacy safely ours—until the next mishap reveals that we relaxed too soon and revives our frenzy. We become again like a tennis player who rushes to the net in order to stop every ball; instead of playing farther back in the court and letting many of those balls fall as they will outside the court, we try to stop the shots our opponent aims too high over the net, and we exhaust ourselves, letting our vigilance drop after a series of volleys. Mobilized for immediate perils, we do not see that time, the intricacies of a highly differentiated world, and a discriminating dose of intervention would take care of a great deal; as a result, we oscillate between lack of attention to the nonvisible sources of trouble, which will force us to take up arms when the pool of trouble has become a sea, and frantic attention to the visible sources. For we are cued only to certain kinds of trouble, and they elicit almost Pavlovian responses of anguish and action; but the more insidious and long-range troubles which would require action of a very different sort, we fail to heed.

Our past, our principles, and our pragmatism breed not only millennial hopes, but an embattled sense that we are the chosen champion of those hopes—and this buoys and harries us in turn. Little do we realize that the international system of today aids the champion on the defense, insofar as the hedges of diversity exhaust our foes' forces. Maybe what keeps making us frenzied is our dim awareness that this very system, those very hedges, will also prevent us from ever giving to the whole world the shape and color of our own ideal. What the system requires from us, as Kennan once said, is more gardening and less militancy. Yet Armageddon is what we seem to need.

*   *   *

As a superpower and as a nation engaged in a worldwide contest with a number of foes, the United States has vital stakes in the international competition of the nuclear age. . . .

Like all great powers in past international systems, the United States has an interest in maintaining (or restoring) a certain degree of *hierarchy* in the system. An international milieu in which the "impotence of power" of the leading states decentralizes power so that the puny and the mighty enjoy the same freedom of action (or suffer from the same paralysis); or a milieu in which the power of smaller states can be used more productively than that of the larger units, in which the latter are Gullivers tied while the Lilliputians roam at will—either would be unacceptable, even if the likely result in both cases were not nuclear proliferation. In the long run, inflation breeds an unhealthy separation between responsibilities and capabilities, in world affairs as in economics. None of this tells us anything about the nature of the hierarchy to be established, but it points to an American interest (and to a Soviet interest as well) in seeing to it that the system does not become more radically equalitarian than the present one.

The United States is locked in a competition with foes that, however divided on means they may be, and engaged as they are in a battle for power of their own, nevertheless agree in their desires to eliminate American power, influence, and interests. The United States naturally wants to *thwart* those designs—how effectively and widely this can be done depends, again, on trends in the international system—and the minimum objective must be to prevent the physical expansion of the power of the two main foes, the Soviet Union and China, and to foil military aggression by minor Communist regimes. In an ideal world, the American objective would be defined as preventing the establishment of any hostile regime that was allied to Russia or China, or even as the elimination of all enemies. Obviously, the range between the minimum and the maximum objective is huge, containing, for instance, the entire area of possible expansion of non-Soviet or non-Chinese Communist influence. But the point here is that there is an incompressible minimum. Some say that the forcible extension of Soviet or Chinese control over some parts of the world would not affect the United States' power position at all, but, as I have indicated, I believe this implies much too complacent an assessment of what is at stake.

The existence of nuclear weapons affects both of these U.S. goals as I have defined them. The national interest in "prevailing" in the international contest is doubly qualified. On the one hand, "victory," or even the kind of defense that involves disproportionate risks, becomes more difficult to advocate, and the interest in thwarting the foe must be reconciled with the interest in survival, which is possible only if armed conflict is strictly restrained. On the other hand, nuclear weapons give an additional reason for deterring a foe's expansion when it is attempted with force, since any resort to force is so dangerous. And the interest in creating or maintaining an international hierarchy is accentuated, since a "unit veto system," where even very small states would dispose of extensive means of destruction, would drastically alter the international hierarchy. Many small nuclear forces would be highly vulnerable, and their vulnerability would increase instability; the possession of nuclear weapons by states that were domestically unstable and poor would make the management of power in international affairs a real nightmare, forcing the superpowers back to a recurrent choice between universal policing (at high costs, both for themselves and in terms of a possible collapse of the taboo on nuclear weapons that has so far prevailed) and letting the world disintegrate into a series of jungles.[4] And it would also condemn the superpowers to a permanent arms race so as to preserve or restore the distance between themselves and minor nuclear states.

Nuclear weapons thus introduce another American interest, namely, in the cultivation of *moderation*—the fleeting characteristic of past balance-of-power systems, the threatened characteristic of the present one. Even sweeping ends must be pursued with prudent means. Since such ends always seem to encourage the selection of incautious means, and we cannot be sure that nuclear sanity will prevail, it is necessary for the chief contestants to define their ends so that the competition can remain within bounds—whether this means a gradual erosion of the more ambitious ends, reduced to rationalized rituals, or a postponement of the more dangerous ends into the increasingly problematic future. This moderation must prevail not only in the "relations of major tension," but also in all other interstate relations; there is a compelling interest in providing effective means of peaceful change or effective means of "peacekeeping and peace-

[4] See the remarks by "Erasmus" in "Polycentrism and Proliferation," *Survey* (January 1966), pp. 70–72.

making" when violence breaks out. To be sure, it takes more than one player to impose moderation on a system. It can be argued that the special circumstances that have created the present paradox of an international system that is both revolutionary and restrained will not recur in the future, however hard the United States tries, either because China's militancy will be far greater than that of Russia under Stalin or his successors or because the proliferation of nuclear powers will undermine the restraints observed now. However, Communist China's actual behavior contrasts with militant Chinese pronouncements, and, although an increase in its supply of power may reduce this gap between words and deeds, the risks of militancy will remain high, and wise American policy would aim at increasing the rewards of moderation. As for the dangers of proliferation, which are very serious, they need not make moderation impossible just at the time when they are making it indispensable.

The United States has another vital interest which encompasses and transcends the ones I have already mentioned. The United States needs not only to protect its material possessions, to preserve its security, to safeguard its power and rank, but also to try to establish a *world order* that will accommodate these concerns. Now which, among likely international systems, is most capable of restoring hierarchy, deterring the main foes of the United States and keeping conflicts moderate? In what kind of world can nations define their goals so that they will be reached, cooperatively or competitively, without large-scale violence, and reconciled without excessive frustrations? The unification of the international system, the shrinking of distance through communications, and the nuclear risks make it imperative to think of foreign policy not exclusively in terms of national strategy and piecemeal objectives, but in systemic terms. And the superpowers are still those most capable of shaping the system—but within its limits.

*   *   *

What is most likely is the emergence of a new type of international system, which I would call "multi-hierarchical."[5] On the one hand, in such a system, as in past multipolar systems, the traditional major

[5] The system described here is in many respects similar to the one outlined by Richard N. Rosecrance in "Bipolarity, Multipolarity and the Future," *Journal of Conflict Resolution*, Vol. X, No. 3 (September 1966), pp. 314–27; to the system advocated by Roger D. Masters in *The Nation is Burdened* (New York: Knopf, 1967); and to the system proposed by Ronald Steel in *Pax Americana* (New York: Viking Press, 1967).

power role would be performed by a number of states, not only by the United States and the Soviet Union. On the other hand, the hierarchy would be more complex. First, there would be more ranks. The relatively simple division between the great powers and the others cannot function any more. The distinction between superpowers and middle powers would remain; the two or (perhaps) three states capable of worldwide destruction would play a major role. But international society has gained in scope and complexity, and just as the hierarchy in a modern factory is more complex than the division between *maîtres* and *compagnons* in an old *métier*, there would be new gradations. Second, there would be a set of hierarchies. Force remains the *ultima ratio*, but insofar as it has become largely unusable and inadequate to deal with many issues, it cannot any longer be the sole yardstick. In a world that must solve internationally the problems once tackled either by domestic or private transnational channels, there will be different hierarchies for different tasks, corresponding to different computations of power. Third, the muting of the competition between the Soviet Union and the United States, the rise of middle powers in various parts of the world, the participation of so many nations, the risk of general destruction through escalation in either extension (number of states involved) or intensity would produce not only a functional diversification of the hierarchy, but also a *regional decentralization* of the international system, i.e., an autonomy of various subsystems under the brooding omnipresence of nuclear deterrence.

This kind of system is the most likely: its rudiments are already with us. The decreasing capacity of lesser allies in each camp, whether they are nuclear powers or not, to trigger the nuclear involvement of Russia or America has begun to fragment the international system.[6] So does those allies' desire to dissociate themselves from more distant ventures—as symbolized by the attitude of most of America's NATO allies toward the war in Vietnam, by the coexistence of stability in Eastern and Western Europe with a war in Asia in which the United States is deeply involved and the Soviet Union moderately committed. Among the nonaligned countries, fragmentation and a tendency to concentrate on regional issues have also affected the earlier notion of a single "Third World." Member states

[6] The Middle East crisis of 1967 has clearly shown that the superpowers' support to their "proxies" falls short even of conventional military involvement.

of the European Economic Community, as well as Japan, whose military power is slight, have a considerable supply of economic power and their acts and opinions matter greatly in questions of trade and international payments. Within the United Nations, some small or middle powers with little economic and military might wield great influence in peacekeeping operations and as diplomatic brokers. But the final shape of such a system is unclear: here is where the policies of the superpowers, particularly of the United States, will be important.

Not every multipolar system of the past has been moderate; it is all too easy to imagine a multi-hierarchical system of dizzying instability. Conflicts, of course, will persist. They are likely to be particularly acute in the "Third World," where states with poor resources, or contested borders, or ethnic grievances, have compelling possession goals as well as ambitious milieu goals and the temptation of interfering in each other's often troubled internal affairs. The rivalry of the superpowers and the contest between each of them and China is likely to feed, as well as to feed on, such conflicts. Nuclear proliferation may not provoke a general nuclear war engulfing the planet, although there exists a risk in the "gray areas" at the fringes of each alliance system, and the new twists of the arms race among the leading nuclear powers may prove dangerously unsettling. But the spread of nuclear weapons could fragment the international system into unstable subsystems, especially in Asia, where the tension between the United States and China could lead to nuclear war, and in areas such as the Middle East. Proliferation may cause the balance of uncertainty to shift, from inciting caution to encouraging rashness and miscalculation. . . .[7]

For the United States, the advantages of a moderate, multi-hierarchical system are considerable. Since there would be several hierarchies, America's nuclear superiority would ultimately count less—but it is hard to imagine any system where the hierarchy was based entirely on unusable power. Yet, fortunately, the United States is not badly endowed in usable power, military and otherwise, and would not suffer in a system that permitted major states to use (non-nuclear) power more freely than happens today. By restoring an international hierarchy and recreating a society of major states, such

---

[7] These points summarize my argument in *A World of Nuclear Powers,* pp. 101–9.

a system would also unfreeze some of the power now frustratingly congealed in the superpowers' storerooms. America's position as a world power would be guaranteed; but, because the responsibilities of world order would be shared by more states and also because of regional diversification, the need to agonize and fret about every incident, to behave as if the United States were an unfortunate Atlas holding up the world, would no longer be so great; selectivity would again be possible.

So would flexibility. The various functional hierarchies, the regional decentralization, the existence of a whole group of powers with interests held partly in common and partly in conflict would allow for supple, shifting alignments. The United States would no longer be torn, in each crisis, between the fear of losing face, security, or power by refraining from confrontation or intervention and the fear of a holocaust if it intervenes or meets the challenge. Crises could more easily be localized and disconnected than is possible when every incident has a potential link to the relationship of major tension.

. . . A moderate multi-hierarchy would reduce the great powers' need for clients and servants and make of the relations among major states the main focus of international politics. Of course, the United States (and the Soviet Union) would no longer enjoy the advantages that leading powers have in bipolar systems—the benefits of domination over a certain group of nations. But, as we know, in the present circumstances, enjoyment has changed to annoyance all too often. The fruits of empire have gone sour, and cannot turn sweet again. And it is hopeless to expect a system where the superpowers would combine the advantages of bipolarity and those of balance-of-power systems.

Can a multi-hierarchical system be moderate? That is the vital question. Any conclusion derived from past balance-of-power systems must be revised. There, the capacity to resort to force provided the yardstick of power and the dynamics of mutual adjustment. The exercise of this capacity could in the future lead to calamity. Since deterrence of major aggression committed by a great power now depends on nuclear weapons, the likelihood of limited wars (like those which agitated balance-of-power systems) decreases, for the risk of their escalation to nuclear war would be too great. On the other hand, the possibility that a coalition of powers could stop a non-nuclear move of one or more great powers by non-nuclear means may be less, since not using nuclear weapons and putting restraints on other military means out of fear of escalation may well result in outcomes quite unproportional to the theoretic force ratios; the regional and functional fragmentation would also tend to "demilitarize" and complicate the traditional calculations of power. The very uncertainty of calculations will put the restraints that have developed in the present international system to a severe test, multiply danger points, and disturb the establishment and operation of mechanisms devised to strengthen the remaining incentives to prudence. "The very flexibility of alignment which brought stability to the balance-of-power system could become a serious threat to the maintenance of deterrence."[8]

As I have said, it is imperative that American foreign policy be focused, beyond the hazards of today's confrontations, on the long-range tasks of moderating a system so complex. It is impossible to give here more than a few general directives:

1. Because "the superpowers predominantly fashion the conventions of the international system" and because "their use of military nuclear technology will crucially influence the behavior of nascent nuclear powers,"[9] it is essential that the United States continue to resist the challenges of its enemies whenever they try to reap gains by using or threatening to use force across national borders; otherwise, revolutionary ideologies will have little incentive to become at least externally moderate. But the United States must also continue to keep its confrontations at a very low level of violence, lest moderation be doomed.

2. In a world with several nuclear states, a hierarchy too prominently based on the yardstick of military nuclear power could wreck moderation, for it could weaken the superpowers' self-deterrence or mutual deterrence which has thus far kept them from exploiting their nuclear and conventional superiority especially against challenging secondary nuclear powers; also, it would encourage more states to acquire nuclear weapons. . . .

3. The temptation that middle and small nuclear powers might have to use their nuclear weapons, or that powers well endowed with

[8] Zoppo, "Nuclear Technology, Multipolarity and International Stability," *World Politics,* July 1966, p. 601. See also Osgood's cautious conclusions in Robert E. Osgood and Robert W. Tucker, *Force, Order, and Justice* (Baltimore: Johns Hopkins Press, 1967), pp. 176 ff.
[9] Zoppo, cited, p. 602.

conventional forces might have to use them in order to make gains, will have to be fought in two ways. They will have to be deterred from, and punished for, resort to force, but in a way that will restore moderation, not encourage escalation. This means, in particular, that nations threatened by a small or middle nuclear power ought to be protected from nuclear blackmail by a nuclear guarantee from the superpowers; but given the limits and uncertainties of such guarantees, protection against non-nuclear attacks and pressures (which are more likely) will have to be insured by the development of the threatened nations' conventional defenses. Also, a moderate international system is one in which "elementary standards of interstate behavior" will have to be observed; for instance, respect for the principle of free passage through international waters, a rule adopted in the interest of all states. Any unilateral violation of such a rule must be resisted, preferably by collective action, worldwide or regional, but, if necessary, by the United States alone—always with the caveat of proportionality, i.e., of employing means that extinguish the fire instead of enlarge it. Thwarting immoderation is not enough; small and middle nuclear powers will have to be rewarded both for having power and for refraining from using it—i.e., they will have to be given a greater role in the management of regional and world affairs.

4. A serious effort will be necessary to decentralize the international system. The superpowers must assure mutual deterrence among themselves and provide a kind of reserve of usable power against lesser delinquents. Deterrence of nuclear war will continue to depend on them, especially on their clear determination to use all methods short of nuclear violence against a lesser power guilty of having broken the taboo on the use of nuclear weapons. Deterrence of other kinds of violence, and the restoration of peace, would have to be assured in priority by regional organizations, in coordination with the United Nations. Such agencies would also be entrusted with the nonmilitary prevention of violence, i.e., with the settlement of disputes. . . . It may take time until such organizations are set up. In the meantime, especially in areas that are too deeply divided to provide regional institutions, moderation will depend, first, on the maintenance of regional balances of power, and, second, on the superpowers' willingness to insure the restoration of peace in regional conflicts, either jointly, or at least under the main responsibility of one of them without destructive opposition from the other, and preferably within

the framework of the United Nations. But this is not a satisfactory solution in the long term.

5. In order to be moderate, the new international system will have to permit a double change in the pursuit of national goals. The pursuit of milieu goals will still be essential—indeed, keeping the milieu moderate through various and diversified arms-control and enforcement measures will be a major concern—but in the future international system, such goals will also have to be more accessible. National power, in its many functional varieties, will have to be geared less to the hectic and frustrating competitive attempts at shaping the milieu in one's own image, less to the paralyzing anguishes of mutual denial, and more to the joint transformation of the milieu. Here again, agencies of international cooperation will be important. On the other hand, nations will also have to be able to pursue possession goals that are accessible without violence. This means that the range of possession goals which can be pursued jointly, according to rules of competition-through-cooperation (rather than competition-in-separate-action), and the range of possession goals which can be reached in separate action but not at the direct expense of other states, must be increased. The whole realm of technology and development offers opportunities which have been curtailed by the concentration on denials.

6. Moderation requires not only the sharpest possible reduction of interstate violence, but also a gradual withdrawal of one state from the manipulation of another's domestic polity. A world in which some leading powers tried to prevent revolutions in other societies and others tried to foment them would be exposed to all the dangers that revolutionary wars create even in today's world. Revolutions are a safety valve of change in an international system in which necessary restraints on force tend to eliminate war (the most effective traditional instrument of change), in which a thwarted revolution would only lead to an uncontrollable explosion, in which new kinds of possession goals and milieu goals create inevitable domestic tensions, and in which the internal conditions of many states will continue to be turbulent. But universal involvement in revolutions would make moderation impossible.

*   *   *

In striving for the future moderate international system, the United States should develop two qualities in its foreign policy—one of which has been destroyed by the present international system and by America's political style and decision-making processes, the other one ruled out by the projection of our institutional habits into foreign affairs. I am referring, of course, to flexibility and the ability to cooperate with others. Flexibility would permit Gulliver to be untied, and would allow the United States to approach the world's issues and conflicts in a way that would not threaten to blow up the planet. The needed kind of flexibility is very different from America's typical technical versatility; or its political ambivalence (the superficially wise choice of a middle course between unattractive extremes, which really conceals an absence of choice and combines the disadvantages, but not the advantages of those extremes); or the coexistence of policies that point in opposite directions and cancel each other out; or the political vacuum (the absence of a policy, other than ritual incantation, because of an incapacity to produce one except under duress or because of undue attachment to principles of small policy relevance). The kind of flexibility that is needed can, in fact, be provided only by the inevitably painful learning of cooperation with others.

What our policy should be can be described by a series of guidelines about discrimination, diversity, and devolution.

Discrimination

The competition the United States faces with its Communist foes is waged on a field that includes many very different and formally independent states. "Communism . . . is not an octopus with one head and a dozen arms, but a hydra with one trunk and a dozen heads, each of them ready to bite the other."[10] As a result, our political strategy can afford to be, and indeed must be, highly discriminating. For the United States, given its values and defensive position, to "win" the competition means not to lose it, whereas for its foes, not to win it means to lose it. The United States can be satisfied with a diverse world in which as few states as possible are under the control of its *main* enemies. The control of many states by national Communists would not be a disaster; what has to (and can) be prevented is their control by the Soviet Union or Red China, or their resort to aggression on their own. Even if there were many independent Com-

10 Ronald Steel, *Pax Americana* (New York: Viking Press, 1967), p. 159.

munist states, all vocally anti-American, dispersing American efforts against them would be a waste of resources, an exaggeration of the degree of harm they could do to us, an underestimation of the detrimental effect fragmentation must have in the Communist world, and a service rendered to the Soviet Union and China, which both would benefit from the dispersal of our efforts and from the leadership opportunity such efforts would provide them. Of course, the control of potentially or presently important nations by Communists, even local ones, would be a calamity because it would raise the number of our main foes; but the way to prevent this happening cannot be military deterrence (external or internal) alone. Instead of acting like a defensive army in classical strategy—ready for a blow anywhere along an interminable front, where the choice of the time and place belongs to the enemy—the United States ought to wage a strategy in depth: it can limit and rank its objectives instead of overexposing itself.

More concretely, this means remembering the internalization of the contest. American strategic power can deter its two major foes from large-scale aggression and help to make the costs of more limited aggressions prohibitive. Hence, the chances of a country being taken over by Communists depend primarily on its domestic circumstances. Even the possibility of preventing by military force a Communist takeover through subversion depends to a degree on the political capacity for resistance in the threatened society. No amount of substitution of American power for missing political forces will do.

It also means the United States must remember that an effective foreign policy uses the art of exploiting differences. Any policy that throws together, even if only as a *de facto* condition, the two main adversaries of the United States (China and the Soviet Union); that consolidates the hold the Soviet Union still exerts on its satellites and clients; that makes Communist movements elsewhere more dependent on one or the other of the Big Brothers; or that throws non-Communist opposition movements in non-Communist countries closer to the Communists, is an absurdity. The division of the world into independent nation-states and the internalization of the international contest make for a kind of natural barrier against the domino effect. In a worldwide defensive contest, some defeats are inevitable; but only if we succeed in convincing ourselves and our friends that the fall of one domino brings down the whole row, will the row indeed be threatened with collapse. In a system as complex as this,

it is necessary to compartmentalize foreign policy, even while per-
suing world-wide objectives—just as on a modern boat, seeping
water in one cabin does not mean the whole vessel will sink. One
only increases the prestige and effectiveness of one's adversaries by
attributing an omnipotent capacity to subvert and start rebellions to
them. "Revolutionary wars" come in all sorts and shapes; countries
cannot be compared to fireplaces where the wood and the paper are
always ready, waiting only for a Communist match to start the fire.
Not even the Red Chinese claim that.

Discrimination also means that the United States must set different
expectations and objectives in different places. In other words, there
must be a range of objectives. To aim for the maximum when it is
out of reach may insure the loss of the minimum. Where the threat
of military invasion or subversion is great, where the domestic society
is reasonably coherent and equipped with fairly reliable institutions
but unable to defend itself by its own means alone, where American
aid in the defense of that society is welcome, and where the military
presence of the United States does not thwart the achievement of
other goals desirable from the viewpoint of international moderation—there the maintenance of the American "presence" is a legitimate objective.

Where the society is weak and much of it discontented, and where
the chances for orderly reform are slight, the objectives ought to be
to keep from turning the United States into a lightning rod. . . .

Diversity

The underlying assumption is that in order to make the world safe
for diversity, diversity must be trusted. And indeed it is true that
when nationalists and Communists clash, the former win, either at
the Communists' expense or by twisting the Communist movement
out of shape. A sound foreign policy would take advantage of our
great asset: the desire of practically all nations, especially the new
ones, to preserve their independence from outside control.

In most countries, the armed forces are inevitably on the side of
national independence; their vigilance, their frequent opposition to
civilian regimes that corrupt or waste national resources, and the
difficulty of modern *coups d'état* in the face of police and military
resistance complicate the Communists' task considerably. The United

States has the means to protect against armed attack the nations situated close to the limits of the Chinese and the Russian domain. If some nations are unable to provide by themselves a sound basis against subversion or civil war, it may be in our interest to help establish such a basis; but American involvement is counterproductive if it (more or less inadvertently) crosses the elusive border between the offer to help consolidate national independence and the presumption to guide the assisted nation in directions we believe wise to follow. For we then lose the benefits of diversity. At worst, such a transgression turns the United States into the target of local discontents, the scapegoat, the Saint Sebastian for nationalist arrows. Thus, while in many cases local armies are our natural allies, deep involvement with them may buy temporary "order" at the cost of future upheavals. At best, a hand both heavy and inept would deprive the assisted nations of a sense of responsibility and self-respect, burden the adviser with perpetual minors, and condemn tutor and tutee alike to all the frustrations of subtly hierarchical relations. . . .

Devolution

The preceding suggestions amount to saying: act in such a way as to let other nations follow their own course; see to it that they are not pushed off their course and that they can follow the course they choose, but do not set the course for them, and if they should stumble and fall, you will not be made responsible.

The only risk in trusting diversity is the risk of chaos in a world of sovereign states skidding on separate courses. This is why the notion of diversity has to be qualified by that of devolution. Many nations, new and old, are engaged in a fight for international recognition—through developing resources that will make them powers that matter, through shrill rebellions against the inequities of past domination or unjust treaties, through attacks on international patterns (such as bipolarity) that deprive them of what they deem their legitimate role. All of this could all too easily make them "turn inward," or turn them into trouble-makers. The United States is caught in a dilemma: if it defines the "constructive enterprises in every corner in the world"[11] that it would like others to undertake and prods them

---

[11] President Johnson, quoted by Walt W. Rostow, in *Department of State Bulletin*, Vol. LX, No. 1412, p. 79.

to start these efforts, it will clash with the profound desire of most peoples for self-determination and self-respect. We need a "rising tide of good sense in the world,"[12] but to define it ourselves is nonsense. Yet to leave diversity to itself may breed immoderation and chaos.

The way out of the dilemma is what I would call devolution. More encouragement should be given to existing international and regional agencies and to the creation of new ones. But it is unlikely that regional and international organizations can become anything but debating societies and limited instruments of technical cooperation unless the United States' attitude changes in two respects. One would be toward a greater willingness to give responsibilities to organizations it does not control or over whose decisions it would have no veto. What often slows down the development of such organizations now (for instance, in Asia and Western Europe) is the fear of some members that they will become trapped in a net held by the United States. The other change would have to be toward a greater willingness to let these organizations handle matters that have so far remained under national control and that will remain so unless the United States gives the decisive impetus by transferring control of various programs to them; this would be particularly appropriate in the realm of foreign aid, but also in that of regional security, especially by giving the organizations of which it is a member greater financial resources.

Second, devolution must consist in placing more responsibilities on the middle powers, such as Japan, India, Britain, or France. They want to play a major role; one must see to it that they can, not as powers concerned only with their own security, expansion, and development, but as partial trustees of world order, interested in the safety, growth, and harmony of a larger area. This means encouraging their diplomatic initiatives for peacekeeping or peaceful change, helping them to defend the area or to initiate schemes for economic cooperation, so that they will have the psychological boost of leadership and contribute to international moderation at the same time. What has often slowed down these developments is our fear that their moves would conflict with our interests or position. We do not seem to realize enough where our higher interest lies. We must

[12] Rostow, same.

understand that our distaste, however justified, for strengthening what we see as "parochial" national ambitions and our preference for collective solutions only prevent the emergence of the latter and reinforces national pettiness by frustrating the designs of states to which the only real alternative is not a collective solution but a for-eign—often an American—one. To be sure, we have encouraged such designs when they coincide exactly with our concerns. But that is not devolution, it is duplication; and, since it violates the impera-tives of diversity, it is no wonder that it repeatedly fails.

Eugene V. Rostow

THE THING WE HAVE TO FEAR IS
FEAR ITSELF

On July 4, 1970, there appeared in The New Yorker _magazine William Whitworth's remarkable interview with Yale law professor and former Under Secretary of State for Political Affairs Eugene V. Rostow. An expanded version is the 1970 volume,_ Naive Questions about War and Peace. _Eugene Rostow is not really a critic of globalism. His recommendations constitute, it was argued in the Introduction, an invitation to a policy of globalism minus the moralism. Readers should ask themselves whether they agree with that charge. They should also ask whether Rostow's rejection of the term "American imperialism," does not land him in a revealing contradiction. On the one hand, he is confident that, forcibly deprived of important trade and investments, the United States could retrench, make the difficult adjustments and pull through. But when it comes to "the fear of hegemony, the fear of being dominated," then Rostow sees the American people as prisoners of their own worst instincts, and American leaders, whom other critics charge with contributing to the psychology of fear in the first place, helpless to educate the nation to view its interests more rationally. Rostow, who is the brother of W. W. Rostow, is also the author of_ Peace in the Balance _(1972)._

[Eugene Rostow:] "Today, we live in a world in which three enormous flows of change are happening at once. First is the liquidation of empire, the withdrawal of the European states to Europe. The second is the rise of Communist powers, and I put that in the plural—there are different forms of communism, and they are dividing, but nonetheless they combine on certain occasions, and the Soviet Union has enormous nuclear strength and conventional strength. And the third is the rise of our own response. The consequence of the withdrawal of Europe from the world has been that the Balkan problem, which used to be a _Balkan_ problem, is now almost universal. We have many nations in Africa and Asia which have been liberated from the control of empire but are weak and vulnerable, both from within and from without.

"Now, our response, starting after the Second World War, when

Reprinted from _Naive Questions about War and Peace_ by William Whitworth, pp. 19–24, 32–33, 36–37, 42–43, 79–81, 108–110. By permission of W. W. Norton & Company, Inc., and International Famous Agency. Copyright © 1970 by William Whitworth.

we began to realize that our earnest and sustained efforts to reach an accommodation with the Soviet Union, to reach a pattern of co-operation with them, based on economic aid and cooperation in eliminating the nuclear threat—when we realized that those efforts had failed, we set about to create a situation of stability in the world; really, to establish a new balance of power. The title of Dean Acheson's great book is *Present at the Creation.* And there is a deep truth in that title, because at the end of the war we faced a situation in which the world political system was in chaos. The system that had kept the peace more or less between 1815 and 1914 disintegrated between 1914 and 1945, and in 1945 it was finished. Russia, China, Japan—these were countries on a new scale, as far as European capacity was concerned, and the Europeans were engaged in a slow, painful withdrawal from their positions of empire, which had preserved a kind of stability in the world political system for a long time. We gradually became aware of a national interest in achieving a new balance of power, within which we could hope to live as a free society, a balance of power which could permit us to survive pretty much in terms of our historic patterns. I like to turn Wilson's remark around: Wilson talked about making the world safe for democracy—we need a world in which American democracy would be safe at home. I don't think we could survive as a democratic nation if we were alone and isolated in a world of hostility, chaos, and poverty. I think our instinct was right shortly after the war, when President Truman finally drew the line and said, 'Thus far, and no further,' about Iran, Greece, Turkey, and Berlin, and later Korea. Now, our rhetoric, our way of talking about problems of national security, hasn't yet caught up with our instincts. We're aware of the fact that the world is much smaller, much more dangerous than it used to be, and that the powers that used to protect us can do so no longer. But we find it extremely difficult to realize that we have a permanent interest in protecting the independence and the territorial integrity of Western Europe, of Japan, and of many other parts of the world which are necessary to constitute a system of order. Many people say this policy is globalism, or it's an anti-Communist crusade. It's neither one. Let me take the second point first. Are we engaged in an anti-Communist crusade? The United States never dreamed of attacking the Soviet Union or of delivering an ultimatum to the Soviet Union at a time when we had the nuclear monopoly. Nor, indeed, did we undertake to change the arrangements which emerged in Eastern Europe, although these arrangements were contrary to agreements that had been made with us at both Yalta and Potsdam. These things happened, they alarmed us and concerned us, but we didn't think of using force to undo them. What happened was that we said, in effect, that the process of outward expansion by the Soviet Union is beginning to threaten the possibility of equilibrium in the world, and that the safest rule is the rule that President Truman laid down—'Thus far, and no further.'

"Now, most people, I think, understand and accept that kind of balance-of-power reasoning about Europe and about Japan, because these are obviously enormous centers of power. And to add them to the Soviet or the Chinese list of resources could be potentially very dangerous, in terms of old instincts about the balance of power. But why do we have to worry about smaller countries, which in themselves don't amount to much in terms of power? Why Korea? Why Vietnam? Why are we concerned about the Middle East? Well, to take the Middle East first—because that's a problem on which I worked hard and long in Washington—manifestly, the United States isn't threatened if Syria or another small country in the Middle East becomes, in effect, a Soviet satellite. There are, of course, implications for the problem of power if Soviet naval bases or airbases are established in Syria or Algeria. Such a dispersion of Soviet power would present problems for us in the nuclear field of targeting and deterrence. The issue is one of degree. In the Middle East, the Soviets are using Arab-Israeli hostility as an engine to stir up terrific political movements in the Arab world—political movements whose goal is to destroy the kind of moderate government that exists in Lebanon, in Tunisia, in Jordan, in Saudi Arabia, ultimately even in Iran. Complete Soviet control in the area, or nearly complete control, would be a genuine threat.

"If you look at this Soviet effort as a military campaign, what do you see? You see, in the first place, that Europe is outflanked. The military arrangements of NATO and of the Warsaw Pact powers in the middle of Europe, facing each other, deterring each other, become almost as irrelevant as the Maginot Line if Soviet power is extended all the way around to Algeria, Tunisia, Libya, and so on. And there are possibilities of explosions in the Middle East, involving Israel or other countries, which could bring us to the kind of panic, the kind of atmosphere of rage, which is the real cause of war. War comes when people feel that the moorings are slipping, when the situation is getting out of hand and there's a slide toward chaos which threatens their sense of safety. I can't imagine that Europe or the United States would stand by and see Israel destroyed, no matter *what* people think now. The actual event, if it began to happen, would precipitate an enormous revulsion, colored, of course, by the Nazi experience. Israel is a country that exists by virtue of a decision made by the United Nations, and by the United States and the Soviet Union, in 1947, and people have lived there, a community has been formed, and we're simply not going to stand by and see these people pushed into the sea.

"Now, this area involves a terrific risk, because arms are being poured into the Middle East, hostility is being mounted. You can say, 'Well, what is our interest there?' Well, our interest is in preventing a convulsion that could threaten the possibility of peace. It's an interest in the people, an interest in the integrity of commitments, but above all it's an interest in the possibility of peace. And if the Soviet Union came to dominate and occupy the whole of the Middle East, we would be threatened strategically in a way that would touch psychological nerves and create the kind of risk we faced in the Cuban missile crisis. You can say, 'Well, why were we so excited by the Cuban missile crisis?' Yes, the Soviet Union had lied to President Kennedy about those missiles. Missiles in Cuba are very close to the United States. On the other hand, there are missiles on Soviet submarines. And missiles can reach the United States from the Soviet Union itself, and from bombers. But the Cuban episode is worth studying because *we were ready to go then.* There was a rage in the country and a sense of threat, and these were extremely dangerous. Was it rational or irrational? Now, I think that one of the main objectives of our foreign policy should be to prevent those risks from developing. Of course, the problem is infinitely more difficult throughout the Third World than it is in Europe or in Japan. Now let me come to Vietnam.

*   *   *

"[W]hat was done [there] was done, I think, in very large part to try to help build Europe and to try to cooperate with France and Britain, and out of concern that [the] smaller states in Southeast Asia would go down like dominoes, in the famous expression, if the process of expansion weren't halted somewhere. It reminds me a little bit of the great debate in the thirties about Danzig. The word went around Europe, 'Why should we die for Danzig?' But if the resistance to Hitler's expansion had come earlier it would have been easier to contain. The phenomenon of a balance of power doesn't depend so much on any particular piece of territory, I think, as on getting acceptance for the notion of equilibrium and for the notion that there can't be expansion through force, expansion by unilateral decision, because you can't tell where it's going to end.

*　　*　　*

"But I think the major concern—at least, my major concern—in this miserable affair is the long-range impact a withdrawal would have on Japanese policy. Japanese policy is a matter of the utmost importance to the future of world politics. Japan is the third industrial nation of the world, and our policy toward Japan has been one of close cooperation, and I think it should remain one of close cooperation. Close and deep cooperation. I think the ultimate question, really, in that whole area, if we're going to try to preserve any kind of balance of power in Asia—which has always been a goal of American policy—is how China is going to be modernized. If we're going to pull away from Asia and let Asia stew in its own juice, then I think one of the things to think about is how this process of modernizing China is going to be organized. Is it going to be carried out in the long run by the whole group of Western nations? By Russia alone? By Japan alone? By everybody working cooperatively, as is now the case, pretty much, in India? That would be the best solution of all. That is a series of questions in which we have an *immense* national interest. And I think the outcome of the Vietnam war has a good deal to do with the calculations that Japan will make about the validity of American guarantees and about the conclusions that can be drawn from American guarantees.

*　　*　　*

"I'm not talking ideologically—about whether a country is Communist or not. I'm talking about a power constellation, about the possibility of peace. Will Japan remain closely associated with us— deeply linked to us in the realm of politics, of the conduct of foreign relations—or will she go off on a course that's totally different, if we pull away?

*   *   *

"If too many strategic areas of the world come under hostile control, that begins to engender the kinds of political fears, the kinds of anxieties, that move men to war. You can say this is irrational. If we just looked at the situation and kept our cool, we wouldn't have to react. That course might be correct sometimes. But there are real risks in such a process nonetheless. The question arises as to when people find the risks intolerable, as we did in the Cuban missile crisis. Now, the Cuban missile crisis wasn't created by the government. It exploded, and the government handled it in a certain way. The information, as you said, became generally available, and it created a wave of panic.

*   *   *

"The trouble is really a deeper one. . . . We know that Soviet policy and Chinese policy are not as benign as all that. We know that they do probe and reach very far—throughout the Middle East, throughout Africa, throughout Asia, of course, and into South America. And in this country there is a fear—which no one can say is irrational—that the aim of their policies is not simply to consolidate power within three great blocks, as you suggest, but to reach all the way."

*   *   *

[William Whitworth]: "As you say, these problems are in some ways more psychological than they are economic, or even military."
[Rostow:] "Absolutely. They're fundamentally psychological. What is security? How do you feel secure, in this kind of world, with this kind of hostility? The changes in the map of the world since 1945 have imposed a great strain on our minds. Americans are now struggling—struggling desperately—to digest the meaning of these enormous changes in the map of the world for their own lives. That's what the turbulence in our universities is really about, I think. That turbulence, and the deep agitation elsewhere in the country, reflects, I believe, the pain and difficulty of this battle between past and present in our minds. It is a demanding process. Can't we free ourselves of the fear of hegemony, the fear of being dominated, which

has led men to war so often in the past? What does the fear of dominance do to people? Perhaps psychiatrists can answer that question.
I can't. All I know is that that kind of fear is a reality in human affairs.
I don't think we are a new breed of men, immune to the diseases and
fears of history. And I remain of the view that foreign policy should
not allow such fears to develop, that the best—the only—cure for
such fears is to prevent the convulsions in the distribution of power
which have always been their cause. That's why I say that the nuclear
bomb doesn't change the problem much, and that we have to continue to struggle patiently and steadily to get the Soviets and the
Chinese to accept the notion of equilibrium which we have been
seeking since 1947. Only on that basis can we hope for the kind of
open, progressive world in which we could flourish as a free people—
a world where energy could be devoted to development, and education, and social advance, and not to the tragedy and brutality of war.
Everything turns on the outcome of the American debate about these
themes."

[Whitworth:] "It seems that the best thing we could do for our
security would be to help our potential enemies feel secure." . . .

[Rostow:] "Of course. I agree completely. But how do you do it?
One of the hardest things for people to realize—to believe—is that
there are people in the world who don't *want* an agreement. . . . Our
politics are politics of compromise, of accommodation, and it's very
difficult for us to imagine that the Egyptians or the North Koreans
or Hanoi or the Russians don't *want* to make an agreement. I was
talking to some students the other day, and one of them said very
earnestly, 'Well, why don't people try to reach an understanding with
the Russians?' I answered, 'What on earth do you think we've been
trying to do?' And I told him about some of our efforts in this direction
—troop reductions in Europe, compromise in the Middle East, a solution in Vietnam, and so on. And he said, 'If I believe what you say,
then I don't know what I believe about the world.' "

*   *   *

[Whitworth:] "What's our concern with the western Pacific? I
mean, then you get back to—"

[Rostow:] "You get back to why we are interested in the first
place. . . . Trade, movement, fear . . . a sense that these—The two
big changes that have occurred, the Communist revolutions in China

and Russia, have cost us an enormous amount. Trying to deter and contain their expansion. The feeling that if they expanded indefinitely, we would face a situation in which we really felt threatened all the time."

[At this point, Whitworth quotes] to Rostow from an article by Robert L. Heilbroner, "Counter-Revolutionary America," which appeared first in *Commentary* and later in a paperback collection entitled *A Dissenter's Guide to Foreign Policy.* [As reported by Whitworth,] "Heilbroner said in the article that even if much of the underdeveloped world turned Communist and became hostile to the United States, the resulting military threat would be slight. We wouldn't be threatened by millions of men who couldn't be deployed, and the armaments capacities of these areas are small. . . . If we lost the entire sixteen billion dollars invested in Latin America, Asia, and Africa, it would be a blow to some corporations . . . but—with our gross national product approaching three-quarters of a trillion dollars and our total corporate assets amounting to more than one and three-tenths trillion—it would be tolerable. Heilbroner went on to say, 'By these remarks I do not wish airily to dismiss the dangers of a Communist avalanche in the backward nations. There would be dangers, not the least those of an American hysteria.'

"Rostow said he didn't disagree with Heilbroner's analysis."

[Whitworth:] "About the economics and the manpower. . . . But you don't agree completely, because Heilbroner says later in the article that much of the motivation for our anticommunism is a fear of our not being the model for world civilization, a fear of losing our place in the sun."

[Rostow:] "I don't agree with that at all . . . I don't think our foreign policy is based on a place-in-the-sun psychology. I don't think we get any pleasure out of our position. I recall George Aiken's remark. He said we've inherited the responsibilities but not the privileges of the British Empire. I don't think any Americans enjoy it. But I think there would be a sense of strategic threat if the changes Heilbroner describes took place. In the emplacement of missiles, for example, just as there was over Cuba and there remains over Cuba. Cuba is a gnawing anxiety in the Congress, really. More than you might think. And the missiles there—we can say very rationally, 'Oh, hell, they have missiles in submarines, why should we fret over whether they have them in Cuba or not? But a threat of being surrounded—

what Heilbroner calls hysteria—I don't think can be discounted. And the strategic space problems, the emplacement of bases all around, can become a major element of politics."

Richard M. Nixon and Henry A. Kissinger

REALISM IN THE WHITE HOUSE

"We must remember that the only time in the history of the world that we have had any extended periods of peace is when there has been a balance of power. I think it will be a safer world and a better world if we have a strong healthy United States, Europe, Soviet Union, China, Japan, each balancing the other, not playing one against the other, an even balance." (Time, January 3, 1972, p. 15.)

The words are President Nixon's, but might not the thought be Henry Kissinger's? Selections from Nixon and Kissinger are placed together because although their writings are separable, their policies are not. Dr. Kissinger wrote the articles collected in American Foreign Policy *while still Professor of Government at Harvard University. Readers will note the parallels, but not of course a complete identity of views with fellow academics Hans Morgenthau and Stanley Hoffmann. Particularly noteworthy is that while Kissinger endorses "equilibrium" as the goal for post-Globalist American policy, he also worries that it may not mesh with America's idealistic style. President Nixon's first State of the World Message (to what extent composed by Kissinger?) offers what may be a solution: Realist (at least in part) policy presented with old-fashioned American hyperbole as the way to a generation of peace.*

HENRY A. KISSINGER, 1969

Wherever we turn, then, the central task of American foreign policy is to analyze anew the current international environment and to develop some concepts which will enable us to contribute to the emergence of a stable order.

First, we must recognize the existence of profound structural

Reprinted from *American Foreign Policy, Three Essays* by Henry A. Kissinger, pp. 91–97. By permission of W. W. Norton & Company, Inc., and George Weidenfeld and Nicolson Ltd. Copyright © 1969 by Henry A. Kissinger.

problems that are to a considerable extent independent of the intentions of the principal protagonists and that cannot be solved merely by good will. The vacuum in Central Europe and the decline of the Western European countries would have disturbed the world equilibrium regardless of the domestic structure of the Soviet Union. A strong China has historically tended to establish suzerainty over its neighbors; in fact, one special problem of dealing with China—communism apart—is that it has had no experience in conducting foreign policy with equals. China has been either dominant or subjected.

To understand the structural issue, it is necessary to undertake an inquiry, from which we have historically shied away, into the essence of our national interest and into the premises of our foreign policy. It is part of American folklore that, while other nations have interests, we have responsibilities; while other nations are concerned with equilibrium, we are concerned with the legal requirements of peace. We have a tendency to offer our altruism as a guarantee of our reliability: "We have no quarrel with the Communists," Secretary of State Rusk said on one occasion; "all our quarrels are on behalf of other people."

Such an attitude makes it difficult to develop a conception of our role in the world. It inhibits other nations from gearing their policy to ours in a confident way—a "disinterested" policy is likely to be considered "unreliable." A mature conception of our interest in the world would obviously have to take into account the widespread interest in stability and peaceful change. It would deal with two fundamental questions: What is it in our interest to prevent? What should we seek to accomplish?

The answer to the first question is complicated by an often-repeated proposition that we must resist aggression anywhere it occurs since peace is indivisible. A corollary is the argument that we do not oppose the fact of particular changes but the method by which they are brought about. We find it hard to articulate a truly vital interest which we would defend however "legal" the challenge. This leads to an undifferentiated globalism and confusion about our purposes. The abstract concept of aggression causes us to multiply our commitments. But the denial that our interests are involved diminishes our staying power when we try to carry out these commitments.

Part of the reason for our difficulties is our reluctance to think in terms of power and equilibrium. In 1949, for example, a State Department memorandum justified NATO as follows:

[The treaty] obligates the parties to defend the purposes and principles of the United Nations, the freedom, common heritage and civilization of the parties and their free institutions based upon the principles of democracy, individual liberty and the role of law. It obligates them to act in defense of peace and security. It is directed against no one; it is directed solely against aggression. It seeks not to influence any shifting balance of power but to strengthen a balance of principle.

But principle, however lofty, must at some point be related to practice; historically, stability has always coincided with an equilibrium that made physical domination difficult. Interest is not necessarily amoral; moral consequences can spring from interested acts. Britain did not contribute any the less to international order for having a clear-cut concept of its interest which required it to prevent the domination of the Continent by a single power (no matter in what way it was threatened) and the control of the seas by anybody (even if the immediate intentions were not hostile). A new American administration confronts the challenge of relating our commitments to our interests and our obligations to our purposes.

The task of defining positive goals is more difficult but even more important. The first two decades after the end of the Second World War posed problems well suited to the American approach to international relations. Wherever we turned, massive dislocations required attention. Our pragmatic, *ad hoc* tendency was an advantage in a world clamoring for technical remedies. Our legal bent contributed to the development of many instruments of stability.

In the late sixties, the situation is more complex. The United States is no longer in a position to operate programs globally; it has to encourage them. It can no longer impose its preferred solutions; it must seek to evoke it. In the forties and fifties, we offered remedies; in the late sixties and in the seventies our role will have to be to contribute to a structure that will foster the initiative of others. We are a superpower physically, but our designs can be meaningful only if they generate willing cooperation. We can continue to contribute to defense and positive programs, but we must seek to encourage and not stifle a sense of local responsibility. Our contribution should not be the sole or principal effort, but it should make the difference between success and failure.

This task requires a different kind of creativity and another form of patience than we have displayed in the past. Enthusiasm, belief in progress, and the invincible conviction that American remedies can work everywhere must give way to an understanding of historical trends, an ordering of our preferences, and above all an understanding of the difference our preferences can in fact make.

The dilemma is that there can be no stability without equilibrium but, equally, equilibrium is not a purpose with which we can respond to the travail of our world. A sense of mission is clearly a legacy of American history; to most Americans, America has always stood for something other than its own grandeur. But a clearer understanding of America's interests and of the requirements of equilibrium can give perspective to our idealism and lead to humane and moderate objectives, especially in relation to political and social change. Thus our conception of world order must have deeper purposes than stability but greater restraints on our behavior than would result if it were approached only in a fit of enthusiasm.

Whether such a leap of the imagination is possible in the modern bureaucratic state remains to be seen. New administrations come to power convinced of the need for goals and for comprehensive concepts. Sooner, rather than later, they find themselves subjected to the pressures of the immediate and the particular. Part of the reason is the pragmatic, issue-oriented bias of our decision makers. But the fundamental reason may be the pervasiveness of modern bureaucracy. What started out as an aid to decision making has developed a momentum of its own. Increasingly, the policy maker is more conscious of the pressures and the morale of his staff than of the purpose this staff is supposed to serve. The policy maker becomes a referee among quasi-autonomous bureaucratic bodies. Success consists of moving the administrative machinery to the point of decision, leaving relatively little energy for analyzing the decision's merit. The modern bureaucratic state widens the range of technical choices while limiting the capacity to make them.

An even more serious problem is posed by the change of ethic of precisely the most idealistic element of American youth. The idealism of the fifties during the Kennedy era expressed itself in self-confident, often zealous, institution building. Today, however, many in the younger generation consider the management of power irrelevant, perhaps even immoral. While the idea of service retains a potent influence, it does so largely with respect to problems which are clearly *not* connected with the strategic aspects of American foreign policy; the Peace Corps is a good example. The new ethic of freedom is not "civic"; it is indifferent or even hostile to systems and notions of order. Management is equated with manipulation. Structural designs are perceived as systems of "domination"—not of order. The generation which has come of age after the fifties has had Vietnam as its introduction to world politics. It has no memory of occasions when American-supported structural innovations were successful or of the motivations which prompted these enterprises.

Partly as a result of the generation gap, the American mood oscillates dangerously between being ashamed of power and expecting too much of it. The former attitude deprecates the use or possession of force; the latter is overly receptive to the possibilities of absolute action and overly indifferent to the likely consequences. The danger of a rejection of power is that it may result in a nihilistic perfectionism which disdains the gradual and seeks to destroy what does not conform to its notion of utopia. The danger of an overconcern with force is that policy makers may respond to clamor by a series of spasmodic gestures and stylistic maneuvers and then recoil before their implications.

These essentially psychological problems cannot be overemphasized. It is the essence of a satisfied, advanced society that it puts a premium on operating within familiar procedures and concepts. It draws its motivation from the present, and it defines excellence by the ability to manipulate an established framework. But for the major part of humanity, the present becomes endurable only through a vision of the future. To most Americans—including most American leaders—the significant reality is what they see around them. But for most of the world—including many of the leaders of the new nations —the significant reality is what they wish to bring about. If we remain nothing but the managers of our physical patrimony, we will grow increasingly irrelevant. And since there can be no stability without us, the prospects of world order will decline.

We require a new burst of creativity, however, not so much for the sake of other countries as for our own people, especially the youth. The contemporary unrest is no doubt exploited by some whose purposes are all too clear. But that it is there to exploit is proof of a profound dissatisfaction with the merely managerial and consumer-oriented qualities of the modern state and with a world which seems to generate crises by inertia. The modern bureaucratic state, for all its panoply of strength, often finds itself shaken to its foundations by seemingly trivial causes. Its brittleness and the worldwide revolution of youth—especially in advanced countries and among the relatively affluent—suggest a spiritual void, an almost metaphysical boredom with a political environment that increasingly emphasizes bureaucratic challenges and is dedicated to no deeper purpose than material comfort.

Our unrest has no easy remedy. Nor is the solution to be found primarily in the realm of foreign policy. Yet a deeper nontechnical challenge would surely help us regain a sense of direction. The best and most prideful expressions of American purposes in the world have been those in which we acted in concert with others. Our influence in these situations has depended on achieving a reputation as a member of such a concert. To act consistently abroad we must be able to generate coalitions of shared purposes. Regional groupings supported by the United States will have to take over major responsibility for their immediate areas, with the United States being concerned more with the overall framework of order than with the management of every regional enterprise.

In the best of circumstances, the next administration will be beset by crises. In almost every area of the world, we have been living off capital—warding off the immediate, rarely dealing with underlying problems. These difficulties are likely to multiply when it becomes apparent that one of the legacies of the war in Vietnam will be a strong American reluctance to risk overseas involvements.

A new administration has the right to ask for compassion and understanding from the American people. But it must found its claim not on pat technical answers to difficult issues; it must above all ask the right questions. It must recognize that, in the field of foreign policy, we will never be able to contribute to building a stable and creative world order unless we first form some conception of it.

RICHARD M. NIXON, 1970

This first annual report on U.S. foreign policy is more than a record of one year. It is this administration's statement of a new approach to foreign policy, to match a new era of international relations.

A New Era

The postwar period in international relations has ended.

Then, we were the only great power whose society and economy had escaped World War II's massive destruction. Today, the ravages of that war have been overcome. Western Europe and Japan have recovered their economic strength, their political vitality, and their national self-confidence. Once the recipients of American aid, they have now begun to share their growing resources with the developing world. Once almost totally dependent on American military power, our European allies now play a greater role in our common policies, commensurate with their growing strength.

Then, new nations were being born, often in turmoil and uncertainty. Today, these nations have a new spirit and a growing strength of independence. Once, many feared that they would become simply a battleground of cold-war rivalry and fertile ground for Communist penetration. But this fear misjudged their pride in their national identities and their determination to preserve their newly won sovereignty.

Then, we were confronted by a monolithic Communist world. Today, the nature of that world has changed—the power of individual Communist nations has grown, but international Communist unity has been shattered. Once a unified bloc, its solidarity has been broken by the powerful forces of nationalism. The Soviet Union and Communist China, once bound by an alliance of friendship, had become bitter adversaries by the mid-1960s. The only times the Soviet Union has used the Red Army since World War II have been against its own allies—in East Germany in 1953, in Hungary in 1956, and in Czechoslovakia in 1968. The Marxist dream of international Communist unity has disintegrated.

Then, the United States had a monopoly or overwhelming supe-

From *U.S. Foreign Policy for the 1970s—A New Strategy for Peace,* A Report to the Congress by Richard Nixon, President of the United States, February 18, 1970.

riority of nuclear weapons. Today, a revolution in the technology of war has altered the nature of the military balance of power. New types of weapons present new dangers. Communist China has acquired thermonuclear weapons. Both the Soviet Union and the United States have acquired the ability to inflict unacceptable damage on the other, no matter which strikes first. There can be no gain and certainly no victory for the power that provokes a thermonuclear exchange. Thus, both sides have recognized a vital mutual interest in halting the dangerous momentum of the nuclear arms race.

Then, the slogans formed in the past century were the ideological accessories of the intellectual debate. Today, the "isms" have lost their vitality—indeed the restlessness of youth on both sides of the dividing line testifies to the need for a new idealism and deeper purposes.

This is the challenge and the opportunity before America as it enters the 1970s.

The Framework for a Durable Peace

In the first postwar decades, American energies were absorbed in coping with a cycle of recurrent crises, whose fundamental origins lay in the destruction of World War II and the tensions attending the emergence of scores of new nations. Our opportunity today—and challenge—is to get at the causes of crises, to take a longer view, and to help build the international relationships that will provide the framework of a durable peace.

I have often reflected on the meaning of "peace," and have reached one certain conclusion: Peace must be far more than the absence of war. Peace must provide a durable structure of international relationships which inhibits or removes the causes of war. Building a lasting peace requires a foreign policy guided by three basic principles:

—Peace requires *partnership.* Its obligations, like its benefits, must be shared. This concept of partnership guides our relations with all friendly nations.

—Peace requires *strength.* So long as there are those who would threaten our vital interests and those of our allies with military force, we must be strong. American weakness could tempt would-be aggressors to make dangerous miscalculations. At the same time, our own strength is important only in relation to the strength of others. We—like others—must place high priority on enhancing our security through cooperative arms control.

—Peace requires a *willingness to negotiate*. All nations—and we are no exception—have important national interests to protect. But the most fundamental interest of all nations lies in building the structure of peace. In partnership with our allies, secure in our own strength, we will seek those areas in which we can agree among ourselves and with others to accommodate conflicts and overcome rivalries. We are working toward the day when *all* nations will have a stake in peace, and will therefore be partners in its maintenance.

Within such a structure, international disputes can be settled and clashes contained. The insecurity of nations, out of which so much conflict arises, will be eased, and the habits of moderation and compromise will be nurtured. Most important, a durable peace will give full opportunity to the powerful forces driving toward economic change and social justice.

This vision of a peace built on partnership, strength, and willingness to negotiate is the unifying theme of this report. In the sections that follow, the first steps we have taken during this past year—the policies we have devised and the programs we have initiated to realize this vision—are placed in the context of these three principles.

1. Peace Through Partnership—The Nixon Doctrine

As I said in my address of November 3, "We Americans are a do-it-yourself people—an impatient people. Instead of teaching someone else to do a job, we like to do it ourselves. This trait has been carried over into our foreign policy."

The postwar era of American foreign policy began in this vein in 1947 with the proclamation of the Truman Doctrine and the Marshall Plan, offering American economic and military assistance to countries threatened by aggression. Our policy held that democracy and prosperity, buttressed by American military strength and organized in a worldwide network of American-led alliances, would insure stability and peace. In the formative years of the postwar period, this great effort of international political and economic reconstruction was a triumph of American leadership and imagination, especially in Europe.

For two decades after the end of the Second World War, our foreign policy was guided by such a vision and inspired by its success. The vision was based on the fact that the United States was the richest and most stable country, without whose initiative and resources little security or progress was possible.

This impulse carried us through into the 1960s. The United States conceived programs and ran them. We devised strategies, and proposed them to our allies. We discerned dangers, and acted directly to combat them.

The world has dramatically changed since the days of the Marshall Plan. We deal now with a world of stronger allies, a community of independent developing nations, and a Communist world still hostile but now divided.

Others now have the ability and responsibility to deal with local disputes which once might have required our intervention. Our contribution and success will depend not on the frequency of our involvement in the affairs of others, but on the stamina of our policies. This is the approach which will best encourage other nations to do their part, and will most genuinely enlist the support of the American people.

This is the message of the doctrine I announced at Guam—the "Nixon Doctrine." Its central thesis is that the United States will participate in the defense and development of allies and friends, but that America cannot—and will not—conceive *all* the plans, design *all* the programs, execute *all* the decisions and undertake *all* the defense of the free nations of the world. We will help where it makes a real difference and is considered in our interest.

America cannot live in isolation if it expects to live in peace. We have no intention of withdrawing from the world. The only issue before us is how we can be most effective in meeting our responsibilities, protecting our interests, and thereby building peace.

A more responsible participation by our foreign friends in their own defense and progress means a more effective common effort toward the goals we all seek. Peace in the world will continue to require us to maintain our commitments—and we will. As I said at the United Nations, "It is not my belief that the way to peace is by giving up our friends or letting down our allies." But a more balanced and realistic American role in the world is essential if American commitments are to be sustained over the long pull. In my State of the Union Address, I affirmed that "to insist that other nations play a role

is not a retreat from responsibility; it is a sharing of responsibility."
This is not a way for America to withdraw from its indispensable
role in the world. It is a way—the only way—we can carry out our
responsibilities.

It is misleading, moreover, to pose the fundamental question so
largely in terms of commitments. Our objective, in the first instance,
is to support our *interests* over the long run with a sound foreign
policy. The more that policy is based on a realistic assessment of
our and others' interests, the more effective our role in the world can
be. We are not involved in the world because we have commitments;
we have commitments because we are involved. Our interests must
shape our commitments, rather than the other way around.

We will view new commitments in the light of a careful assessment
of our own national interests and those of other countries, of the
specific threats to those interests, and of our capacity to counter
those threats at an acceptable risk and cost. . . .

2. America's Strength

The second element of a durable peace must be America's strength.
Peace, we have learned, cannot be gained by good will alone.

In determining the strength of our defenses, we must make precise
and crucial judgments. We should spend no more than is necessary.
But there is an irreducible minimum of essential military security: for
if we are less strong than necessary, and if the worst happens, there
will be no domestic society to look after. The magnitude of such a
catastrophe, and the reality of the opposing military power that could
threaten it, present a risk which requires of any President the most
searching and careful attention to the state of our defenses.

The changes in the world since 1945 have altered the context and
requirements of our defense policy. In this area, perhaps more than
in any other, the need to reexamine our approaches is urgent and
constant.

The last 25 years have seen a revolution in the nature of military
power. In fact, there has been a series of transformations—from the
atomic to the thermonuclear weapon, from the strategic bomber to
the intercontinental ballistic missile, from the surface missile to the
hardened silo and the missile-carrying submarine, from the single to
the multiple warhead, and from air defense to missile defense. We

are now entering an era in which the sophistication and destructiveness of weapons present more formidable and complex issues affecting our strategic posture.

The last 25 years have also seen an important change in the relative balance of strategic power. From 1945 to 1949, we were the only nation in the world possessing an arsenal of atomic weapons. From 1950 to 1966, we possessed an overwhelming superiority in strategic weapons. From 1967 to 1969, we retained a significant superiority. Today, the Soviet Union possesses a powerful and sophisticated strategic force approaching our own. We must consider, too, that Communist China will deploy its own intercontinental missiles during the coming decade, introducing new and complicating factors for our strategic planning and diplomacy.

In the light of these fateful changes, the Administration undertook a comprehensive and far-reaching reconsideration of the premises and procedures for designing our forces. We sought—and I believe we have achieved—a rational and coherent formulation of our defense strategy and requirements for the 1970s. . . .

3. Willingness to Negotiate—An Era of Negotiation

Partnership and strength are two of the pillars of the structure of a durable peace. Negotiation is the third. For our commitment to peace is most convincingly demonstrated in our willingness to negotiate our points of difference in a fair and businesslike manner with the Communist countries.

We are under no illusions. We know that there are enduring ideological differences. We are aware of the difficulty in moderating tensions that arise from the clash of national interests. These differences will not be dissipated by changes of atmosphere or dissolved in cordial personal relations between statesmen. They involve strong convictions and contrary philosophies, necessities of national security, and the deep-seated differences of perspectives formed by geography and history.

The United States, like any other nation, has interests of its own, and will defend those interests. But any nation today must define its interests with special concern for the interests of others. If some nations define their security in a manner that means insecurity for other nations, then peace is threatened and the security of all is diminished.

This obligation is particularly great for the nuclear superpowers on whose decisions the survival of mankind may well depend.

The United States is confident that tensions can be eased and the danger of war reduced by patient and precise efforts to reconcile conflicting interests on concrete issues. Coexistence demands more than a spirit of good will. It requires the definition of positive goals which can be sought and achieved cooperatively. It requires real progress toward resolution of specific differences. This is our objective.

As the Secretary of State said on December 6:

> We will continue to probe every available opening that offers a prospect for better East–West relations, for the resolution of problems large or small, for greater security for all.
>
> In this the United States will continue to play an active role in concert with our allies.

This is the spirit in which the United States ratified the Non-Proliferation Treaty and entered into negotiation with the Soviet Union on control of the military use of the seabeds, on the framework of a settlement in the Middle East, and on limitation of strategic arms. This is the basis on which we and our Atlantic allies have offered to negotiate on concrete issues affecting the security and future of Europe, and on which the United States took steps last year to improve our relations with nations of Eastern Europe. This is also the spirit in which we have resumed formal talks in Warsaw with Communist China. No nation need be our permanent enemy.

America's Purpose

These policies were conceived as a result of change, and we know they will be tested by the change that lies ahead. The world of 1970 was not predicted a decade ago, and we can be certain that the world of 1980 will render many current views obsolete.

The source of America's historic greatness has been our ability to see what had to be done, and then to do it. I believe America now has the chance to move the world closer to a durable peace. And I know that Americans working with each other and with other nations can make our vision real.

III RADICAL-LIBERAL CRITICS

"SHINE, JOE?"

FIGURE 3. A radical-liberal view. (Copyright © *The Chicago Sun-Times;* reproduced by courtesy of Wil-Jo Associates, Inc. and Bill Mauldin.)

J. William Fulbright

THE ARROGANCE OF POWER

Senator J. William Fulbright, Chairman of the Senate Foreign Relations Committee during the foreign policy debate of the 1960s, was at one with Realists in his condemnation of anti-Communist crusading. But while Realists do not shrink from what Stanley Hoffmann called "the processes of politics, the normal patterns of manipulation and force . . . the compromise and shame of an uncertain struggle,"[1] Fulbright seeks a "fundamental change in the nature of international relations," designed to bring the competitive instincts of nations under control of "the morality of decent instincts." Like his old friend Lyndon Johnson, Senator Fulbright may well hope that other nations will come to emulate what is best in American democracy. But if they do so, it must be because they are attracted by America's example and not coerced by her military power.

There are two Americas. One is the America of Lincoln and Adlai Stevenson; the other is the America of Teddy Roosevelt and the modern superpatriots. One is generous and humane, the other narrowly egotistical; one is self-critical, the other self-righteous; one is sensible, the other romantic; one is good-humored, the other solemn; one is inquiring, the other pontificating; one is moderate, the other filled with passionate intensity; one is judicious and the other arrogant in the use of great power.

We have tended in the years of our great power to puzzle the world by presenting to it now the one face of America, now the other, and sometimes both at once. Many people all over the world have come to regard America as being capable of magnanimity and farsightedness but no less capable of pettiness and spite. The result is an inability to anticipate American actions which in turn makes for apprehension and a lack of confidence in American aims.

The inconstancy of American foreign policy is not an accident but an expression of two distinct sides of the American character. Both are characterized by a kind of moralism, but one is the morality of decent instincts tempered by the knowledge of human imper-

From *The Arrogance of Power* by J. William Fulbright, pp. 245–258. Copyright © 1966 by J. William Fulbright. Reprinted by permission of Random House, Inc., and Jonathan Cape Ltd.

[1] *Gulliver's Troubles*, p. 143.

fection and the other is the morality of absolute self-assurance fired by the crusading spirit. The one is exemplified by Lincoln, who found it strange, in the words of his second Inaugural Address, "that any man should dare to ask for a just God's assistance in wringing their bread from the sweat of other men's faces," but then added: "let us judge not, that we be not judged." The other is exemplified by Theodore Roosevelt, who in his December 6, 1904, Annual Message to Congress, without question or doubt as to his own and his country's capacity to judge right and wrong, proclaimed the duty of the United States to exercise an "internal police power" in the hemisphere on the ground that "Chronic wrongdoing, or an impotence which results in a general loosening of the ties of civilized society, may in America . . . ultimately require intervention by some civilized nation. . . ." Roosevelt of course never questioned that the "wrongdoing" would be done by our Latin neighbors and we of course were the "civilized nation" with the duty to set things right.

After twenty-five years of world power the United States must decide which of the two sides of its national character is to predominate—the humanism of Lincoln or the arrogance of those who would make America the world's policeman. One or the other will help shape the spirit of the age—unless of course we refuse to choose, in which case America may come to play a less important role in the world, leaving the great decisions to others.

The current tendency is toward a more strident and aggressive American foreign policy, which is to say, toward a policy closer to the spirit of Theodore Roosevelt than of Lincoln. We are still trying to build bridges to the Communist countries and we are still, in a small way, helping the poorer nations to make a better life for their people; but we are also involved in a growing war against Asian communism, a war which began and might have ended as a civil war if American intervention had not turned it into a contest of ideologies, a war whose fallout is disrupting our internal life and complicating our relations with most of the world.

Our national vocabulary has changed with our policies. A few years ago we were talking of détente and building bridges, of five-year plans in India and Pakistan, or agricultural cooperatives in the Dominican Republic, and land and tax reform all over Latin America. Today these subjects are still discussed in a half-hearted and desultory way but the focus of power and interest has shifted to the politics of war. Diplomacy has become largely image-making, and instead of emphasizing plans for social change, the policy planners and political scientists are conjuring up "scenarios" of escalation and nuclear confrontation and "models" of insurgency and counter-insurgency.

The change in words and values is no less important than the change in policy, because words *are* deeds and style *is* substance insofar as they influence men's minds and behavior. What seems to be happening, as Archibald MacLeish has put it, is that "the feel of America in the world's mind" has begun to change and faith in "the idea of America" has been shaken for the world and, what is more important, for our own people. MacLeish is suggesting—and I think he is right—that much of the idealism and inspiration is disappearing from American policy, but he also points out that they are not yet gone and by no means are they irretrievable:

> . . . if you look closely and listen well, there is a human warmth, a human meaning which nothing has killed in almost twenty years and which nothing is likely to kill. . . . What has always held this country together is an idea—a dream if you will—a large and abstract thought of the sort the realistic and the sophisticated may reject but mankind can hold to.[2]

The foremost need of American foreign policy is a renewal of dedication to an "idea that mankind can hold to"—not a missionary idea full of pretensions about being the world's policemen but a Lincolnian idea expressing that powerful strand of decency and humanity which is the true source of America's greatness.

Humanism and Puritanism

I am not prepared to argue that mankind is suffering from an excess of virtue but I think the world has endured about all it can of the crusades of high-minded men bent on the regeneration of the human race. Since the beginning of history men have been set upon by zealots and crusaders, who, far from wishing them harm, have wanted sincerely and fervently to raise them from benightedness to blessedness. The difficulty about all this doing of noble deeds has not been in its motives but in the perverseness of human nature, in the re-

[2] Archibald MacLeish, Address to the Congress of the International Publishers Association, May 31, 1965.

grettable fact that most men are loutish and ungrateful when it comes to improving their souls and more often than not have to be forced into their own salvation. The result has been a great deal of bloodshed and violence committed not in malice but for the purest of motives. The victims may not always have appreciated the fact that their tormentors had noble motives but the fact remains that it was not wickedness that did them in but, in Thackeray's phrase, "the mischief which the very virtuous do."

Who are the self-appointed emissaries of God who have wrought so much violence in the world? They are men with doctrines, men of faith and idealism, men who confuse power with virtue, men who believe in some cause without doubt and practice their beliefs without scruple, men who cease to be human beings with normal preferences for work and fun and family and become instead living, breathing embodiments of some faith or ideology. From the religious wars to the two world wars they have been responsible for much or most of the violence in the world. From Robespierre to Stalin and Mao Tse-tung they have been the extreme practitioners of the arrogance of power—extreme, indeed, in a way that has never been known and, hopefully, never will be known in America.

There are elements of this kind of fanaticism in Western societies but the essential strength of democracy and capitalism as they are practiced in the West is that they are relatively free of doctrine and dogma and largely free of illusions about man and his nature. Of all the intellectual achievements of Western civilization, the one, I think, that is most truly civilized is that by and large we have learned to deal with man as he is or, at most, as he seems capable of becoming, but not as we suppose in the abstract he ought to be. Our economy is geared to human acquisitiveness and our politics to human ambition. Accepting these qualities as part of human character, we have been able in substantial measure both to satisfy them and to civilize them. We have been able to civilize them because we have understood that a man's own satisfaction is more nearly a condition of than an obstacle to his decent behavior toward others. This realism about man may prove in the long run to be our greatest asset over communism, which can deny and denounce but, with all the "Red Guards" of China, cannot remake human nature.

Acceptance of his own nature would seem to be the most natural thing in the world for a man, but experience shows that it is not.

Only at an advanced state of civilization do men become tolerant of human shortcomings. Only at an advanced level of civilization, it seems, do men acquire the wisdom and humility to acknowledge that they are not really cut out to play God. At all previous levels of culture men seem to be more interested in the enforced improvement of others than in voluntary fulfillment for themselves, more interested in forcing their fellow creatures to be virtuous than in helping them to be happy. Only under the conditions of material affluence and political democracy that prevail in much of the modern West have whole societies been able and willing to renounce the harsh asceticism of their own past, which still prevails in much of the East, and to embrace the philosophy that life after all is short and it is no sin to try to enjoy it.

Our hold on this philosophy is tenuous. There is a strand in our history and in our national character which is all too congenial to the spirit of crusading ideology. The Puritans who came to New England in the seventeenth century did not establish their faith as a major religion in America but the Puritan way of thought—harsh, ascetic, intolerant, promising salvation for the few but damnation for the many—became a major intellectual force in American life. It introduced a discordant element into a society bred in the English heritage of tolerance, moderation, and experimentalism.

Throughout our history two strands have coexisted uneasily—a dominant strand of democratic humanism and a lesser but durable strand of intolerant puritanism. There has been a tendency through the years for reason and moderation to prevail as long as things are going tolerably well or as long as our problems seem clear and finite and manageable. But when things have gone badly for any length of time, or when the reasons for adversity have seemed obscure, or simply when some event or leader of opinion has aroused the people to a state of high emotion, our puritan spirit has tended to break through, leading us to look at the world through the distorting prism of a harsh and angry moralism.

Communism has aroused our latent puritanism as has no other movement in our history, causing us to see principles where there are only interests and conspiracy where there is only misfortune. And when this view of things prevails, conflicts become crusades and morality becomes delusion and hypocrisy. Thus, for example, when young hoodlums—the so-called "Red Guards"—terrorize and humiliate Chinese citizens who are suspected of a lack of fervor for the teachings of Mao Tse-tung, we may feel reconfirmed in our judgment that communism is a barbarous philosophy utterly devoid of redeeming features of humanity, but before going into transports of moral outrage over the offenses of the "Red Guards," we might recall that no fewer than two hundred thousand, and possibly half a million, people were murdered in the anti-Communist terror that swept Indonesia in 1966 and scarcely a voice of protest was heard in America—from our leaders, from the press, or from the general public. One can only conclude that it is not man's inhumanity to man but Communist manifestations of it that arouse the American conscience.

One of the most outrageous effects of the puritan spirit in America is the existence of that tyranny over what it is respectable to say and think. . . ˙ Those who try to look at the country with some objectivity are often the objects of scorn and abuse by professional patriots who believe that there is something illegitimate about national self-criticism, or who equate loyalty to our fighting men in Vietnam with loyalty to the policy that put them there.

Puritanism, fortunately, has not been the dominant strand in American thought. It had nothing to do with the intelligent and subtle diplomacy of the period of the American Revolution. It had nothing to do with the wise policy of remaining aloof from the conflicts of Europe, as long as we were permitted to do so, while we settled and developed the North American continent. It had nothing to do with the restraint shown by the United States at moments of supreme crisis in the cold war—at the time of the Korean War, for example, in the first Indochina war in which President Eisenhower wisely refused to intervene in 1954, and in the Cuban missile crisis of 1962. And it has had absolutely nothing to do with the gradual relaxation of tensions associated with the test ban treaty and the subsequent improvement of relations with the Soviet Union. I am reminded of "Mr. Dooley's" words about the observance of Thanksgiving: " 'Twas founded by th' Puritans to give thanks f'r bein' presarved fr'm th' Indyans, an' . . . we keep it to give thanks we are presarved fr'm th' Puritans."[3]

The crusading puritan spirit has had a great deal to do with some of the regrettable and tragic events of American history. It led us

[3] Finley Peter Dunne, *Mr. Dooley's Opinions* (1900), Thanksgiving.

into needless and costly adventures and victories that crumbled in our hands.

The Civil War is an example. Had the Abolitionists of the North and the hotheads of the South been less influential, the war might have been avoided and slavery would certainly have been abolished anyway, peacefully and probably within a generation after emancipation actually occurred. Had the peace been made by Lincoln rather than the Radical Republicans, it could have been a peace of reconciliation rather than the wrathful Reconstruction which deepened the division of the country, cruelly set back the cause of the Negro, and left a legacy of bitterness for which we are still paying a heavy price.

The puritan spirit was one of the important factors in the brief, unhappy adventure in imperialism that began with the war of 1898. Starting with stirring slogans about "manifest destiny" and a natural sense of moral outrage about atrocities in Cuba—which was fed by a spirited competition for circulation between the Hearst and Pulitzer newspapers—America forced on Spain a war that it was willing to pay almost any price short of complete humiliation to avoid. The war was undertaken to liberate the Cuban people and ended with Cuba being put under an American protectorate, which in turn inaugurated a half century of American intervention in Cuba's internal affairs. American interference was motivated, no doubt, by a sincere desire to bring freedom to the Cuban people but it ended, nonetheless, with their getting Batista and Castro instead.

The crusading spirit of America in its modern form, and the contrast between the crusading spirit and the spirit of tolerance and accommodation, are illustrated in two speeches made by Woodrow Wilson, one preceding, the other following, America's entry into World War I. In early 1917, with the United States still neutral, he declined to make a clear moral distinction between the belligerents, and called on them to compromise their differences and negotiate a "peace without victory." In the spring of 1918, when the United States had been at war for a year, Wilson perceived only one possible response to the challenge of Germany in the war: "Force, Force to the utmost, Force without stint or limit, the righteous and triumphant Force which shall make right the law of the world, and cast every selfish dominion down in the dust."[4]

[4] Speech at Baltimore, Maryland, April 6, 1918.

Even Franklin Roosevelt, who was the most pragmatic of politicians, was not immune from the crusading spirit. So overcome was he, as were all Americans, by the treachery of the Japanese attack on Pearl Harbor that one of America's historic principles, the freedom of the seas, for which we had gone to war in 1812 and 1917, was now immediately forgotten, along with the explicit commitment under the London Naval Treaty of 1930 not to sink merchant vessels without first placing passengers, crews, and ships' papers in a place of safety. Within seven hours of the Japanese attack the order went out to all American ships and planes in the Pacific: "Execute unrestricted air and submarine warfare against Japan." Between 1941 and 1945 American submarines sank 1,750 Japanese merchant ships and took the lives of 105,000 Japanese civilians. So much for the "freedom of the seas."

In January 1943, while meeting with Churchill at Casablanca, President Roosevelt announced that the Allies would fight on until the "unconditional surrender" of their enemies. Roosevelt later said that the phrase just "popped into his mind" but I think it was dredged up from the depths of a puritan soul. Its premise was that our side was all virtue and our enemies were all evil who in justice could expect nothing after their fall but the righteous retribution of Virtue triumphant.

"Unconditional surrender" was an unwise doctrine. Aside from its negativism as a war aim and the fact that it may have prolonged the war, we did not really mean to carry out its implications. As soon as our enemies delivered themselves into our hands we began to treat them with kindness and moderation, and within a very few years we were treating them as valued friends and allies.

The West has won two "total victories" in this century and it has barely survived them. America, especially, fought the two world wars in the spirit of a righteous crusade. We acted as if we had come to the end of history, as if we had only to destroy our enemies and then the world would enter a golden age of peace and human happiness. Some of the problems that spawned the great wars were in fact solved by our victories; others were simply forgotten. But to our shock and dismay we found after 1945 that history had not come to an end, that our triumph had produced at least as many problems as it had solved, and that it was by no means clear that the new problems were preferable to the old ones.

I do not raise these events of the American past for purposes of national flagellation but to illustrate that the problem of excessive ideological zeal is our problem as well as the Communists'. I think also that when we respond to Communist dogmatism with a dogmatism of our own we are not merely responding by the necessity, as we are told, of "fighting fire with fire." I think we are responding in a way that is more natural and congenial to us than we care to admit.

The great challenge in our foreign relations is to make certain that the major strand in our heritage, the strand of humanism, tolerance, and accommodation, remains the dominant one. I do not accept the excuse, so often offered, that Communist zealotry and intransigence justify our own. I do not accept the view that because they have engaged in subversion, intervention, and ideological warfare, so must we and to the same degree. There is far more promise in efforts to encourage Communist imitation of our own more sensible attitudes than in ourselves imitating the least attractive forms of Communist behavior. It is of course reasonable to ask why *we* must take the lead in conciliation; the answer is that we, being the most powerful of nations, can afford as no one else can to be magnanimous. Or, to put it another way, disposing as we do of the greater physical power, we are properly called upon to display the greater moral power as well.

The kind of foreign policy I have been talking about is, in the true sense of the term, a *conservative* policy. It is intended quite literally to conserve the world—a world whose civilizations can be destroyed at any time if either of the great powers should choose or feel driven to do so. It is an approach that accepts the world as it is, with all its existing nations and ideologies, with all its existing qualities and shortcomings. It is an approach that purports to change things in ways that are compatible with the continuity of history and within the limits imposed by a fragile human nature. I think that if the great conservatives of the past, such as Burke and Metternich and Castlereagh, were alive today, they would not be true believers or relentless crusaders against communism. They would wish to come to terms with the world as it is, not because our world would be pleasing to them—almost certainly it would not be—but because they believed in the preservation of indissoluble links between the past and the future, because they profoundly mistrusted abstract ideas, and because they did not think themselves or any other men qualified to play God.

The last, I think, is the central point. I believe that a man's principal business, in foreign policy as in domestic policy and in his daily life, is to keep his own house in order, to make life a little more civilized, a little more satisfying, and a little more serene in the brief time that is allotted him. I think that man is qualified to contemplate metaphysics but not to practice it. The practice of metaphysics is God's work.

An Idea Mankind Can Hold To

Favored as it is, by history, by wealth, and by the vitality and basic decency of its diverse population, it is conceivable, though hardly likely, that America will do something that no other great nation has ever tried to do—to effect a fundamental change in the nature of international relations. It has been my purpose in this book to suggest some ways in which we might proceed with this great work. All that I have proposed in these pages—that we make ourselves the friend of social revolution, that we make our own society an example of human happiness, that we go beyond simple reciprocity in the effort to reconcile hostile worlds—has been based on two major premises: first, that, at this moment in history at which the human race has become capable of destroying itself, it is not merely desirable but essential that the competitive instinct of nations be brought under control; and second, that America, as the most powerful nation, is the only nation equipped to lead the world in an effort to change the nature of its politics.

If we accept this leadership, we will have contributed to the world "an idea mankind can hold to." Perhaps that idea can be defined as the proposition that the nation performs its essential function not in its capacity as a *power,* but in its capacity as a *society,* or to put it simply, that the primary business of the nation is not itself but its people.

Obviously, to bring about fundamental changes in the world we would have to take certain chances: we would have to take the chance that other countries could not so misinterpret a generous initiative on our part as to bring about a calamity; we would have to take a chance that later if not sooner, nations which have been hostile to us would respond to reason and decency with reason and decency. The risks involved are great but they are far less than the risks of traditional methods of international relations in the nuclear age.

If we are interested in bringing about fundamental changes in the world, we must start by resolving some critical questions of our foreign relations: Are we to be the friend or the enemy of the social revolutions of Asia, Africa, and Latin America? Are we to regard the Communist countries as more or less normal states with whom we can have more or less normal relations, or are we to regard them indiscriminately as purveyors of an evil ideology with whom we can never reconcile? And finally, are we to regard ourselves as a friend, counselor, and example for those around the world who seek freedom and who also want our help, or are we to play the role of God's avenging angel, the appointed missionary of freedom in a benighted world?

The answers to these questions depend on which of the two Americas is speaking. There are no inevitable or predetermined answers because our past has prepared us to be either tolerant or puritanical, generous or selfish, sensible or romantic, humanly concerned or morally obsessed, in our relations with the outside world.

For my own part, I prefer the America of Lincoln and Adlai Stevenson. I prefer to have my country the friend rather than the enemy of demands for social justice; I prefer to have the Communists treated as human beings, with all the human capacity for good and bad, for wisdom and folly, rather than as embodiments of an evil abstraction; and I prefer to see my country in the role of sympathetic friend to humanity rather than its stern and prideful schoolmaster.

There are many respects in which America, if she can bring herself to act with the magnanimity and the empathy which are appropriate to her size and power, can be an intelligent example to the world. We have the opportunity to set an example of generous understanding in our relations with China, of practical cooperation for peace in our relations with Russia, of reliable and respectful partnership in our relations with Western Europe, of material helpfulness without moral presumption in our relations with developing nations, of abstention from the temptations of hegemony in our relations with Latin America, and of the all-around advantages of minding one's own business in our relations with everybody. Most of all we have an opportunity to serve as an example of democracy to the world by the way in which we run our own society. America, in the words of John Quincy Adams, should be "the well-wisher to the freedom and independence of all" but "the champion and vindicator only of her own."[5]

If we can bring ourselves so to act, we will have overcome the dangers of the arrogance of power. It would involve, no doubt, the loss of certain glories, but that seems a price worth paying for the probable rewards, which are the happiness of America and the peace of the world.

[5] John Quincy Adams, July 4, 1821, Washington, D.C. Reported in *The National Intelligencer*, July 11, 1821.

Robert L. Heilbroner

COUNTERREVOLUTIONARY AMERICA

"The point I wish to make is not that communism is not a harsh and, to us, a repugnant system of organizing society, but that its doctrine has redeeming tenets of humanitarianism; . . . that some countries are probably better off under Communist rule than they were under preceding regimes; that some people may even want to live under communism; and finally . . . that it is neither the duty nor right of the United States to sort out all these problems for the revolutionary and potentially revolutionary societies of Asia, Africa, and Latin America."

The author of these lines is J. William Fulbright.[1] But for analysis in support of them one can do no better than to turn to economist Robert L. Heilbroner. Heilbroner, it should be noted, is no economic determinist. It is "the fear of losing our place in the sun, of finding ourselves at bay, that motivates a great deal of the anticommunism on which so much of American foreign policy seems to be founded." Nor does he despair about the future so long as "there are strong American currents of humanitarianism that can be directed as a counterforce to this profoundly antihumanitarian view." But is Heilbroner right in his major argument—that "some form of extreme national collectivism or communism" may be "the only chance these [backward] areas have of escaping misery?" Haven't left-wing nationalist regimes also failed at development? Is communism's track record really so impressive? May there not be more possibilities than Heilbroner allows for controlling the population explosion and for fostering democratic approaches to growth?

Is the United States fundamentally opposed to economic development? The question is outrageous. Did we not coin the phrase, "the revolution of rising expectations"? Have we not supported the cause of development more generously than any nation on earth, spent our intellectual energy on the problems of development, offered our expertise freely to the backward nations of the world? How can it possibly be suggested that the United States might be opposed to economic development?

The answer is that we are not at all opposed to what we conceive economic development to be. The process depicted by the "revolu-

From Robert L. Heilbroner, "Counterrevolutionary America," *Commentary* (April 1967), pp. 31–38. Reprinted from *Commentary*, by permission; copyright © 1967 by the American Jewish Committee.

[1] In *Arrogance of Power*, p. 81.

tion of rising expectations" is a deeply attractive one. It conjures up the image of a peasant in some primitive land, leaning on his crude plow and looking to the horizon, where he sees dimly, but for the *first time* (and that is what is so revolutionary about it), the vision of a better life. From this electrifying vision comes the necessary catalysis to change an old and stagnant way of life. The pace of work quickens. Innovations, formerly feared and resisted, are now eagerly accepted. The obstacles are admittedly very great—whence the need for foreign assistance—but under the impetus of new hopes the economic mechanism begins to turn faster, to gain traction against the environment. Slowly, but surely, the Great Ascent begins.

*   *   *

[W]hat our rhetoric fails to bring to our attention is the likelihood that development will require policies and programs repugnant to our "way of life," that it will bring to the fore governments hostile to our international objectives, and that its regnant ideology will bitterly oppose capitalism as a system of world economic power. If that is the case, we would have to think twice before denying that the United States was fundamentally opposed to economic development.

But is it the case? Must development lead in directions that go counter to the present American political philosophy? Let me try to indicate, albeit much too briefly and summarily, the reasons that lead me to answer that question as I do.

I begin with the cardinal point, often noted but still insufficiently appreciated, that the process called "economic development" is not primarily economic at all. We think of development as a campaign of production to be fought with budgets and monetary policies and measured with indices of ouput and income. But the development process is much wider and deeper than can be indicated by such statistics. To be sure, in the end what is hoped for is a tremendous rise in output. But this will not come to pass until a series of tasks, at once cruder and more delicate, simpler and infinitely more difficult, has been commenced and carried along a certain distance.

In most of the new nations of Africa, these tasks consist in establishing the very underpinnings of nationhood itself—in determining national borders, establishing national languages, arousing a basic national (as distinguished from tribal) self-consciousness. Before these steps have been taken, the African states will remain no more than names insecurely affixed to the map, not social entities capable of undertaking an enormous collective venture in economic change. In Asia, nationhood is generally much further advanced than in Africa, but here the main impediment to development is the miasma of apathy and fatalism, superstition and distrust that vitiates every attempt to improve hopelessly inefficient modes of work and patterns of resource use: while India starves, a quarter of the world's cow population devours Indian crops, exempt either from effective employment or slaughter because of sacred taboos. In still other areas, mainly Latin America, the principal handicap to development is not an absence of national identity or the presence of suffocating cultures (although the latter certainly plays its part), but the cramping and crippling inhibitions of obsolete social institutions and reactionary social classes. Where landholding rather than industrial activity is still the basis for social and economic power, and where land is held essentially in fiefdoms rather than as productive real estate, it is not surprising that so much of society retains a medieval cast.

Thus, development is much more than a matter of encouraging economic growth within a given social structure. It is rather the *modernization* of that structure, a process of ideational, social, economic, and political change that requires the remaking of society in its most intimate as well as its most public attributes. When we speak of the revolutionary nature of economic development, it is this kind of deeply penetrative change that we mean—change that reorganizes "normal" ways of thought, established patterns of family life, and structures of village authority as well as class and caste privilege.

What is so egregiously lacking in the great majority of the societies that are now attempting to make the Great Ascent is precisely this pervasive modernization. The trouble with India and Pakistan, with Brazil and Ecuador, with the Philippines and Ethiopia, is not merely that economic growth lags, or proceeds at some pitiable pace. This is only a symptom of deeper-lying ills. The trouble is that the social physiology of these nations remains so depressingly unchanged despite the flurry of economic planning on top. The all-encompassing ignorance and poverty of the rural regions, the unbridgeable gulf between the peasant and the urban elites, the resistive conservatism of the village elders, the unyielding traditionalism of family life—all these remain obdurately, maddeningly, disastrously unchanged. In the cities, a few modern buildings, some-times brilliantly executed, give a deceptive patina of modernity, but once one journeys into the immense countryside, the terrible stasis overwhelms all.

To this vast landscape of apathy and ignorance one must now make an exception of the very greatest importance. It is the fact that a very few nations, all of them Communist, have succeeded in reaching into the lives and stirring the minds of precisely that body of the peasantry which constitutes the insuperable problem else-where. In our concentration on the politics, the betrayals, the suc-cesses and failures of the Russian, Chinese, and Cuban revolutions, we forget that their central motivation has been just such a war *à l'outrance* against the arch-enemy of backwardness—not alone the backwardness of outmoded social superstructures but even more critically that of private inertia and traditionalism.

That the present is irreversibly and unqualifiedly freed from the dead hand of the past is, I think beyond argument in the case of Russia. By this I do not only mean that Russia has made enormous economic strides. I refer rather to the gradual emancipation of its people from the "idiocy of rural life," their gradual entrance upon the stage of contemporary existence. This is not to hide in the small-est degree the continuing backwardness of the Russian countryside where now almost fifty—*and formerly perhaps eighty*—percent of the population lives. But at its worst I do not think that life could now be described in the despairing terms that run through the Rus-sian literature of our grandfathers' time. Here is Chekhov:

> During the summer and winter there had been hours and days when it seemed as if these people [the peasants] lived worse than cattle, and it was terrible to be with them. They were coarse, dishonest, dirty, and drunken; they did not live at peace with one another but quarreled con-tinually, because they feared, suspected, and despised one another. . . . Crushing labor that made the whole body ache at night, cruel winters, scanty crops, overcrowding, and no help, and nowhere to look for help.

It is less certain that the vise of the past has been loosened in China or Cuba. It may well be that Cuba has suffered a considerable economic decline, in part due to absurd planning, in part to our refusal to buy her main crop. The economic record of China is nearly as inscrutable as its political turmoil, and we may not know for many years whether the Chinese peasant is today better or worse off than before the revolution. Yet what strikes me as significant in both countries is something else. In Cuba it is the educational effort that, according to the *New York Times,* has constituted a major effort of the Castro regime. In China it is the unmistakable evidence—and here I lean not alone on the sympathetic account of Edgar Snow but on the most horrified descriptions of the rampages of the Red Guards—that the younger generation is no longer fettered by the traditional view of things. The very fact that the Red Guards now revile their elders, an unthinkable defiance of age-old Chinese custom, is testimony of how deeply change has penetrated into the texture of Chinese life.

It is this herculean effort to reach and rally the great anonymous mass of the population that is *the* great accomplishment of communism—even though it is an accomplishment that is still only partially accomplished. For if the areas of the world afflicted with the self-perpetuating disease of backwardness are ever to rid themselves of its debilitating effects, I think it is likely to be not merely because antiquated social structures have been dismantled (although this is an essential precondition), but because some shock treatment like that of communism has been administered to them.

By way of contrast to this all-out effort, however short it may have fallen of its goal, we must place the timidity of the effort to bring modernization to the peoples of the non-Communist world. Here again I do not merely speak of lagging rates of growth. I refer to the fact that illiteracy in the non-Communist countries of Asia and Central America is increasing (by some 200 million in the last decade) because it has been "impossible" to mount an educational effort that will keep pace with population growth. I refer to the absence of substantial land reform in Latin America, despite how many years of promises. I refer to the indifference or incompetence or corruption of governing elites: the incredible sheiks with their oildoms; the vague, well-meaning leaders of India unable to break the caste system, kill the cows, control the birthrate, reach the villages, house or employ the labor rotting on the streets; the cynical governments of South America, not one of which, according to Lleras Camargo, former president of Colombia, has ever prosecuted a single politician or industrialist for evasion of taxes. And not least, I refer to the fact that every movement that arises to correct these conditions is instantly identified as "Communist" and put down with every means at hand, while the United States clucks or nods approval.

To be sure, even in the most petrified societies, the modernization process is at work. If there were time, the solvent acids of the twentieth century would work their way on the ideas and institutions of the most inert or resistant countries. But what lacks in the twentieth century is time. The multitudes of the underdeveloped world have only in the past two decades been summoned to their reveille. The one thing that is certain about the revolution of rising expectations is that it is only in its inception, and that its pressures for justice and action will steadily mount as the voice of the twentieth century penetrates to villages and slums where it is still almost inaudible. It is not surprising that Princeton historian C. E. Black, surveying this labile world, estimates that we must anticipate "ten to fifteen revolutions a year for the foreseeable future in the less developed societies."

In itself, this prospect of mounting political restiveness enjoins the speediest possible time schedule for development. But this political urgency is many times compounded by that of the population problem. Like an immense river in flood, the number of human beings rises each year to wash away the levees of the preceding year's labors and to pose future requirements of monstrous proportions. To provide shelter for the three billion human beings who will arrive on earth in the next forty years will require as many dwellings as have been constructed since recorded history began. To feed them will take double the world's present output of food. To cope with the mass exodus from the overcrowded countryside will necessitate cities of grotesque size—Calcutta, now a cesspool of three to five millions, threatens us by the year 2000 with a prospective population of from thirty to sixty millions.

These horrific figures spell one importunate message: haste. That is the *mene mene, tekel upharsin* written on the walls of government planning offices around the world. Even if the miracle of the loop is realized—the new contraceptive device that promises the first real breakthrough in population control—we must set ourselves for at least another generation of rampant increase.

But how to achieve haste? How to convince the silent and disbelieving men, how to break through the distrustful glances of women in black shawls, how to overcome the overt hostility of landlords, the opposition of the Church, the petty bickerings of military cliques, the black-marketeering of commercial dealers? I suspect there is only one way. The conditions of backwardness must be attacked with the passion, the ruthlessness, and the messianic fury of a jehad, a Holy War. Only a campaign of an intensity and singlemindedness that must approach the ludicrous and the unbearable offers the chance to ride roughshod over the resistance of the rich and the poor alike and to open the way for the forcible implantation of those modern attitudes and techniques without which there will be no escape from the misery of underdevelopment.

I need hardly add that the cost of this modernization process has been and will be horrendous. If communism is the great modernizer, it is certainly not a benign agent of change. Stalin may well have exceeded Hitler as a mass executioner. Free inquiry in China has been supplanted by dogma and catechism; even in Russia nothing like freedom of criticism or of personal expression is allowed. Furthermore, the economic cost of industrialization in both countries has been at least as severe as that imposed by primitive capitalism.

Yet one must count the gains as well as the losses. Hundreds of millions who would have been confined to the narrow cells of change-less lives have been liberated from prisons they did not even know existed. Class structures that elevated the flighty or irresponsible have been supplanted by others that have promoted the ambitious and the dedicated. Economic systems that gave rise to luxury and poverty have given way to systems that provide a rough distributional justice. Above all, the prospect of a new future has been opened. It is this that lifts the curent ordeal in China above the level of pure horror. The number of human beings in that country who have perished over the past centuries from hunger or neglect, is beyond computation. The present revolution may add its dreadful increment to this number. But it also holds out the hope that China may finally have been galvanized into social, political, and economic attitudes that for the first time make its modernization a possibility.

Two questions must be answered when we dare to risk so favorable a verdict on communism as a modernizing agency. The first is whether the result is worth the cost, whether the possible—by no means assured—escape from underdevelopment is worth the lives that will be squandered to achieve it.

I do not know how one measures the moral price of historical victories or how one can ever decide that a diffuse gain is worth a sharp and particular loss. I only know that the way in which we ordinarily keep the books of history is wrong. No one is now toting up the balance of the wretches who starve in India, or the peasants of Northeastern Brazil who live in the swamps on crabs, or the under-nourished and permanently stunted children of Hong Kong or Honduras. Their sufferings go unrecorded, and are not present to counterbalance the scales when the furies of revolution strike down their victims. Barrington Moore has made a nice calculation that bears on this problem. Taking as the weight in one pan the 35,000 to 40,000 persons who lost their lives—mainly for no fault of theirs—as a result of the Terror during the French Revolution, he asks what would have been the death rate from preventable starvation and injustice under the *ancien regime* to balance the scales. "Offhand," he writes, "it seems unlikely that this would be very much below the proportion of .0010 which [the] figure of 40,000 yields when set against an estimated population of 24 million."

Is it unjust to charge the *ancien regime* in Russia with ten million preventable deaths? I think it not unreasonable. To charge the authorities in prerevolutionary China with equally vast and preventable degradations? Theodore White, writing in 1946, had this to say: . . . "some scholars think that China is perhaps the only country in the world where the people eat less, live more bitterly, and are clothed worse than they were five hundred years ago."

I do not recommend such a calculus of corpses—indeed, I am aware of the license it gives to the unscrupulous—but I raise it to show the onesidedness of our protestations against the brutality and violence of revolutions. In this regard, it is chastening to recall the multitudes who have been killed or mutilated by the Church which is now the first to protest against the excesses of communism.

But there is an even more terrible second question to be asked. It is clear beyond doubt, however awkward it may be for our moralizing propensities, that historians excuse horror that succeeds; and that we write our comfortable books of moral philosophy, seated atop a mound of victims—slaves, serfs, laboring men and women, heretics, dissenters—who were crushed in the course of preparing the way for our triumphal entry into existence. But at least we are here to vindicate the carnage. What if we were not? What if the revolutions grind flesh and blood and produce nothing, if the end of the convulsion is not exhilaration but exhaustion, not triumph but defeat?

Before this possibility—which has been realized more than once in history—one stands mute. Mute, but not paralyzed. For there is the necessity of calculating what is likely to happen in the absence of the revolution whose prospective excesses hold us back. Here one must weigh what has been done to remedy underdevelopment—and what has not been done—in the past twenty years; how much time there remains before the population flood enforces its own ultimate solution; what is the likelihood of bringing modernization without the frenzied assault that communism seems most capable of mounting. As I make this mental calculation I arrive at an answer which is even more painful than that of revolution. I see the alternative as the continuation, without substantial relief—and indeed with a substantial chance of deterioration—of the misery and meanness of life as it is now lived in the sinkhole of the world's backward regions.

*   *   *

[E]ven if for many reasons we should prefer the advent of non-Communist modernizing elites, we must realize that they too will present the United States with programs and policies antipathetic to much that America "believes in" and hostile to America as a world power. The leadership needed to mount a jehad against backward-ness—and it is my main premise that only a Holy War will begin modernization in our time—will be forced to expound a philosophy that approves authoritarian and collectivist measures at home and that utilizes as the target for its national resentment abroad the towering villains of the world, of which the United States is now Number One.

All this confronts American policymakers and public opinion with a dilemma of a totally unforeseen kind. On the one hand we are eager to assist in the rescue of the great majority of mankind from conditions that we recognize as dreadful and ultimately dangerous. On the other hand, we seem to be committed, especially in the under-developed areas, to a policy of defeating communism wherever it is within our military capacity to do so, and of repressing movements that might become Communist if they were allowed to follow their internal dynamics. Thus, we have on the one side the record of

Point Four, the Peace Corps, and foreign aid generally; and on the other, Guatemala, Cuba, the Dominican Republic, and now Vietnam.

That these two policies might be in any way mutually incompatible, that economic development might contain revolutionary implications infinitely more far-reaching than those we have so blandly endorsed in the name of rising expectations, that communism or a radical national collectivism might be the only vehicles for modernization in many key areas of the world—these are dilemmas we have never faced. Now I suggest that we do face them, and that we begin to examine in a serious way ideas that have hitherto been considered blasphemous, if not near-traitorous.

Suppose that most of Southeast Asia and much of Latin America were to go Communist, or to become controlled by revolutionary governments that espoused collectivist ideologies and vented extreme anti-American sentiments. Would this constitute a mortal threat to the United States?

I think it fair to claim that the purely *military* danger posed by such an eventuality would be slight. Given the present and prospective capabilities of the backward world, the addition of hundreds of millions of citizens to the potential armies of communism would mean nothing when there was no way of deploying them against us. The prospect of an invasion by Communist hordes—the specter that frightened Europe after World War II with some (although retrospectively, not too much) realism—would be no more than a phantasm when applied to Asia or South America or Africa.

More important, the nuclear or conventional military power of communism would not be materially increased by the armaments capacities of these areas for many years. By way of indication, the total consumption of energy of all kinds (in terms of coal equivalent) for Afghanistan, Bolivia, Brazil, Burma, Ceylon, Colombia, Costa Rica, Dominican Republic, Ecuador, El Salvador, Ethiopia, Guatemala, Haiti, Honduras, India, Indonesia, Iran, Iraq, Korea, Lebanon, Nicaragua, Pakistan, Paraguay, Peru, Philippines, U.A.R., Uruguay, and Venezuela is less than that annually consumed by West Germany alone. The total steel output of these countries is one-tenth of U.S. annual production. Thus, even the total communization of the backward world would not effectively alter the present balance of military strength in the world.

However small the military threat, it is undeniably true that a Communist or radical collectivist engulfment of these countries would cost us the loss of billions of dollars of capital invested there. Of our roughly $50 billions in overseas investment, some $10 billions are in mining, oil, utility, and manufacturing facilities in Latin America, some $4 billions in Asia including the Near East, and about $2 billions in Africa. To lose these assets would deal a heavy blow to a number of large corporations, particularly in oil, and would cost the nation as a whole the loss of some $3 to $4 billions a year in earnings from those areas.

A Marxist might conclude that the economic interest of a capitalist nation would find such a prospective loss insupportable, and that it would be "forced" to go to war. I do not think this is a warranted assumption, although it is undoubtedly a risk. Against a Gross National Product that is approaching 3/4 of a trillion dollars and with total corporate assets over $1.3 trillions, the loss of even the whole $16 billions in the vulnerable areas should be manageable economically. Whether such a takeover could be resisted politically—that is, whether the red flag of communism could be successfully waved by the corporate interests—is another question. I do not myself believe that the corporate elite is particularly war-minded—not nearly so much so as the military or the congressional—or that corporate seizures would be a suitable issue for purposes of drumming up interventionist sentiment.

By these remarks I do not wish airily to dismiss the dangers of a Communist avalanche in the backward nations. There would be dangers, not least those of an American hysteria. Rather, I want only to assert that the threats of a military or economic kind would not be insuperable, as they might well be if Europe were to succumb to a hostile regime.

But is that not the very point?, it will be asked. Would not a Communist success in a few backward nations lead to successes in others, and thus by degrees engulf the entire world, until the United States and perhaps Europe were fortresses besieged on a hostile planet?

I think the answer to this fear is two-fold. First, as many beside myself have argued, it is now clear that communism, far from constituting a single unified movement with a common aim and dovetailing interests, is a movement in which similarities of economic and political structure and ideology are more than outweighed by divergencies of national interest and character. Two bloody wars have demonstrated that in the case of capitalism, structural similarities between nations do not prevent mortal combat. As with capitalism, so with communism. Russian Communists have already been engaged in skirmishes with Polish and Hungarian Communists, have nearly come to blows with Yugoslavia, and now stand poised at the threshold of open fighting with China. Only in the mind of the *Daily News* (and perhaps still the State Department) does it seem possible, in the face of this spectacle, to refer to the unified machinations of "international communism" or the "Sino-Soviet bloc."

The realities, I believe, point in a very different direction. A world in which Communist governments were engaged in the enormous task of trying to modernize the worst areas of Asia, Latin America, and Africa would be a world in which sharp differences of national interest were certain to arise within these continental areas. The outlook would be for frictions and conflicts to develop among Communist nations with equal frequency as they developed between those nations and their non-Communist neighbors. A long period of jockeying for power and command over resources, rather than anything like a unified sharing of power and resources, seems unavoidable in the developing continents. This would not preclude a continuous barrage of anti-American propaganda, but it would certainly impede a movement to exert a coordinated Communist influence over these areas.

Second, it seems essential to distinguish among the causes of dangerous national and international behavior those that can be traced to the tenets of communism and those that must be located elsewhere. "Do not talk to me about communism and capitalism," said a Hungarian economist with whom I had lunch this winter. "Talk to me about rich nations and poor ones."

I think it *is* wealth and poverty, and not communism or capitalism, that establishes much of the tone and tension of international relations. For that reason I would expect communism in the backward nations (or national collectivism, if that emerges in the place of communism) to be strident, belligerent, and insecure. If these regimes fail—as they may—their rhetoric may become hysterical and their behavior uncontrolled, although of small consequence. But if they succeed, which I believe they can, many of these traits should recede. Russia, Yugoslavia, or Poland are simply not to be compared, either by way of internal pronouncement or external behavior, with

China, or, on a smaller scale, Cuba. Modernization brings, among other things, a waning of the stereotypes, commandments, and flagellations so characteristic of (and so necessary to) a nation engaged in the effort to alter itself from top to bottom. The idiom of ceaseless revolution becomes less relevant—even faintly embarrassing—to a nation that begins to be placed with itself. Then, too, it seems reasonable to suppose that the vituperative quality of Communist invective would show some signs of abating were the United States to modify its own dogmatic attitude and to forego its own wearisome clichés about the nature of communism.

I doubt there are many who will find these arguments wholly reassuring. They are not. It would be folly to imagine that the next generation or two, when communism or national collectivism in the underdeveloped areas passes through its jehad stage, will be a time of international safety. But as always in these matters, it is only by a comparison with the alternatives that one can choose the preferable course. The prospect that I have offered as a plausible scenario of the future must be placed against that which results from a pursuit of our present course. And here I see two dangers of even greater magnitude: (1) the prospect of many more Vietnams, as radical movements assert themselves in other areas of the world; and (2) a continuation of the present inability of the most impoverished areas to modernize, with the prospect of an eventual human catastrophe on an unimaginable scale.

Nevertheless, there *is* a threat in the specter of a Communist or near-Communist supremacy in the underdeveloped world. It is that the rise of communism would signal the end of capitalism as the dominant world order, and would force the acknowledgment that America no longer constituted the model on which the future of world civilization would be mainly based. In this way, as I have written before, the existence of communism frightens American capitalism as the rise of Protestantism frightened the Catholic Church, or the French Revolution the English aristocracy.

It is, I think, the fear of losing our place in the sun, of finding ourselves at bay, that motivates a great deal of the anticommunism on which so much of American foreign policy seems to be founded. In this regard I note that the nations of Europe, most of them profoundly more conservative than America in their social and economic dispositions, have made their peace with communism far more intelligently and easily than we, and I conclude that this is in no small part due to their admission that they are no longer the leaders of the world.

The great question in our own nation is whether we can accept a similar scaling-down of our position in history. This would entail many profound changes in outlook and policy. It would mean the recognition that communism, which may indeed represent a retrogressive movement in the West, where it should continue to be resisted with full energies, may nonetheless represent a progressive movement in the backward areas, where its advent may be the only chance these areas have of escaping misery. Collaterally, it means the recognition that "our side" has neither the political will, nor the ideological wish, nor the stomach for directing those changes that the backward world must make if it is ever to cease being backward. It would undoubtedly entail a more isolationist policy for the United States vis-à-vis the developing continents, and a greater willingness to permit revolutions there to work their way without interference. It would mean in our daily political life the admission that the ideological battle of capitalism and communism had passed its point of usefulness or relevance, and that religious diatribe must give way to the pragmatic dialogue of the age of science and technology.

I do not know how to estimate the chances of affecting such deepseated changes in the American outlook. It may be that the pull of vested interests, the inertia of bureaucracy, plus a certain lurking fundamentalism that regards communism as an evil which admits of no discussion—the antichrist—will maintain America on its present course, with consequences that I find frightening to contemplate. But I believe that our attitudes are not hopelessly frozen. I detect, both above and below, signs that our present view of communism is no longer wholly tenable and that it must be replaced with a new assessment if we are to remain maneuverable in action and cogent in discourse.

Two actions may help speed along this long overdue modernization of our own thought. The first is a continuation of the gradual thawing and convergence of American and Russian views and interests—a rapprochement that is proceeding slowly and hesitantly, but with a discernible momentum. Here the initiative must come from Russia as well as from ourselves.

The other action is for us alone to take. It is the public airing of the consequences of our blind anticommunism for the underdeveloped world. It must be said aloud that our present policy prefers the absence of development to the chance for communism—which is to say, that we prefer hunger and want and the existing inadequate assaults against the causes of hunger and want to any regime that declares its hostility to capitalism. There are strong American currents of humanitarianism that can be directed as a counterforce to this profoundly antihumanitarian view. But for this counterforce to become mobilized it will be necessary to put fearlessly the outrageous question with which I began: is the United States fundamentally opposed to economic development?

Michael Harrington

UP AND ON FROM ALMOST IMPERIALISM

Michael Harrington, past National Chairman of the Socialist Party, represents a nondogmatic brand of Marxism. Imperialism, to Harrington, has not been an economic necessity, but rather a "cruel convenience." It is not fated that a domestic war economy be the main bulwark against depression—provided that Americans are willing to replace arms spending with social spending, and act on the principle that "there is a sort of international Keynesian argument for self-interest in America's doing justice in the world." The massive economic aid program proposed by Harrington would provide, he argues, not only "an economic substitute for the arms economy," but also "an emotional and political substitute for the reactionary passions of rightist anticommunism . . . ." To this, Realist critics might reply: Should we, even if we could, invite a burst of moral fervor whose ultimate direction and consequences cannot be predicted? What makes Harrington think that the deep-seated problems of underdevelopment are susceptible to solution through massive transfusions of money? And do we any more have "the right and the duty" (turning Fulbright's phrase against Harrington) to sort out all these problems by economic means than by military force?

The democratic left must help finish the creation of the world. The world—and I borrow here from Peter Worsley's imaginative way of speaking—is scarcely begun. The globe has, of course, existed for eons, and humans project their various histories more than 4,000 years into the past. But those interrelationships that transcend tribe, nation, and empire, uniting the people of the earth in a common destiny—whether they like it or not—are only a century or so old. The first day of this creation took place when economics, science, and warfare put the planet together. The second day is now, and there might not be a third.

Applying such high-flown biblical imagery to politics strikes most Americans as grandiose; they leave the world to come to the preachers while they pragmatically reconstruct the reality that is. Until World War II the Pacific and Atlantic oceans allowed Americans to disdain foreign entanglements on principle. And being of an anti-imperialist imperialism, a power which usually dominated other lands

From Michael Harrington, "Introduction: American Power in the Twentieth Century," in Irving Howe, ed., *A Dissenter's Guide to Foreign Policy*, pp. 9–10, 27–33, 56–64. Copyright © 1968 by Dissent Publishing Association. Reprinted by permission of Doubleday & Company, Inc.

through the subtlety of money rather than the brutality of force, America burdened its people with an excessively good conscience. For all of these reasons, it is particularly important to insist within the United States that the day-to-day decisions of foreign policy involve the choice of a new order of things for the twenty-first century. So far, America is creating the world very badly—though this need not be.

America is imperialist. To the average citizen, this statement is a patent slander. If the nation has erred, he would say, it has been generous to a fault, and only a Communist could deny the charity and anticolonialism of its historic record. But the United States has been profoundly imperialist in the decades after World War II (and before, but that is another story). Yet, the United States need not be imperialist. This notion strikes most revolutionists, and not just the Communists, as unpardonably tender-minded. To them, fat, prosperous, capitalist America cannot possibly ally itself with the downtrodden and against the international *status quo*; it is fated to be reactionary, the very headquarters of the world's counterrevolution. This trust in the country's inherent evil is, however, almost as naive as the patriotic faith in its goodness. For given a turn to the democratic left, this nation could play a crucial and positive role in finishing the creation of the world.

Anti-utopia seems more possible than a better world. And yet, there is hope. Although there are tremendous social, political, and economic forces urging the U.S. (and the West, and the rich Communist East) to do wrong, this country could take the lead in making a democratic revolution—in finishing the creation of the world in humane fashion. This fragile hope is my point of departure.

*   *   *

Theories on the Fate of Old and New Nations

The theory that the advanced powers are inevitably committed to reaction implies that there is no hope of democracy in the new nations.

The various formulations of America's (or, more precisely, capitalism's) role and fate, from Lenin to Mao, have obvious deficiencies. Yet, it is true that America has displayed a vested interest in at least some of the misery and poverty of the globe, and the defense of such ill-gotten gains could be (and in the past has been) the basis of a world view and foreign policy. There is the tragic possibility that this view might lead America to continue to promote the gap between rich and poor nations. The exploitation of impoverished people, however, is not a necessity for the American economy but only a cruel convenience. The nation could make new international departures without undergoing a sweeping domestic transformation. There would be many motives for such a change, among them enlightened self-interest (the present trends hurry toward more instability and violence which could be disastrous for the wealthy as well as for the hungry)—and that current of democratic idealism which still flows within American society.

So the U.S. embraces an *almost* imperialism. America has the potential of positive change, of helping to create a new world; yet that course would require considerable radicalization of its political life. If, as Aldous Huxley once said pessimistically, a 99 percent pacifist is a 100 percent militarist, then one can optimistically hope that an *almost*-imperialist will become anti-imperialist.

Lenin's belief that capitalism's inability to resolve its internal contradiction drove it to seek imperium over the entire world has become one of the most influential ideas of the twentieth century. And not only those who submit to Communist orthodoxy give lip service to this analysis. (As for the Chinese Communists, it is only lip service; for they have made the most sweeping revisions of doctrine, albeit in a spirit of fanatic fundamentalism.) Beyond that, almost all the nationalist, non-Communist revolutionists and reformers of the ex-colonial world have affirmed one or another version of the Leninist thesis. And even in the advanced countries Lenin's idea has had a profound effect upon intellectual life.

On the whole, the postwar experience violates the letter of the Leninist argument at almost every point—yet leaves much of its spirit intact. Following Marx, Lenin held that capitalism was not simply interested in plunder and booty abroad. The struggle between the various Western powers "for the sources of raw materials . . . and for 'spheres of influence' " was also a fight to avoid crisis at home. Since 1945 and with the single but glaring exception of oil, this assertion has become less true with every passing day. Advances in technology, synthetics, the organization of the market, and a whole host of factors have reduced the importance of the ex-colonies for the big powers; paradoxically, in the short run, the Third World would perhaps be better off if the capitalists were more interested in exploiting it.

But the heart of Lenin's argument was not the simple assertion that there was a greedy scramble for resources and markets. Lenin believed that capitalism was forced to export its capital because it could not invest it profitably within the limits of the advanced economy. As the system became mature and overorganized, the rate of profit fell, and business was thus driven overseas in search for capital outlets. Thus, imperialism was the distinctive and last historical stage of capitalism itself—a final, desperate attempt to postpone the crisis of the system. However, the same maturity that forced the capitalists to war among themselves over the division of global spoils also heightened the revolutionary consciousness of the working class. World War I signalled the beginning of the epoch of "imperialist war and proletarian revolution."

There is no need here to discuss the complex question of how much this analysis applied to events before 1945. Relevant here is that throughout the postwar period, the trend in the export of capital has been to accentuate investment by the affluent powers *in* the affluent powers, rather than competition among them for opportunities in the ex-colonial world. During this time, American "direct investment" abroad (where business sets up a plant in a foreign country rather than exporting American goods to it) more than doubled—and England and Canada absorbed more than 60 percent of the increase. These movements of capital, leaving the oil industry aside for a moment, accounted for a smaller proportion of the national income than similar exports had for Britain in the nineteenth century.[2]

In France, by the mid-sixties, this situation had become a key element in Gaullist economic thinking. The failure of the French computer industry had made that country dependent on American corporations—and allowed the U.S. State Department to veto the sale of machines which might have facilitated the development of the *force de frappe*. As a result, the French government launched a state-subsidized merger movement to create a corporate base large enough

[1] For relevant figures on the trends in international trade, see *Modern Capitalism*, by Andrew Schonfeld, Appendix I, pp. 428–29. For the most recent government figures, see the September 1966 issue of *Survey of Current Business*.
[2] See *After Imperialism,* by Michael Barret Brown, p. 206. This is a fascinating book written from a democratic socialist point of view. It makes more contemporary sense out of Lenin than anything I have read.

to sustain a modern computer technology. There were those on the left who criticized de Gaulle for not having acted earlier and more decisively in this area. The socialist Gaston Deferre, for instance, said that "Europe will be colonized by the United States unless we decide to pool our resources in order to create industrial concerns comparable in size to the American ones and able to compete with them on an equal footing." The British Labor government took much the same line when it reopened its bid for entry into the Common Market in 1966.

Now all of this has a familiar, Leninist ring to it and hardly shows that the world market has been turned into a charitable trust. Gigantic corporations, with the conscious political support of their governments, are engaged in a fierce competition for markets. But the setting is not at all Leninist, for the fight is not conducted so much in Asia, Africa, or Latin America as in Europe and America. Thus, Western business has preserved much of its old-fashioned Leninist spirit, though it has profoundly revised the letter of Lenin's law.

But there is a recalcitrant exception to these trends: oil. For the economy as a whole, the raw materials and capital export markets of the Third World have become less and less important. In economic terms, it is not *necessary* for the U.S. to promote international injustice in order to maintain domestic prosperity. But the huge and politically powerful oil industry thrives on these inequities.

In 1964, there were $44.3 billion of direct U.S. investment overseas, in 1965, $49.2 billion. In both years, net foreign investment was only about 5 percent of gross private domestic investment (the percentage actually declined a bit from 1964 to 1965). In both years, the distribution of this capital was about the same. In 1964, for instance, 31.2 percent of the American money had gone to Canada, 27.2 percent to Europe, 20.1 percent to Latin America, 6.9 percent to Asia, and 3.5 percent to Africa. All these figures support the thesis that exploiting the Third World is a diminishing and noncrucial part of the American economy.

At the same time, however, the petroleum and mining industries accounted for around 40 percent of this total, about the same portion as that of manufacturing. More to the point, the income in 1964 on $14.3 billion of petroleum investment was more than *twice* as great as that realized on the $16.8 billion of investment in manufacturing ($1.9 billion as against $.876 billion). This obviously is a superprofit and it depends on arrangements with countries that are either poor or rich in a distorted way (Kuwait, which has the second highest per capita income in the world, is a balkanized fief for oil and not, as it should be, a source of wealth for Mideast development generally).

In the process of accumulating this enormous wealth, the oil industry works hand in glove with the U.S. government, and vice versa. The companies benefit, of course, from direct production controls within America—the money made in this rigidly *dirigiste* sector of the economy paradoxically seems to create laisser-faire millionaires—and the princely benefits from the 27.5 percent depletion allowance. Import controls are also designed to support the costly, noncompetitive American wells in the manner to which they are accustomed. Indeed, world oil prices are an ingenious and artificial creation; John Strachey once calculated that, were the Arabs to nationalize the petroleum operations in their countries and permit a "market" price to emerge, oil consumers in the West would be able to buy at a much cheaper price than now prevails. However, since a single decision of Royal Dutch Shell was reported by Elizabeth Jager to have affected the balance of payments position of both Britain and Italy, it is unlikely that any such experimentation will be allowed.

But oil politics have also affected American foreign policy. The basic premise was stated in Harry Truman's reminiscences of the 1945 Mideast crisis: "If the Russians were to control Iran's oil, either directly or indirectly, the raw material balance of the world would undergo a serious change and it would be a serious loss for the economy of the Western world."

The oil industry's argument is, of course, that as the producer of a strategic fuel its interest must be protected precisely in the interest of America's common good. Recently, in a Senate speech in May 1966, the late Robert F. Kennedy gave an example of the kind of private self-interest dominating the policy of the nation. In Peru, Kennedy said, President Belaunde had asked for $16 million for a domestic Peace-Corps-type project. The State Department held up these funds in order to "make the Peruvians more reasonable" in the negotiations which they were then carrying on with American oil companies. Kennedy added, "the same was true in Argentina." It should also be noted that when AID threatened to turn off food shipments unless India accepted American price-fixing for fertilizer, it acted as the agent of oil companies.

The oil industry, then, acts according to the classic Leninist scenario. It profiteers in the Third World, supports local reaction, opposes democratic and modernizing movements, and sometimes treats the U.S. government like a hired plant security guard. At almost every point, the result has been to make American foreign policy more reactionary. If the country's international actions were dedicated to reduce the gap between rich and poor nations, the oil industry would suffer. The resultant misery of various millionaires would hardly overturn the American economy; but the catch is, of course, political. Oil is powerful in Washington, therefore any hope of a truly democratic foreign policy would require the defeat of its domestic influence.

With this very important caveat about oil a general and un-Leninist proposition can be restated: the prosperity of the American economy need not depend on the exploitation of the Third World and, to a considerable measure, does not at this moment. The reactionary policies the country has followed in widening the international gap between the rich and the poor are thus not the inexorable expressions of economic and social structure. They are reasonable, businesslike evils perpetrated according to the rules of this world which was so carefully made for us; but these rules could be changed. And that possibility is not to be found in the philosophy of Lenin or his followers.

*   *   *

Planning Toward Internationalized Economic Aid

Perhaps the most positive and dramatic action this nation could undertake would be to internationalize its economic aid. This would lay the basis for the global economic planning which alone can make the notion of "democracy between nations" a meaningful reality. For it is now necessary, as Senator Fulbright has said, to "extend the frontiers of our loyalty and compassion."

As the foregoing has shown, postwar aid, whether capitalist or Communist, has been inspired by almost every motive except one of orderly economic development for the earth's poor. In 1963, the Organization for Economic Cooperation and Development (OECD) reported, 84 percent of aid funds were bilateral—subject to military and political priorities. Thus, France used its disbursements to create a special, and advantageous, relationship with its ex-colonies, and President Kennedy could say, "Our assistance makes possible the stationing of 3.5 million Allied troops along the Communist frontier at one-tenth the cost of maintaining a comparable number of American soldiers." And even when the money was not so blatantly an instrument of the donor's foreign policy, it was regularly tied to the needs of the advanced economy rather than to those of the impoverished economy. And, more recently, the trend has been to loans rather than grants.

For historical reasons normally not of their own making, underdeveloped countries are desperately short on human resources. The tricky political and military vagaries accompanying postwar aid taxed the capacity of a modern country's computerized planning process— and overwhelmed the shaky planning institutions in the new countries. Obviously, funds must now be allocated on some more rational, predictable basis of need and capacity to use them. The U.N. has already begun the ground work of developing econometric models of the world economy.[3] If the goal of closing the gap between the rich and the poor is taken seriously, this tentative undertaking must receive massive support and become the focus of a system of planned, internationalized aid.

Estimates differ as to how much it would cost were the advanced countries to foot the developing nations' deficiency in capital. In 1966, the Council of Economic Advisers optimistically figured that the new nations could only use $3 to $4 billion more than is now available. But there are much higher projections: Jan Tinbergen has set the needed funds at $7 billion, Michael Brower at $12 billion, and the First Committee of the U.N. Trade and Development Conference predicted that the "savings gap" would reach $20 billion in 1970.[4]

However much these computations differ (because of different definitions *and* the fact that so little effort has been devoted to the task), economists consider that there is an objective basis for determining how much capital the developing world needs and how much it can absorb. If massive intellectual and financial resources

[3] *Studies in Long-Term Economic Projections for the World Economy,* United Nations, 1964. This is an example of the kind of work now being done in this area.
[4] Goran Ohlin's study, *Foreign Aid Policies Reconsidered,* Chapter IV (OECD, Paris, 1966), summarizes much of the work already done in computing the capital shortage of the poor nations.

were invested in the task of such an analysis, rational planning and resources could be allocated on a global scale.

Even if the highest estimate is valid—the U.N.'s prediction of a $20 billion savings gap by 1970—the sum at issue is well within the means of the advanced nations. By 1970, Europe, North America, and Australia will have a total GNP of over $1.5 trillion. A deficit of $20 billion would, in that year, be less than the 3 percent of American GNP Harry Truman proposed to spend on the Marshall Plan and would approximately equal the extra appropriation Lyndon B. Johnson asked for the Vietnam War in 1967. Such international economic planning could make long-range policies possible. Capital in the developing lands would no longer be at the mercy of the wild fluctuations of the world market in primary commodities or the vicissitudes of a Cold War. Funds would be guaranteed over a considerable period of years, and this would allow local planners to make more efficient use of their resources. But this massive, steady flow of funds could only be assured if foreign aid by the advanced nations were put on a permanent basis.

There have been proposals to commit all wealthy countries to automatically give 1 percent of their GNP for international economic development. This would be an enormous improvement over the trends of recent years when the ratio has been regularly declining in the U.S. (which possesses more than half of the total GNP of the rich, non-Communist part of the world). This system would yield almost three-fourths of the $20 billion gap the U.N. Conference predicted for 1970.

Yet, there is a much better way of appropriating these funds: a progressive income tax:

1. This notion has an obvious grounding in equity, since the richer a nation (or an individual) the smaller the percentage of income devoted to necessities and the greater the ability to meet social obligations.
2. Such an approach meets the problem of the gap between rich and poor head-on by proposing (if quite modestly) some redistribution of income shares.
3. As Senator Fulbright has emphasized, this would take foreign aid out of the realm of charity and philanthropy and make it a matter of right, like U.S. income tax and Social Security.

Experts, like P. N. Rosenstein-Rodan, have already demonstrated that the details of such an international income-tax system can be worked out if there is the political will.[5]

Aid for Totalitarians?

However, another question in international economic planning is anything but a technicality; this is essentially the same difficulty faced by the Alliance for Progress: what attitude would an international aid agency take toward reactionary governments, toward rightist or Communist dictatorships? Unless this question is answered, the whole enterprise could have the most paradoxical results, and some of these reforms could subsidize local oligarchies, rotten power structures, and economic backwardness. Therefore, some minimal criteria have to be established for these grants.

The U.N., obviously, cannot intervene in the political life of every developing country. Yet it can insist on regional planning in return for its aid; it can disallow dictatorial pyramid-building and old-fashioned thievery; it can insist that nations, and regional groupings, show that there is a "popular consumption criterion" (the phrase is Galbraith's) in their equations—that projects benefit the present, as well as the future, generation.

It is much simpler, of course, to solve these thorny issues on paper than in practice. Even under the best system of international economic planning there will be waste, funds will be appropriated by the corrupt and the dictatorial, etc. It is not that such an approach will work perfectly; but, if one is serious about closing the gap between rich and poor nations, only something like this approach might work at all. Certainly, the defenders of conventional wisdom and the actual aid-and-trade policies of the postwar period have utterly failed in their professed goal of narrowing the chasm which divides the fat North from the hungry South.

Some American right-wing critics are hostile to the present process of foreign aid for the worst of reasons: they want to turn their backs on the people of Asia, Africa, and Latin America—and they are sympathetic to the world's status quo and to military rule. But

[5] In Rosenstein-Rodan's computation, if all the non-Communist advanced nations with per capita GNP of $600 or more were involved, the United States' share of the burden, on the basis of 1961 figures, would be 65 percent of the total. P. N. Rosenstein-Rodan, "International Aid for Underdeveloped Countries," in *The Strategy of World Order*, Richard A. Falk and Saul H. Mendlovitz, ed., Vol. IV, p. 517.

there are others, and they are much more numerous, who are simply bewildered by the seemingly endless and futile appropriations in Washington. There is no use pretending that these people can be easily convinced to support the regular allocation of even larger amounts of money. But this effort in political persuasion must be made. In the doing it is necessary to explain that past programs failed, not because they were so exceedingly generous, but because they were inadequate and manipulative. And international economic planning should not be proposed as a utopia but as the only *practical* way to reach ends Americans have thought they were supporting for over two decades.

International economic planning and a world system of taxation is the simplest and most direct way of achieving redistribution of wealth, and it has the virtue of creating pressure for structural reform in the recipient countries. A change in trade policies would not require sweeping innovations. It would mean a conscious decision to reverse the present reactionary priorities of the world market, to create a mechanism which would automatically transfer some of the profits of the international economy from the rich to the poor. To accomplish this, the tariff policies of the advanced nations would have to be radically changed. Yet, there would be no need for new institutions—only the old arrangement has to be turned upside down.

Basically, what the developing nations need—and want, for they made these demands on GATT in the summer of 1966—is a transition from tariffs which discriminate *against* them to those which discriminate *for* them. They asked the Kennedy Round negotiators to remove their products from the list of items excluded from tariff reduction; to reduce the rate on goods from developing lands more than rates on goods from advanced countries; to make a maximum reduction of tariffs on tropical foods, and to compensate the developing countries for their loss of tariff preferences when this takes place. These demands were basically turned down.

The U.N. economists have come up with an even broader conception. They have suggested a development insurance fund based on the "willingness of advanced countries to contribute, on the understanding that their direct benefits will not equal their contributions." Under this plan, all nations would pay in to a central fund and each would be compensated if there were a drop in export proceeds. In a series of complicated calculations, the U.N. Committee of Experts

which outlined this system concluded that, had it been working between 1953 and 1959, the developing countries' claims would have
ranged between $246 and $466 million a year (and the advanced
countries would have received between $12 and $142 million a year).
Such a program is easily within the bounds of the possible for the
rich powers.

It might, however, be difficult to persuade the well fed to stop
making a profit from the hungry. As noted earlier, Nasser wanted
the 1966 New Delhi summit meeting to advocate a freezing of the
entire debt of the developing countries but, for political reasons,
neither Tito nor Mrs. Gandhi could be persuaded to go along with
this idea. Yet, there is no possibility of justice so long as India must
return about one-quarter of the monies it receives in foreign aid just
to service past debts. New Delhi is afraid to protest this outrage because it might then lose the three-quarters of assistance which does
come through. The advanced economies hardly require this tribute
from the impoverished; the developing countries' debts to the Western powers should be forgiven or else rescheduled and made interest
free. Indeed, it is high time that the Western powers reverse the
scandalous trend toward loans instead of aid which has been pick-
ing up strength throughout the sixties.

This does not mean that the wealthy nations are to choose poverty
in order to fulfill a moral obligation to the world's less fortunate.
But affluent countries might enrich themselves at a somewhat slower
rate and without pushing the majority of the world's population more
deeply into misery. This can be done. Sober, intelligent proposals
have demonstrated the possibility of creating a new world by simply
changing the present injustices of aid and trade. The crucial question
is not technical, but political.

The Politics of Hope

There is a sort of international Keynesian argument for the self-
interest in America's doing justice in the world. For just as the vast
increase in buying power, which developed in the U.S. through the
welfare state and the labor movement, has laid the basis for an advance in the prosperity of the entire nation, so a decent life for the
peoples of Asia, Africa, and Latin America would be to the economic
advantage of the entire world.

There is another paradoxical political case for global decency.

For now that the Cold War is, thank God, coming to an end in Europe, it is possible for the first time to realize the decent values which most Americans thought they had been fighting for all along. To clarify this point requires an analysis of the two anticommunisms.

At the height of the struggle between the NATO West and the Warsaw-Pact East there existed a straightforward version of anticommunism. It was based on reactionary politics, and it viewed the Soviets as only one manifestation of the godlessness and disorder of a world which had taken leave of its fundamental values. From this point of view, anticommunism was one, and only one, way of defending a status quo. The alliances with rightist dictators were, in this perspective, acts of virtue, not of necessity. And lacking any sense of the economic, political, and social roots of both nationalism and communism, these rightist anti-Communists saw the enemy as a conspirator, a subversive, an agent who drove otherwise contented workers and peasants to revolt.

The American symbol of this one-dimensional and paranoid anticommunism was, of course, Senator Joseph McCarthy. And it was no accident that McCarthy's heyday coincided with Stalin's last, demented years, and with the Korean War. The American people were bewildered and fearful in the presence of a megalomaniacal dictator, and involved in a frustrating shooting war only five years after World War II had ended in Tokyo Bay. In this political atmosphere McCarthy rocketed to prominence.

But there was, and is, another anticommunism. It sought some alternative both to communism and to the status quo, for it recognized the right and necessity of revolution but thought it should be democratic, not totalitarian. The views of Galbraith and Robert Kennedy are obviously in this tradition. Indeed, this attitude regularly supplied the official rhetoric for American development in the Cold War itself. "The seeds of totalitarian regimes," Harry Truman said in March 1947, "are nurtured by misery and want. They spread and grow in the evil soil of poverty and strife. They reach their full growth when the hope of a people for a better life ahead has died."

The words were fine enough—but the President uttered them in defense of the Truman Doctrine in Greece, where the United States placed its enormous power at the disposal of conservative forces fighting a popular movement whose leadership had been won over by the Communists. This was typical of the Cold War. Many Americans were committed to the fight against communism for excellent reasons of democratic principle and hatred of injustice. Yet, by far and large, the U.S. could not possibly fulfill the hopes of these decent people; for the essential conservatism of the American economy in this artificially unjust world subverted most of the nation's progressive political aspirations.

In practical terms, as long as America's economic and social policies frustrated its political visions, the country regularly turned to the authoritarian right even as it talked in the words of the democratic left. Thus, the militarization of American foreign policy and its association with so many dictators and antidemocrats is not the result of a particular malevolence of this or that politician, but it is related to massive structural trends both within the U.S. and in its dealings with the world.

In this setting, to put an end to the Cold War allows America to recover its vision, to demilitarize its outlook. A massive commitment to international development does not provide simply an economic substitute for the arms economy. It might serve as an emotional and political substitute for the reactionary passions of rightist anticommunism; it is the one way to implement peacefully the decent values which motivated the anticommunism of the democratic left. However, and most emphatically, this proposal is not primarily "anti." It cannot be, for a new world cannot be constructed out of hostility. One wants to save the workers and peasants of the Third World from the horrors of totalitarian capital accumulation, to be sure, and, in a social and economic sense, that is an anticommunist program. But in an enterprise which requires such far-ranging construction, the stress must be positive and the challenge is, in Fulbright's moving phrase, "to extend the frontiers of our loyalty and compassion."

The United States and the Soviet Union, having brought mankind to the brink of nuclear holocaust, could simply walk away from the Cold War, retreat into their separate self-interests, and respect each other's injustices. Or, America could take the lead in a gigantic international effort to finish the creation of the world. There are economic arguments for such a course, and they must be stated. But ultimately, if this is to be done it will happen because the buried, deep-running force of American idealism bursts out of the channels to which the generals and the executives have confined it, to take its own direction. That will be the politics of hope.

George McGovern

A NEW INTERNATIONALISM

Did George McGovern's 1972 Presidential campaign pose the possibility of a Radical–Liberal foreign policy for America? A complete answer would require examining a broad range of the Senator's speeches and position papers. The selection below is McGovern's most important campaign statement on foreign policy. It challenges Nixon's Realist notion of a five-power balance; far from being realistic, such a principle would "simply resurrect an old world of kings and princes and empires that we will never see again." In good Radical–Liberal fashion, McGovern fears that "our preoccupation with a military balance leaves untouched the deadly imbalance among population, resources and wealth—and they, too, endanger our lives." Yet absent from the speech is a more radical proposal that marked his primary campaign— the pledge to reduce military spending to $55 billion by 1975, in part by withdrawing 170,000 troops from Europe. And to the crucial question, "Where are our vital interests?" the speech answers only with further rhetorical questions which "we had better ask ourselves today rather than later." The tendency to fudge such questions was, we saw, characteristic of Realist criticism. It is also, perhaps inevitably, the way a Presidential candidate broadens his appeal and keeps open his options.

Next week on television I will address the American people on the subject of Vietnam. In that speech I will demonstrate a public plan— as distinct from Mr. Nixon's secret plan—to achieve peace in Indochina. In that same speech I will set forth my own vision of what American society can be once the tragedy of Vietnam is behind us.

But before then, I want to share my more general views of America's role in the world of the 1970s. And I want to contrast my own approach with the record of the Nixon years, so that in this critical area the American people can understand clearly what the choices are.

Mr. Nixon stated his current vision of the world this past January. He declared that:

> *The only time in the history of the world that we have had any extended period of peace is when there has been balance of power. It is when one nation becomes infinitely more powerful in relation to its potential competitor that the danger of war arises. So I believe in a world in which the*

From George McGovern, "A New Internationalism," speech delivered, in part, before the City Club of Cleveland. (Reprinted from *The New York Times,* October 6, 1972, p. 26.

United States is powerful. I think it will be a safer world and a better world if we have a strong, healthy United States, Europe, Soviet Union, China, Japan, each balancing the other, not playing one against the other, an even balance.

But I begin today by asking whether that is all we want. And I ask, too, whether it is relevant and realistic in today's world—or does it simply resurrect an old world, of kings and princes and empires, that we will never see again.

That five-power, balance-of-power thesis attempts to force onto the contemporary world a naive prenuclear view dating back to the 19th century and before.

Today, in the military sense, we have but two superpowers—capable of destroying ourselves and most of humanity many times over.

That will likely be the case for some time. Europe is not one entity yet, and at best, it will be a long time before it functions as one nation. Japan, though clearly a dominant economic and political power, may not seek entry into the military balance at all—and will probably profit from that decision. And we have discovered a China that seems as determined to avoid direct military entanglements outside her borders as she is to assume her proper role as a great society in world diplomacy and commerce.

It is a naive delusion as well to believe that there is some arbitrary number of actors who will determine whether the world has war or peace. There may have been periods of relative peace under a balance of power. But Mr. Nixon forgets that no balance among the giants can eradicate the causes of war among the rest of mankind. Nor can it dispel the demand of some 140 countries to have a say in the issues which determine their survival.

And finally, that balance of power neglects other ominous threats to our safety. On May 9, 1969, the then-Secretary General of the United Nations, U Thant, issued this warning:

. . . the members of the United Nations have perhaps 10 years left in which to subordinate their ancient quarrels and launch a global partnership to curb the arms race, to improve the human environment, to defuse the population explosion, and to supply the required momentum to world development efforts.

If such a global partnership is not forged within the next decade, then I very much fear that the problems I have mentioned will have reached such staggering proportions that they will be beyond our control.

We have lost precious time since 1969, and there are precious few years left. Our preoccupation with a military balance leaves untouched the deadly imbalances among population, resources and wealth—and they, too, endanger our lives.

So we face a much different world from the one we knew as we grew up, or as we served in World War II, or even as we watched our country slip into a disastrous Asian war.

Less than 12 years ago John F. Kennedy was inaugurated, and on that bright January day everything seemed possible. If our sturdy American spirit did not give reason enough for that faith, we had as well a new figure and a new voice, to personify the optimism and boldness of a new generation.

In January, 1961, no one could predict the Bay of Pigs . . . the Cuban Missile Crisis, the tragic murders of John and Robert Kennedy and Martin Luther King . . . the Dominican Intervention . . . the alienation of many in our own society—least of all, the endless minefield in which we would find ourselves in Vietnam.

Yet, in the years that were to follow, we as a people would be buffeted by one shock and disillusionment after another until finally, in Vietnam, we would lose our innocence—and much of our confidence.

And today we are moving toward a mature knowledge that while we are deeply involved and have vast influence in the world, forces beyond our control will have the most to do with shaping the political arrangements of the future. We can see the error of assuming, since World War II, that our actions would be decisive in either "winning" or "losing" China . . . in causing or preventing revolution of the Right or Left in much of Latin America and the rest of the developing world . . . or in determining the outcome of a distant civil war in Southeast Asia.

But at the same time we must be aware that as the richest and most powerful nation in the earth's history, what we do both here and elsewhere will be more important than what anyone else does in moving this planet closer to either its final destruction or a more peaceful and happy future.

Possessed now with a sense of tragedy and of our own limitations, we as a people may finally be ready to play a more responsible and constructive role in the world than we ever have before.

More than 25 years ago, Adlai Stevenson, in his Godkin Lectures at Harvard, offered us these lines—and good advice—from Keats's "Hyperion."

> *For to bear all naked truths,*
> *And to envisage circumstances, all calm,*
> *That is the top of sovereignty . . .*

What shall our role be?

I know of no responsible person who would knowingly call for a return to isolationism.

Modern communications, and the existence of intercontinental weapons systems, have made that a practical impossibility.

Yet, in many ways, the foreign policies of the present administration are isolating us.

We are isolated from our allies and trading partners in Europe and Asia, and even from Canada, because of six-gun economic diplomacy and failure to consult.

We are isolated from the developing nations by a policy which tells them that "what's good for Pepsi-Cola and the First National City Bank is more than good enough for you."

We are isolated from reality by the insistence that tough talk and big Pentagon budgets are somehow synonymous with national manhood.

And most of all, we are isolated from our own ideals as we back a corrupt dictatorship in Saigon, by raining fire and death on helpless people all over Indochina.

I suggest that we must reject this unconscious isolationism in favor of a New Internationalism based not only upon our vital interests, but also upon the kind of nation we can and should be.

Where are our vital interests?

By one measure, they certainly lie in the world's North Temperate Zone.

North America, Europe, the Soviet Union, and Japan do produce some 80 percent of the world's goods. This is where the power—in the sense of wealth, technology, developed human skills, and the capacity to wage modern war—most largely resides.

And this is where both we and the Soviet Union, as the two superpowers, will for the foreseeable future continue to have the highest interest in averting any attempt by the other to threaten or subvert our respective systems of security.

The North Temperate Zone, is in short, where a final World War III would be fought—and where its potential causes must most carefully be guarded against.

But our vital interests go further.

The Arab-Israeli confrontation in the Middle East, with its potential for even more dangerous United States-Soviet confrontation, is an immediate threat to general peace. And we have a firm and deep obligation to the security and integrity of the State of Israel.

Communist China has little power in terms of conventional measurement (by 1975 Japanese per capita GNP will be 12 times that of China's) but she possesses nuclear weapons and a desire to reassert her ancient prestige.

The Indian Subcontinent and Indonesia especially compel our attention in Asia, as do several states in Africa and in our own hemisphere.

What of the hundreds of other sovereign nations existing in the 1970s—including those to the south lying within the purview of the Monroe Doctrine?

All, in one way or another, have some importance to us.

But must we be committed to their armed defense?

Under what conceivable circumstances should we ever become involved in supporting their present governments in the face of domestic turmoil?

These are questions we had better ask ourselves today, rather than later.

I believe that America's New Internationalism in the 1970s must follow several clear guidelines.

First, it must be supported by a strong national defense, but one free of waste, as I have previously outlined; forces fully adequate to defend our own land and to fill vital defense commitments.

Second, it must look toward prudent relaxation of tension with potential adversary powers, such as the Soviet Union and China.

Third, it must look to reestablishment of healthy economic and political relationships with our principal allies and trading partners in Europe, Japan, Canada, and Latin America.

Fourth, it must avoid the kind of reflexive interventionism that has foolishly involved us in the internal political affairs of other countries.

Fifth, it must envision a world community with the capacity to resolve disputes among nations, and to end the war between man and his own environment.

Sixth, it must reassert America's role as a beacon—and friend—to those millions in the human family desperately striving to achieve the elemental human dignity which all men seek.

The kind of interventionism I would favor as President would be agricultural and technical assistance . . . the building of roads and schools . . . the training of skilled personnel, in concert with other nations and through multilateral institutions.

Finally, at the bottom of it all, must lie a just and prosperous domestic society, where all our people—and the people's representatives—are involved in decision making.

As my old friend Senator Humphrey has often said: America's most important foreign policy act in the 1960s was the passage of the Civil Rights Act of 1964.

I agree.

How then, should we proceed?

My first act of American foreign policy on Inauguration Day must be—will be an immediate and total end to our involvement in the Indochina War.

As Richard Nixon said in 1968: "Those who have had a chance for four years and could not produce peace, should not be given another chance."

We have had enough of secret plans to end the war. We need a public plan for peace.

As we look beyond Vietnam, the prevention of nuclear war remains the first charge on America's commitments.

During the 1960s, we built a great arsenal to protect the United States and our allies against a nuclear threat from any quarter. And we must continue to maintain the power we need.

But we also know that too much power is self-defeating.

We have seen the deadly spiral of the arms race, and drawn no comfort from it.

We have seen that if we build weapons we do not need, we only provoke the Soviet Union to follow suit.

The agreements with the Soviet Union to slow the arms race are a significant achievement. Yet they have shortcomings, for they are now used as an excuse not to halt but to escalate the race in nuclear arms. . . .

Let us have the defense we need. But let us not permit the insatiable appetite of our military to replace our good sense, and undermine the prospects of reduction in the balance of nuclear terror.

President Nixon's trip to Moscow this May was historic. It was the culmination of many years of effort that began when President Kennedy signed the Limited-Test-Ban Treaty. This effort continued under three Presidents, both Democratic and Republican.

We must now build upon this effort. That is why it makes no sense for the President to return from Moscow with an arms reduction agreement and then call on the Congress to add another $4-billion to military spending.

We must work to bring the arms race under control.

We must seek areas of agreement with the Soviet Union consistent with the needs and interests of our friends and allies. We should press for justice for Soviet Jews rather than abandon them for a trade agreement. Surely we have learned the lesson at great cost that a free people cannot sit by and merely witness the oppression of a religious minority by a totalitarian society.

We should, of course, encourage expanded trade between our two countries.

And we must spare no effort to build the structure of a lasting peace.

In limiting the arms race we do not begin with excessive trust in the Russians, for we retain more than enough for deterrence.

In reducing our excess we do not rely on Moscow's good intentions, we will remain strong enough to meet any test.

We need only act in our sure defense by seeking areas of genuine mutual interest and by tailoring our armed forces to the reality of the world around us.

If the Soviet Union responds with the cooperation dictated by her own interest as much as ours, then we can build toward a future that is not based on out-dated stereotypes of military confrontation and power politics. Instead we can build toward a world of diversity in which we are secure, a world in which there are new ways of thinking and behaving, and a world where there are real prospects for enduring peace.

I also welcome the progress that the President has made in relations with China—a course I have advocated for 20 years.

We must build on this progress, by encouraging China's full participation in the community of nations, to take part in providing for Asian security, instead of threatening it.

As President, I will begin by recognizing the government in Peking.

The future of Asia will depend in part upon China. But it will also depend upon Japan, the third most powerful economic nation in the world, a nation of vigor and purpose, and a long-standing friend of the United States.

In recent years our relations with Japan have been in steady, but needless decline.

President Nixon announced his trip to China without consulting Japan, betraying the trust that nation had placed in our Asian partnership. He imposed the New Economic Policy without consulting Japan, and then blamed Japan for problems that were largely of his own making. And after these shocks, President Nixon took a year to convene a summit meeting with the Prime Minister of Japan.

This was a diplomacy of insult, and it must not continue. For as we seek new accommodations with our adversaries, we must never neglect old and treasured friends.

We must treat Japan as an equal, consult with her in trust. As President, I would begin the painstaking renewal of our cooperative relationship with this key nation in Asia.

There will be tough negotiations and vigorous competition on important matters of trade and economics, where both our nations have interests to protect. We will expect fair treatment by Japan on matters of trade and investment, and greater understanding of our domestic economic problems. But Japan also expects fair treatment from us, not the patronizing attitude that the President has shown, or the six-gun diplomacy of John Connally.

At the same time, we must recognize that Japan has a chance to become the first great power without a massive military arsenal. We must not crush that hopeful experiment. I will ensure that remaining U.S. forces in Japan serve the original purpose designed for them—

to help provide for the defense of Japan, and not to become involved in military ventures in Southeast Asia.

I will place the support of the United States behind membership for Japan in the United Nations Security Council.

And I will begin laying the groundwork, with Japan, in East Asia that will improve the chances that security in that troubled part of the world will be based on economic cooperation and effort, and never again on the kind of war we have been uselessly and destructively fighting in Indochina.

In Western Europe, there has been great progress toward a relaxation of tensions, and toward resolution of problems left over from World War II.

Much of the credit belongs to Chancellor Brandt of West Germany, despite occasional opposition from the Nixon administration. There is a treaty on Berlin, and there are West German treaties with Poland and the Soviet Union. And we will soon see a Conference on Security and Cooperation.

Our Western European neighbors are fulfilling our mutual hopes and expectations of the past quarter-century.

But in Western Europe's success, there are grave implications for the United States. There will be vigorous economic competition across the Atlantic—and we should welcome it.

The Atlantic Partnership no longer needs single-handed American leadership nor do our partners want it. Nor should we.

But again there are diplomatic failures and challenges to American statesmanship.

President Nixon does not consult adequately with our allies on critical issues of detente, raising fears in Western Europe that we will reach agreements with the Soviet Union at their expense. He talks of cooperation, yet he permitted his Secretary of the Treasury, John Connally, to badger and bully the countries with whom we most need to maintain a cooperative spirit. He talks of the future, but does not understand the importance of good economic relations in preserving and strengthening Atlantic ties.

We must restore good economic and political relations across the Atlantic. And we must restore Europe's faith in our commitment to the success of the European Community.

At the same time I believe in a thorough review of the military aspects of European security.

We no longer need to maintain 319,000 American troops in Europe to deter aggression, 27 years after the Second World War. But the way we reduce our forces—and share burdens more equally—is critical to the future of the Alliance and to European security.

The key to force reductions on the side of the Warsaw Pact does not lie in the number of American troops stationed in the West, rather it lies in the cohesion, cooperation, and common purpose of the Western Alliance.

If we make some force reductions, yet strengthen these attitudes and practices, then there is nothing the Soviet Union can do to weaken us or our allies, or to reduce our security.

We retain a special concern about the Middle East. All Americans have been heartened by the reduction of Soviet involvement in Egypt. But we recognize that this does not end the threat to Israel.

We must remain committed to Israel's future, to her right to live at peace with her neighbors behind secure and recognized borders.

We must continue to supply those arms that will permit Israel to guarantee its own security. In my administration, we will do this because of our deep and abiding concern for Israel, not adopt one policy for election year, and another for the years that follow.

We must continue to retain sufficient American power in the area to ensure that there is no doubt of our commitment to Israel's security.

We must intensify our efforts to end the international terrorism that most recently appalled the world at Munich and that is a threat to us all.

And we must show a deep regard for the economic and human needs of the Palestine refugees.

Today, we have long since met the demands of a world dominated by military concerns. But we are rapidly losing the world in which economic power and relations will have their day.

The international economic system is near collapse—and for a year President Nixon did almost nothing.

Our alliances with Europe and Japan are in disarray over economic issues—and President Nixon does nothing.

The problems of two and one-half billion poor people in the world are insistent and demanding—and President Nixon does nothing.

Under President Nixon, we are becoming a second-rate nation in terms that will really count in the 1970s.

It is more than a year since the New Economic Policy began. Yet, only now has the administration begun an effort to restructure the international economic system, while the United States balance of trade continues in the worst deficit in 100 years, and the United States dollar has been devalued as a result of the Nixon inflation at home. We have still not recovered our sense of responsibility for this economic system, upon which our prosperity, and that of other nations, depends.

We must repair our damaged friendships abroad; we must begin sorting out the difficult problems that must be solved in order to create a new international economic system. We must begin the urgent task of monetary reform not through confrontation, but by restoring and building on the international cooperation and commercial partnership that we had until this administration. We must work out new rules of international conduct in trade and commerce. And we must begin building an awareness and understanding of international economic policy into the councils of government at all levels.

Last week, I made several concrete proposals to begin this effort:

New rules governing changes in exchange rates.

Cooperative arrangements to cushion large disruptive flows of short-term capital.

More special drawing rights—and more of them for developing countries.

Steps to resolve fairly the problem of the dollar "overhang."

We must help businesses that are uncompetitive to shift to new products.

And we must guarantee every working man and woman a good job at good pay in industries that can compete in world markets.

American will is being tested. President Nixon has decided that our will is weak—that we cannot pass the test—that we can survive economically only by having inflated military budgets and by blaming others for our difficulties. But I say this: Give Americans a chance, and we will prove that we can have the strongest economy in the world, and a prosperity in which everyone will share.

In virtually every statement, every act, of this administration, nearly two and a half billion human beings in the world have been left out.

These are the people who have too little power to figure in a new balance of power based on the military giants; they are the people who are too meek to command the attention given to generals and weapons manufacturers producing excess weapons we do not need; they are the people whose crime was to be born poor.

Ten years ago, I was President Kennedy's first Director of Food for Peace.

He declared then: "If we do not help the many who are poor, we cannot hope to save the few who are rich."

Today, this statement is more true than ever.

Today, the ability of people from the rich countries to trade, travel, and invest in the developing countries depends upon our helping them to meet their critical problems of development.

Our future success in preserving the environment will require the help of developing countries. And even the international system of trade and monetary relations is beginning to depend on developing-country cooperation. They deserve and demand a voice, and they desperately need our help.

We have seen little to inspire our confidence in these past four years. Mr. Nixon pledged to untie aid, and then reneged; he talked of the need for development, then slashed the budget and put his lobbying efforts in Congress behind the supply of arms instead of technical assistance to developing countries. He extended the 10 percent surcharge on imports to poor-country products as well as rich. He has used the power of his office to bully and intimidate Latin American nations. He has defied the conscience of mankind by giving up United States opposition to racism in Southern Africa.

He threatened to intervene in the war between India and Pakistan, against our interests, against what was right, and against the conscience of the civilized world. He then waited five months before recognizing the infant, struggling nation of Bangladesh that has suffered so much for so long. And he still has not restored aid to India—aid for schools and roads and health care—that he cut off when the war began. Indeed, the mistaken anti-India pro-Pakistan stand of the Nixon administration while Pakistan was murdering its poor people by the hundreds of thousands was not only morally wrong, it has cost us the goodwill of India—the world's largest democratic nation.

These have been callous displays toward the poor of the world, for fully two-thirds of mankind. As a great nation, America cannot turn its back on their suffering. And we cannot stand aside as development—this great human adventure—goes on.

We cannot continue to abdicate our moral and political responsibility to so many people, and ultimately to the United States itself.

The New Internationalism will chart another course.

We will make a full commitment of the United States to the multilateral institutions that are helping with development, not with military weapons that make war and suffering more likely, but with the economic and technological tools that help men to improve their own lives.

We will put our relations with individual developing countries on a firm footing, not relegate them to an insignificant place in a balance of power.

We will show that we can live up to our commitments to our neighbors in Latin America, not demand that they quietly accept our domination.

We will show that we are concerned for all of Africa, and abandon this administration's support for the racist regimes of Southern Africa. We will show our concern for the racist expulsion of Asians from Uganda.

We will renew our commitment to the efforts of the United Nations for peace and for development. And we will show that we, too, can respond to the demands that membership in the human family places upon us. The United Nations' peace-keeping capacity must be strengthened and utilized. It is an essential framework for international cooperation.

The making of decisions of defense and foreign policy is an awesome task, too great for any one man—or any one branch of government. And here, too, we cry out for reform.

Long ago, we recognized that the powers of the Presidency could isolate the man and his decisions from the American people.

So we protected the nation—and the Presidency itself—from the "man on horseback," by adopting methods for the close scrutiny of foreign and defense policy.

Under President Nixon, these methods have decayed and Congress itself has been thwarted in its efforts to discharge its Constitutional responsibilities.

The executive agreement has often replaced the treaty subject to Senate approval.

Wars are fought in secret, in Laos and Cambodia, and paid for by secret funds in defiance of the will of Congress.

Under President Nixon, however, the Secretary of State has become a minor functionary, and was not even permitted to take part in the most critical negotiations the President had in Peking.

No American President should be permitted to escape the Constitutional restraints on Executive power.

Under my administration, the Congress will be fully informed, it will be fully consulted, and it will have restored to it the full powers set down for it in the Constitution of the United States.

And I will not permit the basic trends of American foreign and defense policy to be set in the inner sanctum of the White House, by men who are hidden from public view and removed from public responsibility.

There will be a Secretary of State of great capability and unquestioned stature.

No foreign policy can be effective if it is backed by weakness at home. President Nixon wants us to believe that talking of America's problems denies its greatness.

But I believe that our greatness lies in part in our ability to look at ourselves, to recognize what we have to do, and then to do something about it.

If we have four more years of the same at home, the wisdom of our foreign policy may not matter very much.

We will be condemned to be a second-rate nation at home.

We must and we can have a strong economy, with a good job at good pay for everyone who wants to work . . . an end to crippling inflation and an end to the Nixon recession.

We must have real tax reform . . . a reduction of crime . . . improved health care . . . and genuine quality education for all our children.

We must resume building a society in which government helps to bring people together, not drive them apart; where it helps to increase opportunity, not limit it; and where it taps the deep roots of the American spirit, not stifles them in indifference to the need for America to grow and change.

I believe that we can have that America, again—a first-rate nation at home and abroad, where American greatness and commitment to international cooperation will again become a thing of wonder in the world.

As a nation, we must bring to an end our time of tragedy: when Americans have lost faith in what their Government tells them; when a bitter and needless war has divided our people, and threatened our spirit and confidence as a nation.

Few other countries have faced what we have in these past few years.

But I believe that we are now prepared to use what we have learned from our past, from success and from failure, to meet our responsibilities both at home and in the world—to the lasting benefit of the American people and all mankind.

In the final analysis, our foreign policy is no more than who and what we are. It is a reflection of our attitudes towards ourselves, towards our country, and towards the rest of mankind. We cannot separate what we do abroad from what we do at home.

How we live in the neighborhoods and communities of America will determine how we live with our international neighbors, and in the broader world community.

Today, we can aspire to a maturity in our actions abroad, and maturity as a great nation—a great people—at home.

This is a challenge appropriate to our ideals, and to all that we have dared and won in the nearly two hundred years of our independence. As Abraham Lincoln once said, in a dark hour for America:

We shall nobly save or meanly lose the last, best hope on earth.

I have faith that we shall nobly save that "last best hope on earth."

IV RADICAL CRITICS

FIGURE 4. A radical view. (Courtesy, Register and Tribune Syndicate.)

Gabriel Kolko

THE ROOTS OF AMERICAN FOREIGN POLICY

Gabriel Kolko is a leading revisionist historian of the Cold War's origins. He concludes that American leaders purposely set out on a road of Globalist expansion, conjuring up as they went a "Soviet threat" with which to justify their course. In the selection below, Kolko has a related aim—to demonstrate that the roots of American globalism are sunk deep into the structure of American capitalism. The military establishment is not master, according to Kolko, but rather a tool of "businessmen and their political cohorts." The fact that the mass of Americans support the foreign policies of "the men of power" may be "less consequential" than that "the economically critical and powerful class endorses the ideology that serves it best."* Could any judgments be more at odds with those of globalism? Yet Kolko shares with W. W. Rostow the conviction that as America goes so goes the world. In Rostow's view, America's mission is to save the world by policing it. Writes Kolko: "The elimination of that American hegemony is the essential precondition for the emergence of a nation and a world in which mass hunger, suppression, and war are no longer the inevitable and continuous characteristics of modern civilization."

For a growing number of Americans the war in Vietnam has become the turning point in their perception of the nature of American foreign policy, the traumatizing event that requires them to look again at the very roots, assumptions, and structure of a policy that is profoundly destructive and dangerous. Vietnam is the logical outcome of a consistent reality we should have understood long before the United States applied much of its energies to ravaging one small nation.

We can only comprehend Vietnam in the larger context of the relations of the United States to the Third World, removing from our analytic framework superfluous notions of capriciousness, accident, and chance as the causal elements in American foreign and military policy. For the events in Vietnam expose in a sustained and systematic manner those American qualities that have led to one of the most frightful examples of barbarism of mechanized man against man known to modern history. The logical, deliberative aspects of

From *The Roots of American Foreign Policy* by Gabriel Kolko, pp. xi–xviii, 27–29, 78–81. Copyright © 1969 by Gabriel Kolko. Reprinted by permission of Beacon Press.

* *The Roots of American Foreign Policy*, p. 11.

American power at home and its interest abroad show how fully irrelevant are notions of accident and innocence in explaining the diverse applications of American power today, not only in Vietnam but throughout the Third World. If America's task of repressing the irrepressible is doomed to failure because it is impossible for six percent of the world's population to police and control the globe, critics of American policy should not attribute the undertaking to omission or ignorance. For if the United States can impose its will on the recalcitrant revolutionaries everywhere it will gain immensely thereby, and its losses will be proportionately great if it fails.

To understand policy one must know the policy makers—the men of power—and define their ideological view and their backgrounds. This means we must better perceive the nature of bureaucracy and state institutions in modern America, and determine whether such organizations carry with them distinctive economic and ideological attributes likely to emerge in the form of specific policies. It is, of course, the dominant fashion in the study of bureaucracy to ascribe to the structure of decision-making bureaucracy a neutral, independent rationale, and to drain away the class nature of formal institutions—indeed, to deny that men of power are something more than disinterested, perhaps misguided, public servants. The fact, of course, is that men of power do come from specific class and business backgrounds and ultimately have a very tangible material interest in the larger contours of policy. And although some are indeed seemingly perfect models of the neutral and disinterested public servant, both, in practice, implement the same policies.

We must confront anew the meaning of the concept of consensus or public opinion and the way it operates in the policy process. On one hand the seemingly shared beliefs, values, and consensus in society appear more critical than any single interest. But the fact that a ruling class makes its policies operate, even when the mass of society ceases to endorse them, and that the voluntaristic and occasionally enforced social goals benefit individuals rather than all of society, is a central reality most analysts perpetually exclude from a descriptive explanation of American society. That the voluntaristic basis of consensus usually justifies the actions of the men of power is less consequential than that, as we see today in the case of the American public and Vietnam, the policy continues when mass agreement withers away and even disappears. For consensus is identifiable with class goals and needs, suitably wrapped in a vague ideology of American nationalism and its global responsibility. These class goals and interests prevail even when the consensus disappears, and it is at this very point we see that administrators base policy on the control of power and interests rather than society's sanction or consent. . . .

In the chapter on American military and civil authority I have attempted to show how pervasive are the assumptions and power of those civilians who run Washington, and how they have freely utilized the Military Establishment as a tool for advancing their own interests rather than the mythical independent goals of the officers. For businessmen and their political cohorts have defined the limits within which the military formulates strategy, extending their values and definitions of priorities over essentially docile generals. A closer look at the nature of the military today only further reveals the pervasiveness of the business-defined consensus, as well as the institutional levers by which the men of power apply their resources and attain their ends. . . . The facts reinforce the point that not a mythical "military-industrial" complex but civilian authority and civilian-defined goals are the sources of American foreign and military policy—and the American malaise. To understand this essential fact is also to reject conspiratorial theories, as well as the liberals' common explanations of the origins of dangerous and destructive policies. It means that in evaluating the responsibility for these policies we must seriously take into account the role of today's respectables—the self-styled liberal realists and businessmen, in and out of the administration, who are the architects of the decades-old premises for the conduct of American diplomacy. It requires, above all, a much clearer definition of the nature of American power and interest in the modern world, an assessment of who gains and loses as a result of the policies Washington pursues.

In my discussion of the United States and world economic power I undertake to outline more precisely the magnitude of American objectives and interests, especially as they lead to global interventionism and give some rational basis for understanding the following description of the United States in Vietnam. I offer this outline on the international economy as an example of the kinds of ingredients and data that must go into a comprehensive portrait of the world role of the United States today. Both critics and defenders of current policy have largely ignored these elements in debates over the motives of American conduct, but such explanations make sense of much that has occurred and is yet to come to pass. Moreover, it is in terms of the world economy that the business and economic backgrounds of the men of power become especially germane, for their perception of the world and United States objectives in it reflects their attempt to apply overseas the structural relations which fattened their interests at home. In brief, they see the role of the state as a servant and regulator of economic affairs, and given the integration of American capitalism with the world economy, particularly with the Third World, their use of the Military Establishment to attain their ends abroad is one of the primary causes of American conduct in the world today.

It is in this setting and with this leadership that the United States has attempted to interact with the Third World both economically and militarily. This painful and insecure relationship is in fact the most important single challenge to confront the United States since the end of the Second World War, and its resolution has defined the course of world politics in the past decades, just as it may limit it in those yet to follow. The American effort has assumed two forms: military and economic.

The military undertaking has, on the whole, failed. As I indicate in my discussion of the Military Establishment, until the end of the Eisenhower administration an overwhelming concern for nuclear strategy forced the United States largely to ignore the far more critical guerrilla and peasant revolutionary movements that it could not reach with missiles or the American ideology. Vietnam was the first serious American effort to relate militarily to the dominant political and social probabilities of the remainder of this century: the graduation of the poor, neocolonial states to a dynamic stage of development via revolutionary nationalist movements dedicated to combating stagnation and misery. This American encroachment into Vietnam took, . . . I maintain . . . , the character of an international intervention rather than, as is commonly suggested, United States alignment with one side in a civil war.

The American failure to destroy quickly the Vietnamese revolution has now begun to erode the impressive successes the United States has had in defining an immensely profitable relationship to most Third World economies. But ultimately, as many in Washington well realize, the major cost of Vietnam will not be its impact on gold and trade balances, but the weakening of United States resolve and ability to interfere in the domestic affairs of nations everywhere, making both increasingly possible and plausible to others the revolutionary path, one that even the greatest intervention in history by the strong against the seemingly weak could not bar. To the oppressed peasants in Brazil or Peru the outcome in Vietnam will not influence their ultimate actions, but where leadership cadres may play a vital role the many lessons of Vietnam will not be lost. Immediately, however, the war in Vietnam has accelerated certain latent weaknesses that the United States, sooner or later, would have had to face in its dealings with European capitalism.

In this book I concentrate mainly on the economic strength of the United States in relationship to the Third World because it is here, for reasons which I make clear, that the United States has intervened continuously in numerous, diverse ways in regions where abstract questions of internal political forms are irrelevant to American security, save as they threaten United States economic interests. The precise nature, extent, and importance of those interests I will specify in an effort to give some larger content and meaning to American global interventionism. However, . . . despite America's great power over the Third World economies, for over a decade its competition with Europe for domination in many key aspects of the world economy has consistently undermined its supremacy. Combined with the seemingly endless cost of the Vietnam war, this competition has seriously, and perhaps fatally, sapped whatever decisive advantages the United States holds in the total world economy. The result is reflected in what is superficially called the "gold" or "dollar" crisis. In fact what is at stake is the long-term future of American economic power as it overextends itself in the hopeless, openended task of policing the world.

United States mastery over the world economy, especially in the decade after 1945, was due more to Europe's political follies and rival imperialisms from 1900 to 1945, and less to inherent American economic talent and resources than most analysts would care to admit. Insularity and caution, in effect, combined to allow the United States to avoid most of their consequences while Europe engaged in two massive, prolonged bloodlettings and orgies of destruction. After the mid-1950s, however, the Western European nations began achieving

. . . significant economic gains in industry and export . . . , and the United States committed itself to costly and increasingly bloody policies that further benefited European power in global trade. The so-called gold and dollar crisis is the combination of all these postwar factors leading to a new distribution of world economic power in which Europe will, at this rate, increasingly define the rules of the game. The acrimonious GATT tariff and trade negotiations expressed this competition between the United States and Europe for some years. Today the controversy is over the value of a dollar which makes possible United States military bases everywhere, a relatively cheaper Vietnam war, and greater American investment in Europe and the world than the other capitalist nations now care to see. The devaluation of the dollar will make increasingly expensive and implausible Washington's application of all these financial and military policies at one and the same time, further strengthening Europe's advantage in the world economy.

The gold crisis, the deeper and more fundamental shifts in power beneath it, and the Vietnam debacle have begun to reveal not only the limits of United States power in the world but also the structure, content, and purposes of American policy. A coherent social theory must take into account both the sources and objectives of American diplomacy and also its capacity to achieve its goals. Any assessment of the future of American society which fails to relate power and class, domestic and foreign policy, does not do justice to the integrated nature of the existing social system, the manner in which the Cold War gave a temporary respite to the system's internal economic problems of poverty, automation, and the like, and how the failure of America's global strategy will open up new options and tensions at home. No one can predict the scope, intensity, and timing of this constriction of American might, but it is sufficient that the very existence of these weaknesses creates new possibilities for social change at home, and in any event reveals the inexorable lesson of modern history: that no nation can guide the destinies of the entire world.

Vietnam is both the most dramatic reflection and a cause of the United States' present malaise. It sharpens the character and reveals the potential danger and inhumanity of American globalism as no other event has in our lifetime. It is a futile effort to contain the irrepressible belief that men can control their own fates and transform their own societies, a notion that is utterly incompatible with an integrated world system ordered to benefit the United States' material welfare. Vietnam exposes the inability of Washington to restrain the overflowing national revolutionary movements. In the context of what the United States has to lose should its immense undertaking fail, Vietnam grotesquely highlights, as does no other event, the interests and objectives of those men of power who today direct this nation's foreign policy.

* * *

In the United States the civilians, the self-styled "liberals" and "democrats," finally direct the application of American power in all its forms throughout the world. Despite the dramatic and sinister overtones in the phrase "military-industrial complex," or C. Wright Mills' vision of "the military ascendancy," the fact is that the nature of global conflict and the means of violence are so thoroughly political and economic in their essential character, so completely intricate technologically, that it is probably more correct to argue the case for the declining importance of the military in the decision-making structure. For military power is the instrument American political leaders utilize to advance their enormous and ever-growing objectives, and that they require a vast Military Establishment is the logical, necessary effect rather than the cause of the basic objectives and momentum of American foreign policy since 1943. Civilians formulated that policy, in the context of the critical postwar period, when the Military Establishment was docile and relatively starved. Belligerence requires generals and arms as tools for the advancement of permanent objectives.

The critics of America's policies in the world have focused their attacks on the visibility of the military, as if its "liberalization" would transform the reality of America's global role. The notion of an independent military dynamic and ethic occludes the real interests and purposes of American foreign policy, which is not to fight wars but to gain vital strategic and economic objectives that materially enlarge American power everywhere. That the military is a neutral instrumentality of civilian policy is inherent in the fact that increasingly the major object of strategic military policy is how to avoid using suicidal nuclear armaments while successfully advancing American economic and political goals. These ends are active, the struggle for them the potential cause of nuclear conflict that could destroy the world; only the most extreme imperatives ever led the civilians to consider this risk and option. If a distinctive military ethic, a regenerative theory of blood-letting and heroism, has ever existed, it has not caused a war in which civilian men of power did not first conceive of some more rational, material goals. This is no less true of the Cold War than of the Spanish-American War, when Washington used an essentially civilian-inspired theoretical school of heroism, which Theodore Roosevelt, Henry and Brooks Adams, and their friends led, as an ideological frosting for advancing American colonialism and global economic power.

Modern warfare is utilitarian to the furtherance of present American objectives, but only so long as it is combat between unequals and excludes great nuclear powers. This means, in brief, that in a world of revolutionary nationalist movements there are many small wars that the United States may choose to fight without confronting the U.S.S.R. or China, and that the strategic and most expensive section of the American Military Establishment will remain restrained and passive, as it has in a disciplined fashion in the past. What is left, from the numerous alternatives to antipeasant, antirevolutionary warfare with tiny powers, is a choice of political options for relating to the Third World, policies that civilian political leaders and their experts always determine and often call upon the military to implement. In some instances, such as Iran, Indonesia, Greece, and Cuba, the half-political, quasi-military CIA has offered policy makers more graceful-appearing means for attaining goals while skirting the more cumbersome and overt regular military. Indeed, the very existence of the CIA, completely removed from the military services, has increasingly strengthened the total control of the civilians over physical power and military intelligence. If the constantly changing technological escalation of the arms race has given the Military Establishment a dynamic and ever-growing appearance, we must never forget the fact that this is an effect rather than a cause of political policy, an appearance and instrumentality rather than the full nature of reality. If this were not the case, and the American military were all that the naive element of the Left has blandly claimed, it would have destroyed the world some years ago.

*   *   *

The United States and the Price of Stability

Under conditions in which the United States has been the major ben-
eficiary of a world economy geared to serve it, the continued, invari-
able American opposition to basic innovations and reforms in world
economic relations is entirely predictable. Not merely resistance to
stabilizing commodity and price agreements, or non-tied grants and
loans, but to every imperatively needed structural change has characterized United States policy toward the Third World. In short, the
United States is today the bastion of the *ancien regime,* of stagnation and continued poverty for the Third World.

There was never any secret in the decade and a half after the war
that the basic foreign economic policy of the United States posited
that "The U.S. is convinced that private ownership and operation of
industrial and extractive enterprises contribute more effectively than
public ownership and operation to the general improvement of the
economy of a country. . . . It is therefore a basic policy of the I.C.A.
to employ U.S. assistance to aid-receiving countries in such a way as
will encourage the development of the private sectors of their economies." Both personally and publicly, American leaders felt, as Doug-
las Dillon "most emphatically" phrased it, ". . . aid to a foreign
country is no substitute for the adoption of sound economic policies
on the part of that country."

Invariably, this meant opening the doors of developing nations to
American investments and the support for pliable *comprador* elements wherever they could be found, in the belief, to cite Secretary
of Treasury George M. Humphrey, that "There are hundreds of ener-
getic people in the world who are better equipped than governments
ever can be to risk huge sums in search, exploration, and development wherever the laws of the country will give them half a chance."

The implications of such a policy were great, requiring intervention to save American investors and friendly conservative governments, and above all the maximization of raw materials production
for export to the fluctuating world market. "Our purpose," Percy W.
Bidwell wrote in his studies for the Council on Foreign Relations,
"should be to encourage the expansion of low-cost production and
to make sure that neither nationalistic policies nor Communist in-
fluences deny American industries access on reasonable terms to
the basic materials necessary to the continued growth of the Ameri-

can economy." Hence nationalism and modest but genuine reform were quite as great an enemy as bolshevism. This meant that via diplomatic pressures and contingent loans and aid the United States engaged in what Eugene Black has called "development diplomacy" throughout the world, a strategy that attempts to show that "The desire for autarky will not be tempered until there is more awareness of how, by underemphasizing exports, the leaders of these nations are prolonging the poverty of their people." That fluctuating raw materials prices and immense foreign profits were crucial handicaps to the problems of development was of no consequence, since the primary objective of the United States was to serve its own interests.

The advancement of American capitalism and an open field for development in the Third World were the guiding principles of American diplomacy, both on the part of government and business leaders. This has required, in turn, specific opposition to every measure likely to alleviate Third World misery at the expense of the industrial nations. Land reform, especially in Latin American nations, is now regarded essentially as a problem of increasing productivity rather than broadening tenure or redistributing land. The United States has opposed measures to stop the so-called "brain drain" which now brings 30,000 professionals and technically trained migrants to the United States each year (not counting nonreturning foreign students who are educated here), about one-third of them from Third World countries. In fact this also represents the annual transfer of hundreds of millions of dollars of educational investment to the United States.

Global efforts to revise the terms of trade go beyond commodity agreements, but the United States opposed such reforms at the United Nations Conference on Trade and Development at Geneva in March 1964, where the American delegation found itself in the uncomfortable position of disputing nearly all Third World proposals. At the Delhi session in March 1968 the United States position was seemingly more liberal, but geared to the unattainable precondition that France and England give up their preferential agreements with former colonies, even though the United States has its own with the Philippines and Puerto Rico. Significantly, the United States has also consistently opposed the creation of a meaningful Latin American "free trade" area. In principle, if such blocs lower costs of production, conserve scarce exchange, or improve the terms of trade, they can develop into effective means for development. In fact, both the

Common Market and European special agreements in Africa and Asia have filled the United States with profound reservations concerning all new exclusionary trade blocs, for in practice they have tended to close off United States trade. Indeed, a Latin American trade zone would not make sense if it qualified as a true free-trade bloc into which the United States could export and invest without planned economic development, and since only restrictionism in one form or another will improve Latin economic conditions the United States has ranged itself against meaningful Latin American economic integration.

The numerous American interventions to protect its investors throughout the world, and the United States ability to use foreign aid and loans as a lever to extract required conformity and concessions, have been more significant as a measure of its practice.

* * *

In today's context, we should regard United States political and strategic intervention as a rational overhead charge for its present and future freedom to act and expand. One must also point out that however high that cost may appear today, in the history of United States diplomacy specific American economic interests in a country or region have often defined the national interest on the assumption that the nation can identify its welfare with the profits of some of its citizens—whether in oil, cotton, or bananas. The costs to the state as a whole are less consequential than the desires and profits of specific class strata and their need to operate everywhere in a manner that, collectively, brings vast prosperity to the United States and its rulers.

Today it is a fact that capitalism in one country is a long-term physical and economic impossibility without a drastic shift in the distribution of the world's income. Isolated, the United States would face those domestic backlogged economic and social problems and weaknesses it has deferred confronting for over two decades, and its disappearing strength in a global context would soon open the door to the internal dynamics which might jeopardize the very existence of liberal corporate capitalism at home. It is logical to regard Vietnam, therefore, as the inevitable cost of maintaining United States imperial power, a step toward saving the future in something akin to its present form by revealing to others in the Third World what they too may encounter should they also seek to control their own development. That Vietnam itself has relatively little of value to the United States is all the more significant as an example of America's determination to hold the line as a matter of principle against revolutionary movements. What is at stake, according to the "domino" theory with which Washington accurately perceives the world, is the control of Vietnam's neighbors, Southeast Asia and, ultimately, Latin America.

The contemporary world crisis, in brief, is a by-product of United States response to Third World change and its own definitions of what it must do to preserve and expand its vital national interests. At the present moment, the larger relationships in the Third World economy benefit the United States, and it is this type of structure America is struggling to preserve. Moreover, the United States requires the option to expand to regions it has not yet penetrated, a fact which not only brings it into conflict with Third World revolutions but also with an increasingly powerful European capitalism. Where neocolonial economic penetration via loans, aid, or attacks on balanced economic development or diversification in the Third World are not sufficient to maintain stability, direct interventions to save local *compradors* and oligarchies often follow. Frequently such encroachments succeed, as in Greece and the Dominican Republic, but at times, such as Vietnam, it is the very process of intervention itself that creates its own defeat by deranging an already moribund society, polarizing options, and compelling men to choose—and to resist. Even the returns to the United States on partial successes have warranted the entire undertaking in the form not just of high profit ratios and exports, but in the existence of a vast world economic sector which supplies the disproportionately important materials without which American prosperity within its present social framework would eventually dry up.

The existing global political and economic structure, with all its stagnation and misery, has not only brought the United States billions but has made possible, above all, a vast power that requires total world economic integration not on the basis of equality but of domination. And to preserve this form of world is vital to the men who run the American economy and politics at the highest levels. If some of them now reluctantly believe that Vietnam was not the place to make the final defense against tides of unpredictable revolutionary change, they all concede that they must do it somewhere, and the logic of their larger view makes their shift on Vietnam a matter of expediency or tactics rather than of principle. All the various American leaders believe in global stability which they are committed to defend against revolution that may threaten the existing distribution of economic power in the world.

When the day arrives that the United States cannot create or threaten further Vietnams, the issue at stake will be no less than the power of the United States in the world. At that point, both the United States and the rest of the world will undergo a period of profound crises and trauma, at home as well as abroad, as the allocation of the earth's economic power is increasingly removed from American control. *If,* in the process of defending their prerogatives, the leaders of the United States during those trying years do not destroy the globe, piecemeal as in Vietnam or in a war with China or Russia, we shall be on the verge of a fundamentally new era for the United States and mankind. The elimination of that American hegemony is the essential precondition for the emergence of a nation and a world in which mass hunger, suppression, and war are no longer the inevitable and continuous characteristics of modern civilization.

Harry Magdoff

THE LOGIC OF IMPERIALISM

Economist Harry Magdoff is the author of a book-length study of The Age
of Imperialism. *The selection below has the merit of presenting his major
arguments in a boiled-down version, and has the additional virtue of framing
the argument as a reply to critics who, like others considered in this book,
do not agree that the U.S. economy requires imperialism. How would less
radical analysts reply to Magdoff's reply? Readers, including both those who
share Magdoff's perspective and those who do not, might pose that question
to themselves.*

How a question is formulated usually defines the limits of its answer.
Hence, a most important aspect of scientific inquiry is discovering
the right questions to ask. In this context, the very formulation of the
question about imperialism by S. M. Miller, Roy Bennett, and Cyril
Alapatt takes us off the path of understanding modern imperialism.

Their article is directed to the question, "Is imperialism really
necessary?" Imperialism, however, is so intertwined with the history
and resulting structure of modern capitalist society—with its economics, politics, ruling ideas—that this kind of question is in the
same category as, for example, "Is it necessary for the United States
to keep Texas and New Mexico?" We could, after all, return these
territories to the Mexican people and still maintain a high-production
and high-standard-of-living economy. We could import the oil, mineral
ores, and cattle from these territories and sell U.S. goods in exchange. Any temporary decline in our gross national product would
surely be a small price to pay for social justice. And given our
growth rate and supposed ability to regulate our economy, continued
economic growth should soon make up any losses resulting from the
return of stolen lands.

Or one might ask, "Is Manhattan necessary for the United States?"
It would surely be equitable to return land obtained from the Indians
in a sharp deal. Such a transfer might at first have some small downward economic effect, but eventually should make for more prosperity.

Manufacturing on the island is an insignificant percentage of total U.S. output. The profitable port activity could be shifted to New Jersey or other excellent Atlantic ports. Other economic functions—stock and commodity exchanges, investment and commercial banks, headquarters of large corporations—could be transferred lock, stock, and barrel to the interior. Such a move to wipe out a terrible blot on the conscience of white America could be socially useful. Moreover, a new financial headquarters of the United States (and the capitalist world) could be designed to avoid slum, smog, pollution, and traffic crises; the demand for buildings, housing, and transportation and communication equipment in the new "Manhattan" might spur the economy to new heights.

Such questions might be useful in the classroom to help stimulate students' imagination and to illustrate the contradictions of a capitalist economy. But they will not contribute to an understanding of the role of territorial expansion in the evolution and functioning of the economy, or the unique role of a financial center in the operations of a capitalist economy.

Our Critics[1] no doubt justify their questions on the grounds that some popularizers on the Left formulate the issue purely in terms of "economic necessity"—as if every political and military action were in response to an immediate economic cause or to a telephone call from a corporation executive. Such a mechanical cause-effect approach is an obvious oversimplification, an inadequate guide to history, and more rhetoric than analysis. But when one merely meets an exaggerated rhetoric head on and makes the rhetoric the focus for debate, one departs from the tasks of scientific inquiry: one may thus be at a ball park, but not where the game is being played. The major task, in my opinion, for the study of imperialism is to discover and understand what Bernard Baruch described as "the essential one-ness of [U.S.] economic, political, and strategic interests." In such a study, we have to seek the key roots—the mainsprings—of this "one-ness" as well as to understand the interactions and interdependence of the economic, political, and military drives.

It takes no deep perception to recognize the limits of the "neces-

---

[1] To avoid the awkwardness of listing the three authors at each reference, and to somewhat depersonalize the controversy, we will refer to them as the "Critics." We trust they will not take offense. "Critic," to our way of thinking, is an honorable designation.

sity" formula. Thus, a substantial part of the world, notably the Soviet Union and China, has chosen the path of economic independence and therefore broken the trade and investment ties with the imperialist network. The advanced capitalist countries adjusted to these changes and have in recent decades achieved considerable prosperity and industrial advance. However, important as it is to recognize that such adjustments can take place, it is equally important to understand the route that these adjustments take: via wars, depressions, and huge armament programs. The economic adaptations emerged in the midst of recurrent struggles for control over spheres of influence—over other advanced countries as well as over Third World areas, it should be noted. And, most important, these adjustments have in no way lessened the intensity of the counter-revolutionary thrust of imperialist states, by wars and other means, directed (a) to preventing a further narrowing down of the territory in which they can freely trade and invest, and (b) to reconquering the space lost to the imperialist world. Nor has this counter-revolutionary activity, which began during the first days of the Bolshevik Revolution, diminished since the United States took the reins as leader and organizer of the capitalist world.

The relevant question is not whether imperialism is necessary for the United States, but to discover the "rationality" of the historic process itself: why the United States and other leading capitalist nations have persistently and recurrently acted in an imperialist fashion for at least three quarters of a century.

The contrast between speculative hypotheses about the "necessity" of imperialism and the actual course of history is excellently demonstrated by the Critics themselves when they illustrate their interpretation of imperialism by referring to, and endorsing, the theoretical position of Karl Kautsky in his debate with Rosa Luxemburg. Kautsky argued, they point out, that imperialist expansion was sustained by only a small and powerful group of capitalists and that such expansion conflicted with the interests of the capitalist class as a whole. Because of this, Kautsky believed that the majority of the capitalist class would increase its opposition to, and eventually prevent, armed imperialist expansion.

It is strange indeed, in this day and age, to come across a revival of Kautsky's theory—a theory that has been devastatingly refuted by events. Our Critics refer to Kautsky's exposition at the 1907 Stuttgart Conference of the Second International. But only seven years later the First World War broke out, to be followed at the earliest practical opportunity by the Second World War. It doesn't take much insight to recognize the role that Germany's expansionist aims played in both wars: Kautsky's optimism turned out to be mere illusion.

The Critics remind us of the current dissatisfaction of some U.S. businessmen with the Vietnam War. That there are shrewd businessmen who recognize that at times one must cut one's losses should hardly come as a surprise. The surprise is that it has taken them so long to awaken to the reality of a lost war and its social and economic consequences. However, the acid test of Kautsky's and the Critics' position would be: how many of these businessmen would agree (1) to an immediate pullout of U.S. forces from Vietnam, leaving the fate of Vietnam to the Vietnamese people, and (2) to a complete withdrawal of all U.S. military forces and equipment from all of Asia?

The major weakness of Kautsky's theory was precisely its concentration on "necessity." By casting his argument within this sterile framework, he distinguished between capitalists who "need" and those who "don't need" expansion. He thus ignored what was most important in explaining the course of militarism and imperialism: the industrial and financial structure of the economy, the strategic elements of change, and the special nature of the political system associated with successful monopoly capitalism. (It should go without saying that a full explanation of, say, German imperialism would have to take into account the special socioeconomic features and history of Germany.)

On their part, the Critics in effect adopt for their own economic analysis the same limited and crude economic interpretation of imperialism that they are criticizing. Accordingly, they look at only some of the relevant economic elements; those that they examine are treated as isolates, not as part of a social and economic organism; and then they whittle down even these isolates. This shrinking process takes on the following forms: (1) They eliminate from the realm of imperialism U.S. economic activity *in other advanced capitalist nations;* (2) they restrict the field of economic penetration in underdeveloped countries to *exports and direct private investment;* and (3) *concerning foreign mineral resources,* they deal only with the so-called *national interest,* ignoring the drive for control over sucn resources by monopolistic interest groups.

Imperialism and Relations between Developed Countries

A large part of the Critics' article is devoted to statistical computations based on the assumption (and argument) that U.S. trade with, and investment in, other advanced capitalist nations have nothing to do with imperialism. Imperialism, they claim, concerns only the relations between advanced and underdeveloped countries.

This assumption misses an essential distinguishing feature of modern imperialism. The occupation and/or manipulation of a weaker by a stronger nation and the building of empires by powerful military states have occurred frequently in human history, in ancient, medieval, and modern times. Moreover, the birth and adolescence of capitalism were marked by military penetration of noncapitalist areas to bring the latter into the trade and investment sphere of the dominant capitalists.

Because empire-building has been prevalent over long stretches of history, the use of the term *imperialism* to cover all such activities leads to definitions that stress the superficial and avoid the essential. The value of distinguishing different periods of history, to which convenient labels are attached, is to provide a useful analytical framework for discovering and understanding the main operating levers of the particular stage under study. For that reason, it seems to us, the term *imperialism* is best used to designate the international practices and relations of the capitalist world during the distinct stage of mature capitalism that begins in the last quarter of the nineteenth century.

But even if one disagrees with this terminological approach, it still has to be recognized that the international economics and politics of the past seventy to ninety years have certain unique features. Hence some historians follow the practice of calling the new stage *modern* or *new* imperialism, to distinguish it from that of mere empire-building. The rationale for this should become clearer if we spell out some of the major features of this new or modern imperialism:

(1) As noted above, capitalism from its earliest days sank its roots in the noncapitalist world. It prospered by adapting (through force and economic pressure) the rest of the world to fit the needs of the more advanced capitalist nations. However, it is in the stage of modern imperialism that its "historic task" is fulfilled: the entire globe

is fitted into the world capitalist system (until, in more recent years, parts of this system break away). Prices of commodities produced around the world become dominated by one world price established in the major financial centers. In this period of modern imperialism, there is a sharp step-up in the international flow of commodities, men, and capital—in response primarily to pressures emanating from the most advanced centers of capitalism, including the pressures of competition among the advanced capitalist countries themselves.

(2) The resulting world capitalist system of modern imperialism comprehends an intricate and interdependent set of relations between countries at various stages of industrial development. The most striking aspect of this world system is the freezing of the so-called Third World countries as industrial and financial dependencies of key metropolitan centers—a dependency that is continuously reproduced by the normal behavior of capitalist markets. In addition, among the more advanced capitalist nations, there are a variety of relations of dependency of weaker nations on stronger ones.

(3) The technical underpinning of the modern international world economy is the growth of what Veblen called the "technology of physics and chemistry": steel, electricity, oil refining, synthetic organic chemicals, internal combustion engines, etc. The technology of modern imperialism became the material base of decisive concentration of economic power in large industrial corporations and large financial institutions. The maturation of this economic concentration of power (called, for convenience, *monopoly capital*) affected the whole economic and political structure of advanced capitalist nations. On the economic side, in contrast with the earlier stage of competitive capitalism, economic change and economic policy are primarily determined by the imperatives of monopolistic-type industries (oligopolies, to be technical). The latter, to protect their assets and maintain their leading positions, are impelled to seek control over supplies of raw materials and over markets—wherever these raw materials and markets may exist. Furthermore, the evolution of an economic structure based on monopolistic firms limits the alternatives open to the political regimes of these countries. Governments, whether liberal or conservative, can operate with a successful economy only if they support, and help make more efficient, the major determinants of the economy: the monopolistic

firms and the international financial arrangements with which these firms operate.

(4) Finally, a distinctive feature of the new imperialism is the rise of intensive competitive struggle among advanced capitalist nations. It is this competitive struggle which helps determine the new world-economic arrangements and which is a major source of continual turbulence in the world capitalistic system. Before the era of modern imperialism, Great Britain was the undisputed dominant nation in foreign trade, investment, and finance. The rise of industrialized nations, based on advanced technology that permitted economic and military competition with Britain, led to the hectic struggle for conquest of those parts of the globe not yet incorporated into the global capitalist arrangements. It also led to struggles for re-division of colonies and spheres of influence. But, it should be noted most especially, the competitive struggle is not restricted to dominance over the underdeveloped world. It also entails struggle for dominance and/or special influence over other advanced capitalist nations, as was seen in two world wars. Present also as a major element in the power struggle between nations and between monopolistic firms of these nations is the use of investment in one another's territories and/or cartel arrangements for the division of markets.

Thus, if one sees modern imperialism in historical perspective, it should be clear that there are two attributes of the power struggles of this period: (1) the struggle for economic power vis-à-vis other industrial nations, and (2) the struggle for economic power over the underdeveloped nations. Furthermore, to understand the imperialist drives since the Second World War, and the strategic alternatives confronting the decision-makers of U.S. foreign policy, one must take into account the past and potential rivalries of the industrialized nations. Not the least aspect of the latter is the maneuvering of U.S. government policy, and of U.S. firms, to take over trade and investment outlets of former allies (as well as former enemies) in the underdeveloped world.

Narrowing down imperialism to trade with, and investment in, the Third World thus eliminates a vital sector of international economic and political activity: the imperialist rivalries associated with the investment operations of advanced capitalist nations across one another's borders. In addition, the Critics do not face up to the reality of world economic interdependence and the significance of U.S. international financial and military preeminence. The latter might be better appreciated if we focus on the balance of payments situation.

The United States has had a deficit in its balance of payments for all but one or two of the past twenty years, and that deficit shows no signs of disappearing. This is unique in capitalist history. Any other country—and the United States itself prior to its post-Second World War dominance—would have had to submit to the discipline of the international marketplace long, long before the twenty years were up. What would this discipline of the marketplace imply? Adoption by the U.S. government of such measures as would produce deflation: a sharp rise in unemployment and downward economic adjustment. Instead, the United States has been able to maintain its kind of prosperity through the 1950s and 1960s without undertaking effective measures to eliminate the international payments deficit. Quite the opposite: its prosperity was sustained by the very kind of activities which have generated the persistent deficit.

Why the deficit? As a rule, U.S. exports of goods and services (on current account) exceed imports. The deficit therefore arises because the U.S. government and investors spend in international markets over and above their "means." The government spends huge sums for its military establishment around the globe, for its wars, and for military and economic assistance to other countries. Corporations spend on investment in foreign business undertakings—in advanced as well as underdeveloped countries. All of these activities, independently of the motives which induce them, contribute to the prosperity of the economy as it is constituted.

The nub of this whole development is that it is made possible by the fact that the other capitalist nations have, willingly and unwillingly, accepted the U.S. dollar as if it were as good as gold.

One need not follow too carefully the financial news to be aware that the other industrialized nations are not too happy about the necessity to accept the U.S. dollar as a substitute for gold; indeed, considerable friction has resulted, and still exists. Yet they do accept it, for several reasons. First, they fear that if they rock the boat too much, all the central bankers will sink in a sea of financial difficulties. Second, they are impressed with U.S. economic strength, though this confidence is being increasingly shaken. Finally, and not the least of the considerations, is U.S. military might and its global presence.

In fact, the United States has undertaken the major responsibility for maintaining the world imperialist system. It first supplied the armaments, armies, and Marshall Plan aid to prevent social revolution in Western Europe. It has furnished naval and air bases around the world, sufficient not only to encircle the Soviet Union and China but to act as a threat of military intervention or for actual intervention in the Third World.

Thus the United States provides the main military might for the "security" of the Western world, including Japan. The *quid pro quo* has been the reluctant acceptance of the U.S. dollar as a reserve currency, despite the inability of the United States to provide adequate gold coverage for its dollar debts. And one of the results of this *quid pro quo* is that U.S. business can keep on investing in Western Europe and buying up European firms, in effect paid for by credit extended by other advanced capitalist nations to the United States.

Suppose, however, one does not accept this analysis of the interrelationship between U.S. investment in advanced capitalist nations, on the one hand, and (1) the actual and incipient tensions between imperialist nations, and (2) the maintenance of control and "stability" in the Third World, on the other. Would the Critics then be correct in isolating U.S. investments in advanced countries as a thing apart from economic and political concern with the Third World? In our judgment, they would still be mistaken in such a narrowing down of imperialism. The reason is simple: when firms invest in advanced countries they become directly involved in the ties between those countries and "their" parts of the Third World. The larger U.S. investments in Europe and Japan become, the more extensively are U.S. interests bound up with the spheres of influence and neocolonial arrangements of *the entire capitalist world.*

The simplest and most direct illustration is the oil industry. Some 24 percent of U.S. direct private investment in Europe is in oil: oil refining, production of by-products, and the marketing of these products to Europeans and their foreign customers. But where do the U.S. subsidiaries get the oil to refine? From the Middle East, of course. Note especially that the rapid rise in U.S. oil investments in Europe was accompanied by a decisive change in U.S. ownership of nearby oil deposits: before the Second World War, U.S. firms controlled some 10 percent of Middle East oil reserves; by 1967, this percentage rose to 59. The success and prosperity of U.S. investment in the European oil industry depends on access to the oil extracted from Third World countries. Conversely, U.S. companies increase their profits on Middle Eastern oil by investing in oil refining and distribution in nearby Europe.

In less dramatic fashion, yet equally relevant, is the growing interest in the Third World entailed by other investments in the advanced nations. Thus, half of all U.S. direct investments in Europe and Japan is in manufacturing other than petroleum refining. Where do these firms get the raw materials to process? A significant portion comes from the Third World.

On top of this is the growing involvement of U.S. firms in the markets of the other advanced nations in the Third World. Manufacturers in the advanced countries have special positions and privileges in some of these markets through treaties and currency arrangements. Some of these preferred market outlets exist because of tariff barriers and distribution channels established in colonial days. U.S. firms thus extend their markets, getting a foothold in the preserves of other advanced countries, by investing in and thus becoming business "citizens" of the mother countries.

We have by no means exhausted the number of ways U.S. investment in advanced nations extends U.S. involvement in the economic affairs of the Third World. Let us look at just one other way. Quite recently, three U.S. banks made investments in England (a developed country, to be sure): Mellon National Bank and Trust Co. acquired a 25 percent stake in the Bank of London and South America Ltd. (BOLSA); New York's First National City Bank obtained a 40 percent share of National & Grindlay's Bank Ltd.; and Chase Manhattan Bank acquired a 15 percent interest in Standard Bank Ltd. Note, however, that while all three of these U.S. bank affiliates are based in London, "their main operations are in broad chunks of the underdeveloped world. National & Grindlay's operates in India, Pakistan, and the Middle East, Standard is in Africa, and BOLSA concentrates on Latin America." (The data and the quotation are from the *American Banker*, January 28, 1970.)

Investment in Underdeveloped Countries

Having disposed of U.S. investment in advanced countries as unrelated to imperialism, the Critics train their guns on the relative smallness of U.S. business interests in underdeveloped countries. In the statistical process of estimating the degree of U.S. economic interests, they reduce the dimensions of this involvement by restricting the discussion to exports and direct private investment. Perhaps they do so because of the availability of export and investment data and the lack of other adequate data. Whatever the reason, this concentration on direct private investment and exports results in overlooking other major involvement. For example:

(1) Licenses of patents, processes, and trademarks granted to foreign manufacturers by U.S. manufacturing firms. This represents a growing business interest in the Third World as well as in advanced countries—in part a by-product of the worldwide distribution of U.S. movies, TV, and advertising. One finds, for example, such ordinary products as inks and paints manufactured in the Philippines under licenses from U.S. manufacturers.

(2) An important source of income to U.S. business is profit derived from shipping food and raw materials from the Third World to the United States, and the reciprocal trade. A considerable number of these ships are U.S. ships flying the flags of Liberia and Panama. Investments in such shipping companies are included in the Department of Commerce statistics under the category "International Shipping" and are excluded from statistics on direct private investments in underdeveloped countries. (Incidentally, control over shipping and related insurance required for Third-World trade are important elements of the dependency relation between the peripheral countries and the metropolitan centers.)

(3) Excluded from direct private investment statistics are such significant and expanding areas of economic involvement as: (a) direct loans by U.S. banks to foreign governments and businesses, (b) many types of foreign bonds floated in the United States, and (c) loans made in foreign countries by Edge Act corporations (subsidiaries of U.S. banks). It should also be noted that a favorite form of financing by Edge Act corporations is the convertible bond, a financial instrument whereby the U.S. banking corporation can convert the bond to shares of ownership in the foreign company if the latter proves profitable.

(4) The data on direct private investment do not include or measure the degree of diffusion of U.S. business interests in the eco-

nomic life of underdeveloped countries. This is especially evident in the case of the operations of foreign branches of U.S. banks and foreign banks owned by U.S. banks. (This is over and above items referred to in the preceding paragraph.) For example, direct private investment in banks abroad shows up in the catchall category of "other investments," which takes in a wide variety of activities, including such investments as those in sugar and banana plantations. Thus, direct private investment in Latin America under the category "other investments" amounted to $1,057 million in 1968. Since bank investments are only one component of this category, investments in banks as counted by the Department of Commerce would be considerably below $1,057 million. But the assets of the branches of U.S. banks alone in that year amounted to $1,736 million. And this does not include the extent of financial involvement of U.S. banks through (a) Edge Act corporations owned by U.S. banks, (b) finance companies owned by U.S. banks and other financial institutions, (c) assets controlled directly via equity holdings in Latin American banks, or (d) indirect control over Latin American financial assets through branches of European banks, such as noted above in the case of the Mellon Bank stake in BOLSA. The financial assets controlled and influenced represent a diffusion of U.S. interests throughout the interstices of the Third World economies far beyond direct investments —in the day-to-day activities of the native firms as well as of other U.S. investors.

The importance of U.S. business interests in Latin America, for example, is indirectly reflected in the reason given for the partnership arrangement that Mellon National Bank made with BOLSA to enter the Latin American markets:

> By 1961 it was becoming obvious to the bank's management . . . that because of its lack of international banking facilities Mellon's share of the domestic market was being threatened. Huge banks from New York, California, and Chicago were taking advantage of their international expertise to obtain larger shares of the domestic business of Mellon's traditional customers. (American Banker, January 28, 1970.)

In this we can see several important aspects of U.S. involvement in the underdeveloped world: (1) it is becoming increasingly important—important enough for banks to be able to win customers from each other based on the services they can give businesses operating abroad; (2) there is an interconnection of domestic and international business activities, one that exists in nonfinancial business too; and (3) competition within an industry spurs further penetration into the underdeveloped economies—also a factor in promoting pressure for investments other than banking in the Third World.

. . . [T]he Critics base their interpretation of the current state of U.S. imperialism on what they consider to be the relative smallness of private investment in the underdeveloped world. We have tried to show that the economic involvement is considerably larger than one would infer merely from the statistics on direct foreign private investment. However, one needs to dig deeper. While the relative size of a particular economic sector is important, it is by no means the only consideration. It is necessary to understand the influence of the sector on the dynamics of an economy in motion. For example, the stock market in and of itself is a relatively small part of the U.S. economy. Yet what goes on in the stock market far exceeds its insignificant "statistical" contribution to the gross national product. The availability of this gambling casino is of the very essence of an advanced capitalist system. In addition, speculative fervor on the upside of the market can act as a goad and prop to boom and inflation, while panic among speculators can spark and intensify a major economic decline.

The vagaries of the balance of payments are a significant illustration of the potential "bigness" of a statistically small category. The chronic deficit in our balance of payments since 1950 has ranged roughly between $1 billion and $4 billion a year. Now this is obviously an insignificant portion of GNP. Statistically, it is hardly worth mentioning: just the statistical error involved in measuring GNP is surely much larger than the balance of payments deficit. Yet this "statistically insignificant" deficit, due to its unique function and its cumulative effect, contains all the potentials of a major international crisis. Lack of cooperation by the governments and central banks of the other advanced industrial nations—that is, their decision to go off the "dollar standard" and back to the "gold standard"—would undoubtedly lead to a breakdown of the existing international payments system and consequently of international trade, with obviously serious consequences to the world capitalist economy. (Central bankers understand this; it is, in fact, an important reason for their reluctant endurance of U.S. financial hegemony. But such cooperation is a slim reed to depend on in a world of aggressive, competitive, national and business interests.)

Once we recognize the role of the balance of payments deficit in maintaining U.S. prosperity and international financial stability, we can better appreciate the special advantages accruing from business involvement in the Third World. As noted earlier, the United States is able to sustain its wars, military posture, foreign investment, and military and economic assistance for two reasons: (a) the large surplus in the balance of its transactions on goods and services (technically, the "current account"), and (b) its relative freedom to accumulate deficits. We have already dwelt briefly on the politics of the latter. Let us now look into the former. Taking the last five years (1964–1968) for which complete annual data are available at the time of writing, we find that the surplus of goods and services in trade with the underdeveloped countries (including the profits on foreign investments) represented 66 percent of the total U.S. surplus on this account. For the last three of these years (years of full-scale war in Vietnam), the U.S. export balance on goods and services with the Third World was no less than 85 percent of the total U.S. surplus.

Examination of the ramifications of the balance of payments issue (for example, the interrelations between current and capital transactions and the ensuing contradictions) would take us too far afield. Suffice it to note here that business dealings with the Third World, from the perspective of the balance of payments, are an especially strategic element of the current capitalist economy of the United States. The balance of payments data, however, are a summation of many thousands of transactions. If we look into these "small" transactions, we will also find areas of significance that far outweigh statistical "smallness."

The business of individual firms in the Third World arises usually in response to the following motives: (1) to obtain and maintain enlarged markets; (2) to get higher profit rates by taking advantage of lower production costs; and (3) to achieve control over sources of raw materials and food. Given the international maldistribution of income, it is only natural—indeed, inevitable—that trade (and investment for better access to a country's markets) will be much larger in the case of the rich than in that of the poor nations, despite the great disproportion of population in the two. But this does not mean that interest in the markets of the poor nations has slackened or will diminish in the future—any more than one would expect a waning of business interest in the "peripheral" areas within the United States (e.g., Mississippi) in contrast with the metropolitan centers of the country (e.g., New York). Nor would the business community take with better grace the shutting off of lesser foreign markets than they would countenance the secession of poorer regions of the United States.

The economics of the business firm is dominated by the growth imperative: growth of profits, growth of sales, and growth of capital investment. In the early stages of the evolution of a firm or a product, it is usually found that speediest results are obtained by concentrating on the upper-income segments of the native country and on those foreign countries that have a large upper-income population. However, no successful firm can afford to rest there. Under the pressure of competition, it must seek out additional and, if possible, more profitable markets. While these additional markets may be relatively small, their marginal effect can be unusually important because of their role in sustaining growth. This role of the marginal increase in the export market applies also to the marginal investment in a foreign country.

To liberal-minded observers, like our Critics, some of the percentages of business contributed by exports and investments may look small and unimportant. But these small percentages necessarily loom large in the eyes of the owners and managers of a business. The realities of the business world are such that these owners and managers must struggle doggedly not only to hang on to their share of the market but constantly to maneuver to increase it. Their logic is necessarily shaped by these realities. And it is the logic of the owners and managers of business that insists on keeping as much of the world as possible free for capital investment and trade—to provide at least the possibility of still another marginal boost in sales, profits, and investment. By the same token, the closing down of any area to "free enterprise" is a threat to growth potential.

When the "free world" remains free for private enterprise, opportunities do in fact arise for a new spurt in one business field or another—for a new source of growth. Thus the sober-minded *Business Week* (December 6, 1969) in its forecast for the 1970s recognized the differences between trade with the developed and underdeveloped nations, but it also showed that it understands the new opportunities:

As in the past, exports to industrial nations will rise faster than those to developing countries. In the 1960s, sales to industrial nations climbed from $13 billion to $24 billion, sales to developing countries rose from $7 billion to $11 billion. An exception will be a boom in U.S. export and import trade with East and South Asia, *excluding Japan. (Emphasis added.)*

It would be illuminating if the authors of this projection were to spell out their assumptions concerning the continuation or end of the Vietnamese War and the nature of the U.S. military presence in Asia in the 1970s, as for example, the replacement by the United States of British bases in Southeast Asia.

Raw Materials and the Third World

The Critics give two reasons for brushing aside the crucial question of the raw materials factor and the ties with the Third World: (a) they themselves have not studied the question of dependency on foreign raw materials in depth, and (b) they think it is necessary to recognize the possibility of substituting one material for another. Their straightforward acknowledgment of limited acquaintance with the facts is commendable; by all means, they should look into these facts. We would suggest, though, that they not restrict their study to the "dependency" angle. Imperialism is not so much a question of dependency on raw materials as of the compulsive behavior of monopolistic-type business organizations.

That the drive for control of foreign resources extends beyond dependency can be seen in the way U.S. corporations sought, fought for, and obtained exploration and development rights for oil, copper and other minerals *when the United States was blessed with a surplus of these minerals.* A major reason for the oil industry to invest abroad was specifically to protect its foreign markets. (In the 1870s two thirds of U.S. oil production was exported.) Here is how Professor Raymond Vernon summarizes the early history of the global expansion of the U.S. oil industry:

The more remote sources of crude oil, such as those of the Middle East and the Far East, were needed by the U.S. companies because of their proximity to established export markets in Asia and the Mediterranean basin. While these markets had been developed by U.S. companies in the latter part of the nineteenth century on the basis of U.S. exports, they were never wholly free from challenge by others. . . . For two decades

before 1900, the American companies tried to counter this threat by cap-
turing downstream facilities in some of the main markets in which they
were challenged. By 1900, however, they seem to have decided that
control of marketing facilities was not the appropriate strategy and that
control of the crude oil was the key. It was then that the U.S. firms began
aggressively to try for acquisition of foreign crude oil sources. More
generally, however, the major oil companies had to take some interest
in any potential source of oil, wherever there was a risk that the source,
when developed, might undersell existing supplies. . . . In economic
terms, the cost of development could better be attributed to the hedging
of risk—the risk of losing control of the price structure in established
markets. . . . The early history of the major oil companies suggested
another principle of a prudential sort. A well-diversified supply of re-
sources, they rapidly discovered, was especially useful in dealing with
blockages of supply, whether threatened or actual. ("Foreign Enterprises
and Developing Nations in the Raw Materials Industries," in Allied Social
Science Associations, Papers and Abstracts to be Presented at the Annual Meeting of the ASSA, *New York, N. Y., December 28–30, 1969.)*

Foreign investment for the development and extraction of resources took place for many reasons. Just profit alone has been
a sufficient motive for starting many plantations and mines in the
underdeveloped world. But the investment in raw materials by monopolistic-type firms has added a new dimension—a dimension which
goes a long way to explaining what the era of modern imperialism
is all about.

The concentration of economic power in a limited number of giant
firms became possible in many industries precisely because of the
control by these firms over raw materials sources. The ability to maintain this concentrated power, to ward off native and foreign competi-
tors, to weaken newcomers, and to conduct affairs in accordance
with monopolistic price and production policies depended on the
alertness and aggressiveness of the giant firms to obtain and maintain control over major segments of the supplies of raw materials—
on a world scale. This has been the underlying rationality of foreign
investment in the extractive industries during the whole era of modern imperialism: not only in oil but in a spectrum of products, especially minerals.

The issue, therefore, is not dependency of the United States on
foreign mineral supplies, but the dependency of monopoly industry
qua "monopolies" on the control of these supplies. The data on the
extent to which minerals used in the United States are obtained

abroad are merely one measure of the far-flung interests of U.S. monopolies. Necessarily, large firms that process "scarce" raw materials must be vitally concerned about the *world* production, distribution, and prices of these supplies, not merely the demand for the products in the United States.

On this subject, too, the issue of "smallness" raised by the Critics has little relevance. They point out that only the investment in foreign oil is large; the investment in other minerals is relatively small. The fact that the proportion of foreign investment in other minerals is small compared with oil has no bearing whatsoever on the depth of the concern and involvement of the firms using these other minerals. The proportion of foreign investment in iron ore, bauxite, and copper ore (among others) to investment in oil has little if any meaning to the steel, aluminum, and copper producers who seek to secure their leading positions and their special profit advantages by controlling a major segment of the foreign (as well as domestic) supplies of their products.

The second point on raw materials raised by the Critics concerns the possible substitution of one product for another in order to reduce the "dependency" on foreign supplies. Obviously, they do not mean the substitution of some ore other than iron to make steel or a bauxite substitute to make aluminum. Our alchemists have not learned these tricks yet. What the Critics dwell on is the substitution of, say, aluminum and/or plastics for some uses of steel and of aluminum for copper. To a considerable extent substitution has been going on for years, if not centuries and millennia. Where technical substitution is feasible, competition between raw materials for the same or similar uses has been heated. This competition, however, has been accompanied not by a lessening of "dependency" on foreign sources but by an increase of such "dependency." The reason is quite simple. One cannot substitute at will—even if the price is right or even if the cost of the raw material is unimportant. For example, copper used in electric wire and cable can be replaced only by a material that conducts electricity. Steel, paper, and wood are therefore not usable as substitutes for wire requiring electrical conductivity. However, whereas aluminum is a possible substitute, the result of such substitution is an increase in "dependency" on foreign sources of supply: the proportion of foreign to domestic bauxite is considerably higher than the foreign-to-domestic ratio of copper ore.

Another reason for not relying on substitutability for removing or diminishing the use of foreign sources can be seen in the case of steel. Steel has been on the losing end of many competitive battles, including the competition of plastics made from purely domestic sources. Nevertheless, the weakening competitive position of steel has been accompanied by an *increase* in the use of foreign ore. The reason is the depletion of the great Mesabi iron ore deposit. Furthermore, even though technical breakthroughs have made the conversion of domestic taconite ore economically feasible, the interest of U.S. steel firms in iron ore reserves in Canada, South America, Africa, and Asia has increased.

The upshot is that the problem of substitution of minerals, on the whole, is quite different from that of butter vs. margarine or synthetics vs. silk/cotton. At rock bottom, the replacement of one mineral by another is a technical problem. Economics is often involved, but the economic maneuverability is severely restricted by the technical determinants. One cannot, at the present stage of technology, send an electric current through matter that lacks the properties to transmit it. Nor can one make airplanes that carry passengers and freight without aluminum. Moreover, we don't know how to make an effective jet engine without getting columbium, tungsten, nickel, chromium, and cobalt from the four corners of the earth. Nor do politics and economics stand still, waiting on the sidelines for future imaginative technological breakthroughs.

The Critics, though, make a still more daring hypothesis on the substitution question: "The question of substitutability is affected by possible shifts in the end-products of American industry which, in turn, determine what materials are needed. The main possibility is, of course, a reduction in military production." But why stop at military production? We could, for example, have our commercial jet airplanes made in France, England, Germany, and Japan. These countries would be happy to get the business, and we would reduce our dependency on foreign raw materials. Better still, we could shift the end-products of our society by restricting the use of automobiles in our crowded cities and reducing truck traffic through vastly increased use of the railroads. We would thereby lower the demand for cars, cut down on our dependence on foreign sources of minerals, and improve the air we breathe.

It is interesting to indulge in speculations on what a rational society would do to simplify the problem of foreign raw-material dependency. Such speculation might even have educational value in exposing the limits and contradictions of a capitalist society whose *primum mobile* is the profit motive. But if we want to understand what capitalist imperialism is all about, we had better pay attention to the mechanics and dynamics of capitalism as it really is, i.e., *capitalism as a world system.*

Fundamental Changes?

The Critics summarize their argument in a section entitled "Fundamental Changes"—changes which, in their opinion, point to the plausibility of a U.S. capitalist economy without imperialism. We do not have the space to tackle all the points made, but we shall comment briefly on a few.

First, they invoke the authority of John Kenneth Galbraith's *New Industrial State* to support their contention that fundamental changes have occurred in capitalism which depart from the "necessity" of imperialism. But what are the changes that Galbraith deals with? The "new" capitalism, he claims, is and must be dominated by a limited number of giant corporations; the success of the "new industrial state" depends on the success of these giants. These industrial giants, in turn, have three imperatives: they must keep on growing; they must control their raw material supplies at consistent prices; and they must control their markets. Precisely. Galbraith, whether he knows it or not, is explaining the mainspring of the imperialism of monopoly capitalism.

Second, the Critics see a fundamental change in the absence of a major economic crisis since the end of the Second World War. If, however, one of the most important reasons for this "fundamental change" is the huge military machine built up and maintained by the United States, then such a change is hardly an opener of a new dawn of a peaceful modern capitalism. Quite the contrary. It is a harbinger of wars and revolutions. The internal and external conflicts generated by such a "success" do indeed foretell the end of imperialism and the decline of the U.S. empire—but not by a peaceful reform of monopoly capitalism.

Third, the Critics contrast the more rapid growth of "nonimperialist" Germany and Japan with the slower growth of imperialist United States and Great Britain. (Incidentally, they refer to "the tempestuous

growth of Japan and Germany in the postwar period, without foreign
investments. . . ." They may wish to argue that foreign investments
were not *important* for the growth rate, but they are mistaken if they
think there have not been considerable foreign investments by Germany and Japan.) What is missing in this sort of correlation is an
appreciation of the way the world capitalist system has been working
in recent decades.

Under *Pax Americana,* the United States supplies the main military
power and the police action to keep as much of the world as possible
safe for "free" enterprise. In this arrangement, Germany and Japan,
as major and strategic components of world capitalism, are special
beneficiaries of the economic and military strategy of the United
States. Japan, in particular, has benefited not only from the advantages of a prosperous U.S. market but also from U.S. purchases for
the Korean and Vietnamese wars. There are, of course, special factors which have contributed to the German and Japanese growth
rates, but the very possibility of growth is intimately related to *Pax
Americana* and a relatively successful U.S. economy based on militarism.

In sum, the Critics' analytical method is to separate out the various
parts of the U.S. and world economy and to sever economics from
politics. They arrive at the conclusion that, by tinkering with some
of the parts through political pressure, capitalism can be reformed
so that it can live and grow without imperialism. Our point of view
is that the separate parts must be understood in the context of their
interrelations with the social organism of world monopoly capitalism.
Further, it is important to recognize the essential unity of the economics, politics, militarism, and culture of this social organism. We
reach the conclusion that *imperialism is the way of life of capitalism.
Therefore, the elimination of imperialism requires the overthrow of
capitalism.*

Suggestions for Additional Reading

The American foreign policy debate of the 1960s ranged widely over events and issues of the entire post-World War II era. Books offering more or less traditional overviews of that period include Seyom Brown, *The Faces of Power* (New York, 1968); Louis J. Halle, *The Cold War as History* (London, 1967); John Spanier, *American Foreign Policy Since World War II* (New York, 1965); Paul Y. Hammond, *The Cold War Years: American Foreign Policy Since 1945* (New York, 1969); Charles L. Robertson, *International Politics Since World War II* (New York, 1966). Volumes covering the same period from a more radical or "revisionist" perspective are D. F. Fleming, *The Cold War and Its Origins* (Garden City, 1961; 2 vol.); Stephen E. Ambrose, *The Rise to Globalism: American Foreign Policy Since 1938* (Baltimore, 1968); David Horowitz, *The Free World Colossus* (New York, 1965); and Walter LaFeber, *America, Russia and the Cold War* (New York, 1967). Adam Ulam's *The Rivals: America and Russia Since World War II* reassesses Soviet-American relations from an explicitly Realist point of view.

An indispensable source for the whole period but particularly for the 1960s is *The Pentagon Papers,* available both in a short version originally published by *The New York Times* (New York, 1971), and in two longer editions, one released by Senator Mike Gravel and published by Beacon Press (Boston, 1971), the other officially cleared by the United States Government (Washington, 1971). There are, one should note, differing interpretations of *The Pentagon Papers.* Daniel Ellsberg argues, in *Papers on the War* (New York, 1972), that five American presidents extended America's involvement in Vietnam mainly to avoid right-wing electoral retribution for having "lost Vietnam to Communism." Leslie H. Gelb agrees but places greater stress on external reasons for "staying the course" in "The System Worked," *Foreign Policy* (Summer 1971), pp. 140–167. Both Ellsberg and Gelb are the targets of Arthur M. Schlesinger Jr.'s "A Disagreement with Daniel Ellsberg," *The New York Review of Books* (October 21, 1971), pp. 23–32, an article which triggered a further exchange in Gelb, "On Ellsberg and Schlesinger," *The New York Review* (December 2, 1972), pp. 31–33; and Schlesinger, "The Quagmire Papers (Cont.)," *The New York Review* (December 16, 1971), pp. 41–42. Also pertinent is Hannah Arendt's interpretation in the first chapter of her *Crises of the Republic* (New York, 1972).

Since most of the selections in this book deal with the 1960s little additional reading need be suggested on the period per se. It is important, however, to note the debate about the foreign policy of President John F. Kennedy. Among books in praise of President Kennedy are Arthur M. Schlesinger Jr., *A Thousand Days: John F. Kennedy in the White House* (Boston, 1965); and Roger Hilsman, *To Move a Nation: The Politics of Foreign Policy in the Administration of John F. Kennedy* (New York, 1967). More recently, some writers have been more critical. An early example is George Kateb's review of the Schlesinger and Sorenson volumes in "Kennedy as Statesman," *Commentary* (June 1966), pp. 54–60. A full-dress revisionist analysis is Richard J. Walton, *Cold War and Counterrevolution: The Foreign Policy of John F. Kennedy* (New York, 1972). For a general overview plus a series of contrasting views, see Earl G. Latham, ed., *John F. Kennedy and Presidential Power* (Lexington, Mass., 1972).

Globalist voices are found less in books and articles and more in state papers and official pronouncements including Congressional testimony. Of such sources the most important are the *Public Papers* of Presidents Kennedy, Johnson, and Nixon, the *Department of State Bulletin,* and Congressional hearings including those before the Senate Foreign Relations Committee, the House Foreign Affairs Committee, plus the annual "military posture" statement of the Secretary of Defense before the Armed Services and Appropriations Committees. Memoirs revealing Globalist assumptions include Lyndon B. Johnson, *The Vantage Point: Perspectives of the Presidency, 1963–1969* (New York, 1971); Maxwell D. Taylor, *Swords into Plowshares* (New York, 1972); and, although devoted primarily to the early postwar years, Dean G. Acheson, *Present at the Creation* (New York, 1969). Other books by writers included in this one are George Liska, *Imperial America: The International Politics of Primacy* (Baltimore, 1967); and W. W. Rostow, *The Diffusion of Power* (New York, 1972). For a study of the foreshadowing of globalism in Woodrow Wilson's Presidency, see N. Gordon Levin, Jr., *Woodrow Wilson and World Politics* (New York, 1968). For a blast at a whole flight of Vietnam hawks, portrayed in a veritable cornucopia of anecdotes, see David Halberstam, *The Best and the Brightest* (New York, 1972).

Perhaps the best presentation of the contrast between Realism and Idealism in international relations is Robert E. Osgood, *Ideals and Self-Interest in America's Foreign Relations* (Chicago, 1953). For incisive analysis of the Globalist versus Realist debate see Robert W. Tucker, *Nation or Empire?* (Baltimore, 1968). Hans J. Morgenthau's Realist approach is most fully laid out in his *Politics Among Nations* (New York, 1967); his comments on American policy are scattered throughout the periodicals of the 1960s. An equally trenchant and prolific Realist writer is former Ambassador to the Soviet Union, George F. Kennan, whose two volumes of *Memoirs* (New York, 1967–1972; 2 vol.) are a most valuable resource. Those who wish to understand the diplomacy of Henry Kissinger must consult his early work, *A World Restored* (New York, 1964). Kissinger and other Realists and Radical–Liberals debate the origins and significance of America's Vietnam involvement in an important volume, Richard M. Pfeffer, ed., *No More Vietnams? The War and the Future of American Foreign Policy* (New York, 1968). Readers *In Search of Nixon* may consult a psycho-historical study of that name by Bruce Mazlish (New York, 1971) plus a number of more traditional studies, plus the President himself as revealed in his *Public Papers* and his annual *State of the World Messages.*

Of the critiques into which this book has been divided, the Radical–Liberal is perhaps the most difficult strictly to delimit. For Arnold Kaufman's effort to do so across a broad range of issues, see his *The Radical Liberal: New Man in American Politics* (New York, 1968). Other volumes which belong under this rubric include Robert W. Tucker, *A New Isolationism: Threat or Promise* (New York, 1972); Noam Chomsky, *American Power and the New Mandarins* (New York, 1969); Ronald Steel, *Pax Americana* (New York, 1967) and *Imperialists and Other Heroes: A Chronicle of the American Empire* (New York, 1971); Marcus Raskin and Richard J. Barnet, *After Twenty Years: Alternatives to the Cold War in Europe* (New York, 1965); Richard Barnet, *Intervention and Revolution: America's Confrontation with Insurgent Movements Around the World* (New York, 1968), *The Economy of Death* (New York, 1970), and *The Roots of War* (New York, 1972).

Radical criticism of globalism often, but not always, undergirds what have been called "revisionist" accounts of the Cold War and its origins. Two massive volumes in which this is the case are Gabriel Kolko, *The Politics of War: The World and United States Foreign Policy, 1943–1945* (New York, 1968) and Joyce and Gabriel Kolko, *The Limits of Power: The World and United States Foreign Policy,*

1945–1954 (New York, 1972). Other accounts in which a largely economic explanation of American imperialism plays an important role are William A. Williams, *The Tragedy of American Diplomacy* (New York, 1962); Carl Oglesby and Richard Shaull, *Containment and Change* (New York, 1967); David Horowitz, *Containment and Revolution* (Boston, 1967); N. D. Houghton, ed., *Struggle Against History* (New York, 1968); Gar Alperovitz, *Cold War Essays* (New York, 1971); and Michael Parenti, ed., *Trends and Tragedies in American Foreign Policy* (Boston, 1971). Less historical and more topical are Harry Magdoff, *The Age of Imperialism: The Economics of United States Foreign Policy* (New York, 1969); Richard C. Edwards et al., *The Capitalist System* (Englewood Cliffs, N.J., 1972); G. William Domhoff, *Who Rules America?* (Englewood Cliffs, N.J., 1967); John Gerassi, *The Great Fear: The Reconquest of Latin America by Latin Americans* (New York, 1963); and Paul A. Baran and Paul M. Sweezy, *Monopoly Capital: An Essay on the American Economic and Social Order* (New York, 1968). Useful articles include Mark Pilisuk and Tom Hayden, "Is There a Military-Industrial Complex That Prevents Peace?" in Robert Perucci and Mark Pilisuk, eds., *The Triple Revolution* (Boston, 1968); Gareth Stedman Jones, "The Specificity of U.S. Imperialism," *New Left Review* (March–April 1970), pp. 59–86; and Thomas E. Weisskopf, "Capitalism, Underdevelopment and the Future of the Poor Countries," Economic Development Report No. 174, December, 1970, Center for International Affairs, Harvard University. An overview written by a non-Radical, but not without sympathy and respect, is Robert W. Tucker, *The Radical Left and American Foreign Policy* (Baltimore, 1971).